Business and Management in Asia: Disruption and Change

Tobias Endress · Yuosre F. Badir
Editors

Business and Management in Asia: Disruption and Change

Springer

Editors
Tobias Endress
School of Management
Asian Institute of Technology
Bangkok, Thailand

Yuosre F. Badir
School of Management
Asian Institute of Technology
Bangkok, Thailand

ISBN 978-981-99-9370-3   ISBN 978-981-99-9371-0 (eBook)
https://doi.org/10.1007/978-981-99-9371-0

© The Editor(s) (if applicable) and The Author(s), under exclusive license to Springer Nature Singapore Pte Ltd. 2024

This work is subject to copyright. All rights are solely and exclusively licensed by the Publisher, whether the whole or part of the material is concerned, specifically the rights of translation, reprinting, reuse of illustrations, recitation, broadcasting, reproduction on microfilms or in any other physical way, and transmission or information storage and retrieval, electronic adaptation, computer software, or by similar or dissimilar methodology now known or hereafter developed.
The use of general descriptive names, registered names, trademarks, service marks, etc. in this publication does not imply, even in the absence of a specific statement, that such names are exempt from the relevant protective laws and regulations and therefore free for general use.
The publisher, the authors, and the editors are safe to assume that the advice and information in this book are believed to be true and accurate at the date of publication. Neither the publisher nor the authors or the editors give a warranty, expressed or implied, with respect to the material contained herein or for any errors or omissions that may have been made. The publisher remains neutral with regard to jurisdictional claims in published maps and institutional affiliations.

This Springer imprint is published by the registered company Springer Nature Singapore Pte Ltd.
The registered company address is: 152 Beach Road, #21-01/04 Gateway East, Singapore 189721, Singapore

Paper in this product is recyclable.

Preface

The emerging markets in the Asian region are changing fast and have the potential for high growth but are also prone to various risks. The Asian business world constantly faces new global and regional challenges (such as climate change, pandemic, technology change, and regional conflicts, to name a few) which directly influence how businesses operate and are managed. Strategies are needed to address these challenges and explore the opportunities inherent to disruption. This book presents innovative ideas and valuable managerial solutions produced by the region's managers and decision-makers who think and act creatively. Each chapter in this book series contains different contributions that deal with new ideas of strategic orientation, organizational issues as well as technical and methodical approaches.

The book at hand is the second volume in the "Business and Management in Asia" series. The prior publication, titled "Business and Management in Asia: Digital Innovation and Sustainability," received widespread recognition and positive feedback. It became a vital resource for both scholars and professionals alike. The focus of the 2023 edition is on "Disruption and Change" in the Asian region. In this context, managers and policymakers face a fast transformation of existing structures and business environments. From a business perspective, *change* is the adoption of business strategies, activities, and operations that meet the needs of the firm and its stakeholders today while protecting, sustaining, and enhancing the human and natural resources that will be needed in the future. *Disruption* refers to the radical changes in existing industries or markets due to technological innovation breakthroughs. There is a consensus among scholars and practitioners that organizations must manage the change well to flourish in a competitive business environment. Many business models need to be rethought to establish new ways to stay competitive. The book, with its practical examples, gives the reader impulses for fresh Asian approaches and encourages them to dare to think and act in new ways.

This book comprises 11 chapters.

Chapter one is entitled "Disruptive Business Climates". This chapter discusses how disruptive business proposals, driven by innovative technology and changing demographics, have transformed traditional approaches to the business world.

Chapter two "The Best Change Models for Asian Business and Management", highlights the importance of change management in growing businesses, emphasizing the need to consider cultural, economic, and political factors in Asia's diverse region.

Chapter three is named "Driving Success in Asia: The Essential Role of Disruption". It explains how disruption goes beyond change, transforming entire systems and bridging the gap between advanced and developing digital economies in Asia.

Chapter four entitled "Frontier Technologies Supporting Sustainable Development in Business", is dedicated to sustainable technology, shedding light on innovative solutions that consider the environment, ecological risks, and sustainable products.

Chapter five "Cultural Change at a Shipbuilding Joint Venture in Vietnam: Hard or Soft Value for Partnership?", delves into the complexities of cultural change within international joint ventures, focusing on the intercontinental shipbuilding industry in Vietnam. The chapter explores how cultural differences can inspire innovative solutions and drive organizational and individual changes.

Chapter six named "Digital Transformation and Resilience: Navigating Disruptions in Asian Emerging Markets", examines the implications of digital disruption in Asia's emerging markets. It provides a comprehensive analysis of the Fourth Industrial Revolution (4IR) and its impact on Asian developing economies.

Chapter seven "Disruption and the Gig Economy: What's Next?", explores the transformative impact of the gig economy, which has disrupted traditional industries but is now struggling to find sustainable business models. It delves into the challenges and benefits of the gig economy, discussing issues such as labor rights, job security, and regulatory control.

The title of chapter eight is "Adopting Tele-migration in Developing Asian Market: Exploring Drivers in the Face of Change". It explores the emerging trend of tele-migration, enabling individuals to work remotely from foreign countries. This chapter utilizes the diffusion of innovation theory to examine the internal and external factors that drive individuals in developing Asian markets to embrace tele-migration.

Chapter nine is entitled "Back to Work or Remote Work: Trends and Challenges" and investigates the evolving working mode policies in Asian countries, particularly in the context of the post-pandemic return to work.

Chapter ten is about "Managing the 3 Ps in Workplace Disruption: People, Place and Process in the Case of Co-working Space". It explores the impact of digitalization and the pandemic on workplace design, particularly the rise of co-working spaces. It also offers recommendations for designing co-working offices that meet users' needs.

Chapter eleven entitled "Organizational Resilience, Innovation Capabilities, and SME Performance in High-Risk Contexts", focuses on the relationship between innovative capabilities and SME performance in high-risk contexts, such as emerging Asian economies. It emphasizes the importance of both explorative and exploitative innovation capabilities in helping SMEs thrive.

Asia stands at the precipice of immense transformation. As the world's largest and most diverse continent, its growth trajectories are inextricably linked with the tides of global change. In "Business and Management in Asia: Disruption and Change," we dive deep into the pressing challenges and boundless opportunities that lie ahead for the Asian business landscape. By shedding light on strategies, technological advancements, and novel approaches to business, this book equips readers with the knowledge and tools to navigate an era characterized by rapid disruption and change. In essence, this book serves as a compass, guiding readers through the complex world of Asian business and management. Through meticulous research and insightful analysis, we hope to inspire readers to embrace change, harness disruption, and craft a brighter future for Asia and the world at large.

Bangkok, Thailand   Tobias Endress
November 2023   Yuosre F. Badir

Contents

Disruptive Business Climates 1
Archana Parashar

The Best Change Models for Asian Business and Management 19
Ayşe Meriç Yazıcı

Driving Success in Asia: The Essential Role of Disruption 39
David Galipeau

Frontier Technologies Supporting Sustainable Development
in Business 53
Anjali Malik, Deepika Dhingra, and Seema Sharma

Cultural Change at a Shipbuilding Joint Venture in Vietnam:
Hard or Soft Value for Partnership? 73
Que N. Tran, Chuyen T. Nguyen, and Cat-My Dang

Digital Transformation and Resilience: Navigating Disruptions
in Asian Emerging Markets 91
Mohamad Zreik

Disruption and the Gig Economy: What's Next? 109
Tobias Endress

Adopting Tele-migration in Developing Asian Market: Exploring
Drivers in the Face of Change 123
Tayyaba Irum Shakil, Adeel Tariq, Mumtaz Ali Memon,
and Marko Torkkeli

Back to Work or Remote Work: Trends and Challenges 139
Anita Maharani

Managing the 3 Ps in Workplace Disruption: People, Place,
and Process in the Case of Co-working Space 151
Aqilah Yaacob, Goh See Kwong, Gu Manli, and Karen Tsen Mung Khie

ix

Organizational Resilience, Innovation Capabilities, and SME Performance in High-Risk Contexts 171
Nadia Zahoor, Ahmad Arslan, Donman Miri, and Zaheer Khan

Disruptive Business Climates

Archana Parashar

Abstract Disruptive business proposals have revolutionized the traditional ways of approaching the business world. Novel business models have emerged with diversified methods of value creation that have varied drivers of disruption ranging from innovative technology to demographic shifts. Internet and social media have facilitated disruptive innovations, allowing the development of creative business models that cater to emerging customer expectations effectively and efficiently. The present chapter is formulated with the objective of comprehensively analysing how social media has innovatively disrupted the existing business models by citing relevant research studies and real-world applications. To specify the positive effects of disruptive technologies, constructive catalytic innovations in the educational sector have been highlighted. Further, the existing executives' preferred managerial skills and key strategies are identified that assist them in managing the aftereffects of business disruption. These contemporary business trends have immense practical implications, encouraging business leaders to adapt creatively to the prevalent paradigm shift.

Keywords Business disruption · Social media · Catalytic innovations

Introduction

The present chapter aims to provide an in-depth understanding of disruptive innovations in the contemporary business world, with special emphasis on the role of social media. A comprehensive narrative review was conducted to analyse how social media and the internet have disrupted the prevalent business models in the most innovative ways. The phenomenon has been explained using empirical research studies and real-world instances to highlight the changes these disruptive technologies have brought about in the functioning of novel business approaches. Given the prevalence of business disruption, the chapter also provides useful insights about how

---

A. Parashar (✉)
Indian Institute of Management, Raipur, India
e-mail: archana@iimraipur.ac.in

© The Author(s), under exclusive license to Springer Nature Singapore Pte Ltd. 2024
T. Endress and Y. F. Badir (eds.), *Business and Management in Asia: Disruption and Change*, https://doi.org/10.1007/978-981-99-9371-0_1

present business leaders successfully handle the challenges resulting from disruptive technologies to their advantage. Further, with the objective of highlighting the positive impacts of disruptive innovations, constructive disruptions were analysed in the educational sector. In light of the above objectives, practical implications and research opportunities have been discussed.

Disruptive Innovations

Christensen and Bower formally introduced the disruptive-innovation model in their 1995 Harvard Business Review article 'Disruptive Technologies: Catching the Wave' and categorized innovations as sustainable and disruptive. Sustainable innovations were identified as serving an organization's most-demanding customers by providing better quality products and services, such as incremental improvements (for example, different versions of the iPhone). In contrast, disruptive innovations were identified as relatively simple, convenient, inexpensive products and services appealing to novel or less demanding customers. For instance, Southwest Airlines' cheaper and no-frills flights serve leisure travellers. Disruptive business approaches majorly impact existing industry frameworks and produce social change in their advent (Christensen et al., 2006). Hence, disruptive business models fundamentally transform and replace the traditional models, thereby impacting the business value of products and services (Horváth, 2016).

The digital revolution has evolved the business world, wherein the complete standstill of COVID-19 facilitated consumer preference for e-commerce. The aftereffects of digitalization are witnessed in altered product/service portfolios and integrated communication and networking systems (Evanschitzky et al., 2020). Excessive advancement in digital technology is reflected in the innovations of artificial intelligence (AI), social media apps, smart sensors, and the internet of things (IoT), which present products and services in a modified form. The well-established business models stand disrupted in the face of digitalizing products and services. The traditional business dynamics of taxi and hotel services received immense shock with the introduction of the online platform models of Uber and Airbnb, respectively. In other words, the unfolding of digital technologies results in the rapidly growing phenomenon of digital disruption (Thakur et al., 2021).

Business Disruption

Disruption creates new business models wherein varied and novel knowledge and intellectual capital result in value creation (Neilson et al., 2017). They are characterized as having "novel revenue logic and new customer benefit" (Matzler et al., 2018). Disruptive business models are "a process whereby a smaller company with fewer resources can successfully challenge established incumbent businesses" (Christensen et al., 2015). Cozzolino et al. (2018) highlight that disruptions challenge the efficacy of existing models, as evidenced by Polaroid's failure to transition from a "razor-blade" chemical films business to a "hardware-based" business model. The authors have centered their propositions around the news publishing industry, referring to the traditional business model as a closed model wherein internal knowledge was responsible for value creation and value capture depended on having specific complementary assets. Conversely, the disruptive, relatively open model holds internal and external knowledge responsible for value creation and development of knowledge exchange (including customer data) platforms responsible for value capture.

Lang and Rumsey (2018) have addressed business disruption as the new normal facilitated by the rapid progress in technology and globalization. Often, businesses stand disrupted due to the competitive climate that allows the development of cheaper, innovative products and services. Accenture's (2018) survey reported that among 1440 executives, the respondents had attributed the advent of business disruption to innovations enabled by technology (68%), new competitors (55%), new regulations (53%), socio-cultural issues (51%), and demographic shifts (46%). Start-ups and new market entrants accompany them with disruptive business models that modify or eliminate the existing foundations (Matzler et al., 2018). Whole disruptive technologies are likely to proceed with the innovation of a disruptive model, but this is not always the case, as displayed by Ryanair's inexpensive, no-frills model (Cozzolino et al., 2018).

Businesses like Apple's iTunes have been disrupted as they utilize customer data to build useful insights about customer behaviour and enhance business intelligence. For instance, Apple fulfilled the customer expectations of wishing to pay for only those songs one wished to listen to instead of the whole CD. Products such as Amazon's Alexa, Google Home, and Microsoft Cortana that are characterized by a combination of two or more digitized technologies have disrupted business fields. Digital disruption positively impacts the customer experience and firm performance as it results in personalized user experiences (Thakur et al., 2021).

The prevalent digital businesses such as Uber, Airbnb, and Spotify have disrupted many dominant firms by eroding the boundaries of existing methods of production organization and value capture. Digital disruption is understood as a combination of digital innovation (novel business models/products/services), digital ecosystem (socio-technical network of interdependent technologies), and value logic (foundational logic behind a digital innovation creation). Digital disruption can shake the foundation of all existing industries if the potential risks are managed properly (Skog et al., 2018).

Business Models as Disrupted by Internet

The Internet positively disrupted the trade-off between the amount of knowledge (the richness) that could be communicated and the size of the audience attending to it (reach), shaking the foundation of many businesses that used the trade-off as a competitive advantage, such as those producing newspapers and encyclopedias. Micheal Porter concluded that the internet has the potential to fuel competition whilst decreasing profit margins, as demonstrated by Napster, Amazon, and the Apple Store takeover of Tower Records and Musicland and the rise of smartphones brewing trouble for camera creators (Ovans, 2015).

The world rapidly embraced the internet due to its wide range of services and information it gave people at just a click. The internet sowed the seeds of the new e-business or e-commerce business model, which disrupted the traditional brick-and-mortar business model. Consequently, a novel distribution channel came into being, getting businesses access to the global market that promoted the sustainable development of world economies. The domestic supply chains became the current global supply and value chains that provide customers with needs-specific products and services. As evidenced through Reddit, Instagram, Twitter, and Facebook, these online businesses allow customers to readily access information about opportunities and simultaneously provide means to access them. Online businesses have extensive unstructured streaming data incoming from websites and internet-connecting sources such as smartphones, machine data, video, audio, and the like. The interconnectivity results in shortened supply chains as the internet becomes the single, direct carrier of logistics, purchasing strategies, and supply management (Sheriff, 2018).

The Internet evolved the climate of business-to-business communications and business-to-customer relationships by lowering the operational cost and, thereby, increasing cost-effectiveness, efficiency, and profits. Consequently, the attitude towards the business world has transformed, positing that drive and motivation help companies to climb up the steps to success rather than just huge capital in isolation (Sheriff, 2018). The trend of online shopping displays the disruptive potential of the internet, facilitating greater speed and convenience, an expanded array of products and services, and the use of word of mouth through customer reviews (Sheppard, 2017).

Social Media Disruption of Traditional Donor Engagement Models

Social media displayed its disruptive potential by chipping away at the principles of existing donor engagement and outreach models. The traditional donor-engagement models were designed as pyramids, ladders, or funnels, proclaiming that any donor exists at a single level in a given time and progresses towards the top as their commitment towards and investment in the product/service/organization increases through the suppliers' outreach efforts. Professionals have realized that large masses depend on social media channels to gather and process information. Organizations have integrated social media into the lower levels of their business pyramids to build awareness and initiate donor relationships with diverse populations. Donor interactions are witnessed as liking posts, blogging/ tweeting, or adding the brand logo to one's profile. Social media disruption has rendered the static pyramid and ladder models ineffective, demanding new models of donor engagement (Dixon & Keyes, 2013).

The 2010 survey conducted among 2,000 American adults by Georgetown University's Centre for Social Impact Communication and Ogilvy Public Relations Worldwide revealed the impact of social media on consumer interaction based on the premise of traditional models' inability to keep up with the communication demands. The survey reported that donors display multiple levels of engagement. While social-media-driven actions such as joining online groups, blogging, or posting were not primary donor engagement signs, these activities later replaced or supplemented traditional engagement styles such as volunteering or donating. Such donors are popularly known as "slacktivists" who progressed down the ladder to use social media to engage with organizations. The traditional models hardly had any room for such downward movements and multiple engagement platforms, which have been in demand given the broad range of activities made available by social media to potential supporters (Dixon & Keyes, 2013).

Similarly, social media opened the avenues for novel donor-communication methods such as e-newsletters, personal outreach, and other automated channels. Organizations must utilize various channels to increase the opportunities to introduce and reinforce messages likely to result in what Jennifer Wayman defines as a "surround sound" experience. Social media comes with the advantage of providing consistent and scheduled communication. It also accounts for peer-to-peer influence on donors' decisions. For instance, Americans (39%) reported that their motivation to get involved in an organization is dependent if the promoted causes have impacted someone known or if it is important to their family and peers (Dixon & Keyes, 2013).

The newer social media-based donor engagement models have distinct features such as allowing donors to be engaged at multiple levels and to move easily within these levels, having no fixed entry point, donor-engagement footprint expansion or contraction as per convenience and accounting for peer-to-peer influences to strengthen donor-organization relationships. This business outreach disruption is represented as a vortex with the donor at the centre, and their commitment to the organization is represented as a continuous field around them which expands as their commitment depth increases. The vortex, representing continuous communication and engagement flow, recognizes multiple methods of maximizing donor support for any issue (Dixon & Keyes, 2013).

Implementing this disruptive innovation requires altered outreach tactics and employee training manuals. Social media has made continuous communication an essential component of the disruptive shift. The disruption demands defining donor contributions beyond financial donations (e.g. experience sharing) and diversifying the types of action calls (e.g. forwarding messages and leading fundraisers). Successful organizations such as Little Lights Urban Ministries use identical calls, encouraging donors to share email appeals. Slacktivists participate in nearly twice as many varied support activities (walk or an event) as the average American and are more likely to "solicit donations" on behalf of the cause. The vertex model provides donors with a tailored portfolio of engagement that allows them to pick and choose those activities that suit their strengths and ability to make a difference. Hence, social media has completely disrupted traditional donor-engagement models by transforming donor-organization interactions (Dixon & Keyes, 2013).

Disruptive Potential of Social Media

Social media has been an evolutionary advancement, altogether transforming the approach towards the internet. It is perceived as a collection of online applications and technologies that facilitate connectivity, user-generated content, information-sharing, and community interaction. It has been extensively used in business-to-consumer climates for brand promotion. Recently, the field of supply chain management has begun exploring its disruptive potential for monitoring chain events, keeping everyone up-to-date and providing insights about potential risks, enabling the implementation of timely corrective measures (Cox & Atkinson, 2018). Social media has transformed how customers consume media content, disrupting incumbent media industries. The platforms serve as novel information distribution channels while providing superior information checks and within-organization content exchange (Flew, 2018).

Disruptive Journalism Industry

Flew (2018) reported that traditional journalism industries are disrupted by the new online sites such as Huffington Post, VICE, and Buzzfeed that cater to the younger generations. Social media has disrupted the longstanding business model that worked on three main revenue sources: direct sales, advertising, and classified. Currently, the revenue is dependent on the extent of content availability, accessibility, and user engagement. Phenomena such as click baits and churnalism have been trending, especially to build brand identity.

Laurell and Sandström (2014) have examined the disruptive potential of social media in the fashion journalism industry. They have described how entrant fashion bloggers have taken over incumbent fashion journalism. Using a netnographic lens, the authors studied Swedish fashion bloggers and reported that entrant bloggers had infiltrated the field in such a way that the topmost four entrant bloggers have an audience four times larger than that captured by incumbent journalist bloggers. The entrant bloggers were reported employing a disruptive business model that allowed them varied value creation means and personal ways of appropriating it. Social media interactivity facilitated the generation of low-cost content characterized by readers' involvement in content production, thereby overcoming the journalist-reader distance barrier traditional print journalists face.

Targeting Environmental Disasters

Dwivedi et al. (2022) highlight enterprise social media as another disruptive trend which includes how organizations utilize social media platforms diversely to fulfil objectives such as brand campaigning, knowledge transfer, building relationships, gaining market insights, and spreading awareness. Interestingly, social media platforms proved helpful during environmental disasters such as the Haiti earthquake and the Harvey hurricane. Hence, disaster management organizations have realized the potential of such platforms in managing internal tasks such as enhancing knowledge exchange, internal communication and collaboration during emergencies and external operations such as marketing and customer interaction monitoring. The authors emphasize that disaster management organizations' use of social media to make decisions during prevention and mitigation, preparedness, response and recovery enhances their decision-making effectiveness as mediated by social media structure, organizational agility, and knowledge sharing. Increased decision-making effectiveness positively impacts organizations' operation and social performance, such as delivering quick, result-oriented, real-time decisions.

Similarly, Van Wyk et al. (2023) have examined social media, specifically Twitter data, as a resource to understand disaster-related adaptations during Hurricanes Irma and Maria. Impacted individuals turn to social media to gather news, spread awareness, and collaborate to make sense of the events. Such analysis provided future insights into how individuals behave in real-time events, which can be further utilized to make necessary modifications and preparations for emergencies to have adequate communication strategies.

Influencing Small and Medium Enterprises

Zhang and Zhu (2021) emphasize using social media to promote disruptive innovations in small and medium enterprises. Using a strategic capability perspective, the authors emphasize using social media platforms to make strategic decisions, formulating market insights and timely innovative solutions based on extensive information. Social media has facilitated new product development, accessible to a wider audience, through expanded visions regarding industrial development and resource utilization and widened knowledge base. Hence, social media strategic capability has provided small and medium enterprises with an advantageous opportunity to benefit from disruptive innovations.

Disruptive Marketing

The COVID-19 pandemic trapped the world in four walls, but disruptive innovators could not be stopped from fulfilling the demands of many distraught couples. Using the disruptive technologies of artificial technology and augmented reality, virtual dressing rooms appealed to huge masses who were apprehensive about leaving the safety of their homes but wished to shop. Along similar lines, efficient and feasible digital shelves, such as mobile shopping applications, have transformed the marketing world, resolving customer complaints about standing in queues, time wastage, and exposure to a limited product range. Disruptive innovations such as IKEA Place, providing a virtual home experience and Lego Hidden Side, providing a virtual gaming experience, have created new customer markets (Kumar, 2021).

Disruptive marketing is appreciated and feared for creating new markets by increasing product functionality and prestige (Djakeli, 2018). Toyota car advertisements shifted their focus from product features to product sustainability, immensely influencing customers. Similarly, Nike stressed how their product facilitated the customers' comfort and fitness (Parth, 2020). The entertainment sector was disrupted by Netflix, the world's first streaming service, with binge-watching (Cohen, 2022). Such a strategy carries risk as it challenges the prevalent marketing rules intending to attract new customers and enhance the brand loyalty of existing customers. Hence, it may backfire as thinking out of the box may not be appreciated (Parth, 2020). Conversely, disruptive marketing facilitates meeting customer demands and keeping up with the ongoing competition with adequate technological updates (Walters, 2023).

Disruptive Versus Conventional Marketing

Disruptive marketing differs from traditional marketing on several grounds. Traditional marketing strategy moves from products and services to seeking buyers, whereas disruptive marketing strategy tailors products and services as per customer expectations and wants. Disruptive marketing has moved away from the generic messaging traditionally used to advertise by highlighting how customer challenges are resolved when they engage with their products and services. Traditional marketing follows brick-and-mortar distribution and uses spreadsheet analysis, whereas disruptive marketing has adapted to e-commerce and uses advanced business intelligence technologies to measure multiple success variables. According to the marketing consulting firm McCarthy Group, 84% of millennials overlook traditional marketing services and prefer personalized services; a demand disruptive marketing aims to fulfil (Wysseier, 2019).

Colon (2016) reports that disruptive marketers focus on four major marketing goals, namely developing those products, services, solutions, or causes that meet the demands of emerging consumer markets; reengineering the existing products and services to fulfil the demands of unsatisfied customers; achieving customer-centricity; and employing emotional intelligence to build strong customer-employee communication. A disruptive marketer is a hybrid professional who performs diverse functions simultaneously, such as search engine optimization, social media management, web development, inbound marketing, web and social analytics analysis, and the like. In contrast, conventional marketing hires individuals who perform any one task. Unlike conventional marketing, disruptive marketing focuses on building ongoing customer conversations over product marketing.

Constructive Disruptive in Education

Catalytic Innovations

The contemporary period demands expanded support for organizations addressing social-sector issues through novel approaches by developing "scalable, sustainable, system-changing solutions" (Christensen et al., 2006, p. 1). Catalytic innovations, a subset of disruptive innovations, are identified by their major focus on social change by developing effective solutions to overcome the established status quo by adequately addressing social problems. Catalytic innovations use scaling and replication to produce social change, aim to meet over-served or underserved needs sustainably, offer simple and inexpensive products and services, and generate useful resources (donations, volunteer workforce or intellectual capital). Such attractive characteristics result in the existing incumbent competitors ignoring these innovations. Catalytic innovation in education allows people to access various goods and affordable resources they were denied earlier, such as degree opportunities (Christensen et al., 2006).

Christensen et al. (2006) have exemplified online learning and community colleges as catalytic innovations in education. Online classes catered to the needs of small student groups interested in learning certain languages and taking advanced placement courses to increase college credit. However, they were denied the opportunity because of constrained budgets. Platforms such as Apex Learning, Virtual High School, and Florida Virtual School have utilized the catalytic innovation of online learning to provide these specialized classes, allowing school systems to offer informative courses at a much lower cost. Online education has served as an adequate alternative for the underserved sectors. It is based on beneficial, disruptive business models that focus on providing affordable and widely accessible education that the existing systems fail to achieve.

Similarly, community colleges have immensely transformed higher education systems by offering inexpensive alternatives to four-year universities and measuring quality based on job placement rates and access convenience to attending classes, resulting in widened access and redefined goals. Community colleges are considered a viable option for the disadvantaged sectors for whom traditional education systems are inaccessible. They also serve as "feeder schools" for four-year institutions as many first- and second-year students consider community colleges as a cheap and good-enough alternative for the first two years before saving up to transfer to four-year institutions (Christensen et al., 2006).

Accessible Knowledge for All

Disruptive technologies have transformed the educational models by replacing the existing models and consequently impacting the role of the suppliers of higher education, educational service value, and business life (Horváth, 2016). Sousa and Rocha (2019) list digital learning, mobile learning, and e-learning as the contemporary disruptive businesses emerging from information technology in the education sector. Around 30 universities from all over America, Europe, and China responded to an international survey concerning introducing disruptive technologies in higher education learning material. The lecturers reported that blending disruptive technologies in the learning material facilitates student creativity, problem-solving, and employment opportunities, allowing education to gain a novel outlook. The disruptive technologies, namely Big Data, Cloud Computing, Private Cloud Computing, Gamification, HTML5, Internet of Things, 3D printing, and virtualization, were included at bachelor's and master's training levels. The disruptive potential of these technologies is reflected in their capacity to build a common and multidisciplinary knowledge source accessible to all by reducing the gap between the digital lives of lecturers and students and consequently facilitating the efficiency of educational success marked by creative student innovations (Horváth, 2016).

Kaplan and Haenlein (2016) highlight the disruptive potential of the pedagogical tool, distance learning, supplemented with MOOCs (Massive Open Online Courses) and SPOCs (Small Private Online Courses) that have revolutionized the existing education system landscape. Firms like Coursera and Udacity facilitate distance learning by providing customers with pre-planned and prepared educational material. Disruptive innovation is cost-effective and highly flexible, a combination suitable for the prevalent fast-paced lifestyle.

Facilitative Social Media

Social media has quickly expanded over the years, as witnessed by its overwhelming advent in the education society displayed by students' increased utilization of web-based lifestyles. Social media and networking sites offer students a combination of instruments blended to suit their learning styles best and increment their academic achievements. Social media platforms have disrupted the educational stream by focusing on building such person-to-person web networks that intensely center around the audience's basic interests. The student community has a platform to express creativity, acquire administrative skills, and expand their social networks globally (NeelaKandan et al., 2020).

Social media reinforces educational incentives in higher education by facilitating scholarly interactions based on academic behavior and constructive discourse, resulting in a knowledgeable learning atmosphere (Rambe, 2012). For instance, Fincham (2011) took the example of Storify to demonstrate the creative intent of social media applications. Storify allowed journalists and others to provide relevant context to information by adding suitable images, tweets, statuses, and the like. Such innovations captured the focus of those with limited attention spans, enhancing users' imagination and reconstruction abilities. Similarly, Stanford University reported a Wi-Fi-supported classroom embedded in collaborative Social Media tools such as forums, wikis, video conferring and the like, enabling live lectures and widened learning exposure wherein the readily available curriculum material challenges traditional teaching instructions (Rambe, 2012). Teachers may even utilize applications such as Celly and Poll Everywhere to set up a student update schedule concerning quizzes, feedback and study groups (Watters, 2014). Social media has fostered constructive engagements, producing valuable knowledge (King, 2012).

Rambe (2012) examined lecture-student and peer-based Facebook postings to study social media's impact on meaningful academic learning and pedagogical instruction and concluded that Facebook acted as a "Third safe space" encouraging democratic student expression and collaborative knowledge formulation. The social presence facilitated open communication and honest expression of personal challenges and associated emotions. The platform activated widespread conceptual applications in response to increased useful information exchange and peer-based engagements. Lastly, introducing Facebook enhanced the teaching presence by making teacher-student dialogue much more constructive, wherein conflict resolution had a practical basis.

Kaplan and Haenlein (2016) have talked of connectivist MOOCs (Massive Open Online Courses), which implies a combination of MOOCs with social media platforms, referred to as "cMOOCS." Such innovations allow the creation of educational material via social media applications subjected to comments and harbor the possibility of further enhancement. It has given rise to a novel teaching strategy wherein peer collaboration and cooperation drive learning wherein the teacher embodies a facilitative role rather than serving as the primary knowledge transmitter.

In the GPT World

Most recently, OpenAL-powered ChatGPT gained about one million followers in mere five days. The disruptive potential of the artificially intelligent tool lies in its creativity and reliability to replicate and respond to human language by offering customized and interactive support, most likely altering the students' approach to education and especially serving the autodidactic customers. ChatGPT facilitates the self-reliant learning style of autodidacticism by offering personalized and interactive assistance and real-time feedback, allowing the customers to meet their needs for conventional teaching support. Moreover, it is highly accessible, effectively guiding students to utilize open educational resources. It has added the features of convenience and flexibility to self-directed learning whilst simultaneously allowing users to self-evaluate and reflect on their progress (Firat, 2023).

Given these disruptive features, ChatGPT targets creative engagement and innovation potential among teachers and students. ChatGPT has increased the quality of virtual teaching, impacting the lecturers' teaching approaches. Students and academic researchers constituted the two major groups of ChatGPT users in the first few weeks. Scientific writing and software development are the recognized potential disruptive fields for ChatGPT. The current educational departments are mulling over the possible issues of curriculum adaptation, regulation, and plagiarism checks concerning this artificial disruptive technology (Neumann et al., 2023).

Facing Business Disruption

Required Skill Set

The management of disruptive businesses depends on specific skill sets to bring about market evolution. Sousa and Rocha's (2019) online survey analysis listed innovation, leadership, and management skills as necessary to manage disruptive businesses. The innovation skills included creativity, the ability to identify and generate new opportunities, project and risk management, efficiency and efficacy, and building national and international networks. The leadership skills were characterized by high-performance teams, careers and talent management, motivation and satisfaction, effective communication, and multicultural sensitivity. The management skills included adaptation to new work organization models, emergent technology and organizational change, effective use of decision-making tools and big data analysis, strategic management, and social and relational knowledge. Developing these skills will likely induce emerging disruptive businesses to align the company strategies accordingly to effectively respond to market challenges and reach the horizons of success.

Similarly, California State Automobile Association's (CSAA) chief strategy and innovation officer, Debra Brackeen, lists unconventional thinking, autonomy and proactivity, business awareness and risk-taking as the basis for scouting out potential customers and their needs and, accordingly, developing a business culture adaptable to the ongoing disruption (Outthinker, 2018). Thakur et al. (2021) reported that managerial skills of adaptability, dynamic vision, and innovation facilitate digital disruption, allowing executives to maximize their success.

Key Strategies

Wessel and Christensen (2021) rightly said, "It is not enough to know that a threat is coming. You need to know whether it is coming right for you." The two have offered a strategic getaway in disruptive times as a three-fold path: identification of disruptive businesses' strengths, followed by identification of the existing businesses' relative advantages and then a comparison between the two to pinpoint those conditions that would facilitate or obstruct the disruptor from overpowering the relative advantages in near future. One must pay close attention to the disruptive businesses' extendable core that allows them to expand their customer base whilst maintaining performance strengths. The existing business must make an overall assessment before being reckless and engaging in price competition or worse by giving into the sunk-cost fallacy and increasing their investments in a lost cause.

Businesses surviving disruption are characterized by a persistent pursuit of customer satisfaction as indicated by the desired customer experience based on product quality, price, and associated convenience and services. Such insights are built through deep customer engagement. Customer satisfaction may require reinvention in modernization and creativity to build innovative competencies. Satisfying customers requires businesses to treat their employees and stakeholders as partners so that they play an instrumental role in deepening customer intimacy. Successful businesses make long-term commitments and manage their financial resources well, for sustainability protects against disruptive business changes (Biltz, 2019).

Practical Implications

The literature review highlighted the advent of business disruption that has shaken the foundation of long-standing traditional methods of marketing and business. Social media and the internet have played a key facilitative role in business disruption. Catalytic innovations highlight the constructive potential of business disruption that must be utilized to benefit the customers in every way possible. However, such innovations may carry deliberated risks, as discussed in the case of the artificially intelligent tool, ChatGPT. A consensus has been reached that adaptation rather than prevention is the mode to survive business disruption. Such adaptation is dependent on specific executive skills and key strategies that the current business players have advocated.

The COVID-19 pandemic emphasized the natural accelerators of business disruption, in addition to the manufactured foundations of digitalization and the industrial revolution. Such contributors impact the existing business models and sow the seeds of futurist trends, for instance, the ongoing requests to work from home. In response, a hybrid model has been infiltrating the business world wherein employees harvest the perceived advantages of working at home and in office spaces (Barnes et al., 2021). Yet another trend is the advent of artificial intelligence, especially in the marketing field, which has resulted in various promising research themes. Taking social media as an instance, scholars should dive into how such platforms can be employed to analyse and predict customer expectations to highlight the most engaged population segment and, accordingly, design marketing pitches. Artificial intelligence indulgence requires scholars to explore the consequent ethical and social implications (Chintalapati & Pandey, 2022).

The rapid emergence of business disruption models has opened up many research opportunities. Scholars may benefit from empirically analysing business sectors yet to be explored in the context of business disruption and then highlighting similarities and differences among business sectors by comparing the findings. Similarly, scholars may investigate corporate behaviour in response to business disruption and identify the factors resulting in resisting or adopting transforming business principles. Such investigation may also centre around customer experience and how it acts as a social motive to fuel business disruption. The academic sphere can further study the incumbents' struggle between maintaining existing business models and accepting the innovative business disruption approach to provide exemplary guidance to present business players for making an effective decision (Schiavi & Behr, 2018).

While business disruption is currently perceived as inevitable, business players are still struggling to identify its origin to respond appropriately. It has been proposed that business disruption is not only limited to innovative technology or how businesses evolve in response but is accompanied by a transforming worldview regarding the contextuality of key concepts, core entities, and associated problems. Further research should investigate the pathways that would allow business incumbents to overcome defensive tendencies when faced with paradigm shifts and actively invest in the meaning-making process of the evolved paradigm to survive disruption advantageously. On the practical forefront, business incumbents will likely benefit from attempting to understand the transformed industry principles with open-mindedness. These attempts must be followed by being experimental, which implies proactively playing with the so-assumed "crazy" propositions or providing a supportive platform to novices who can provide innovative alternatives to successfully battle disruption (Riemer & Johnston, 2019).

Conclusion

In this chapter, the process of business disruption has been highlighted with respect to the disruptive innovation model. Many businesses have utilized the disruptive power of the Internet to evolve the climate of business-to-business communications and business-to-customer relationships. Similarly, the disruptive potential of social media has been utilized to transform donor-engagement models and encourage disruptive innovations. Even business marketing has taken a disruptive turn to meet customer expectations. The educational world has also been struck by disruptive catalytic innovations, bringing about excessive advancement as facilitated by social media.

There is an overwhelming need for current executives to harness adequate managerial skills and utilize strategic getaways to adapt to the ongoing business disruption.

When faced with business disruption, one's response to it determines whether the disruption will impact their business positively or negatively. As per Gans (2016), business incumbents may react in three possible ways: proactively beating it, reactively joining it or passively outlasting it. Adapting to disruption may resemble embracing paradox to generate useful insights. It means letting go of defensive stances when approached with business disruption to harness the value creation potential of evolved business landscapes advantageously. It involves perceiving threats as opportunity-bearing chances to research enduring business foundations. For instance, the fragmented business economy, erupting from disruption, may be profitable for the scale and scope businesses. Business disruption paradoxically correlates to zooming out to future possibilities for zooming in to maximizing current initiatives. Taking on a pragmatic approach, existing businesses can adapt to disruption by studying patterns of disruption, investing in effective opportunities that will likely concentrate over time, designing impactful responses that resonate with the future, and continuously learning from ongoing transformation (Hagel et al., 2016).

References

Accenture. (2018). Disruption need not be an enigma. Retrieved from https://www.accenture.com/_acnmedia/pdf-72/accenture-disruptability-index-pov-final.pdf.

Barnes, L., Long, W., & Williams, P. (2021). Purpose built offices replaced by work from home (WFH) in a time of business disruption: Hybrid office model (HOM). *Frontiers of Contemporary Education, 2*(1), 56–74.

Chintalapati, S., & Pandey, S. K. (2022). Artificial intelligence in marketing: A systematic literature review. *International Journal of Market Research, 64*(1), 38–68.

Christensen, C. M., Baumann, H., Ruggles, R., & Sadtler, T. M. (2006). Disruptive innovation for social change. *Harvard Business Review, 84*(12), 94.

Christensen, C. M., Raynor, M. E., & McDonald, R. (2015). What is disruptive innovation? *Harvard Business Review*.

Cohen, B. (2022). Netflix disrupted entertainment with binge viewing. *Now Can It Avoid Disruption Itself? The Wall Street Journal*.

Colon, G. (2016). *Disruptive marketing: What growth hackers, data punks, and other hybrid thinkers can teach us about navigating the new normal*. Amacom.

Cox, S. R., & Atkinson, K. (2018). Social media and the supply chain: Improving risk detection, risk management, and disruption recovery. *SAIS 2018 Proceedings*.

Cozzolino, A., Verona, G., & Rothaermel, F. T. (2018). Unpacking the disruption process: New technology, business models, and incumbent adaptation. *Journal of Management Studies, 55*(7), 1166–1202.

Djakeli, D. K. (2018). From the disruptive marketing to the new model of prestigious branding. *Quality-Access to Success, 19*(166).

Dixon, J., & Keyes, D. (2013). The permanent disruption of social media. *Stanford Social Innovation Review*. Retrieved from https://ssir.org/articles/entry/the_permanent_disruption_of_social_media.

Dwivedi, Y. K., Shareef, M. A., Akram, M. S., Bhatti, Z. A., & Rana, N. P. (2022). Examining the effects of enterprise social media on operational and social performance during environmental disruption. *Technological Forecasting and Social Change, 175*, 121364.

Evanschitzky, H., Bartikowski, B., Baines, T., Blut, M., Brock, C., Kleinlercher, K., ... & Wünderlich, N. V. (2020). Digital disruption in retailing and beyond. *SMR-Journal of Service Management Research, 4*(4), 187-204.

Fincham, K. (2011). Storify. *Journal of Media Literacy Education, 3*(1), 15.

Firat, M. (2023). *How chat GPT can transform autodidactic experiences and open education.* Open Education Faculty, Anadolu University.

Flew, T. (2018). Social media and the cultural and creative industries. *The Sage Handbook of Social Media*, 512–526.

Gans, J. S. (2016). Keep calm and manage disruption. *MIT Sloan Management Review, 57*(3), 83–95.

Hagel, J., Brown, J. S., de Maar, A., & Wooll, M. (2016). *Approaching disruption: Charting a course for new growth and performance at the edge and beyond.* Deloitte University Press.

Horváth, I. (2016). Disruptive technologies in higher education. In *2016 7th IEEE International Conference on Cognitive Infocommunications (CogInfoCom)* (pp. 000347–000352). IEEE.

Kaplan, A. M., & Haenlein, M. (2016). Higher education and the digital revolution: About MOOCs, SPOCs, social media, and the Cookie Monster. *Business Horizons, 59*(4), 441–450.

King, K. P. (2012). Social media as positive disruption in education, e-learning and b-learning. In *Handbook of Research on Business Social Networking: Organisational, Managerial, and Technological Dimensions* (pp. 434–452). IGI Global.

Kumar, V. (2021). Emergence of disruptive technologies & their impact on marketing of products and services. In *Proceedings of the International Conference on Advances in Management Practices (ICAMP 2021).*

Lang, D., & Rumsey, C. (2018). Business disruption is here to stay—what should leaders do? *Quality-Access to Success, 3*(19), 35–40.

Laurell, C., & Sandström, C. (2014). Disruption and Social Media—Entrant firms as institutional entrepreneurs. *International Journal of Innovation Management, 18*(03), 1440006.

Matzler, K., Friedrich von den Eichen, S., Anschober, M., & Kohler, T. (2018). The crusade of digital disruption. *Journal of Business Strategy, 39*(6), 13–20.

Neelakandan, S., Annamalai, R., Rayen, S. J., & Arunajsmine, J. (2020). Social media networks owing to disruptions for effective learning. *Procedia Computer Science, 172,* 145–151. https://doi.org/10.1016/j.procs.2020.05.022

Neumann, M., Rauschenberger, M., & Schön, E. M. (2023). "We Need To Talk About ChatGPT": The Future of AI and Higher Education.

Outthinker. (2018). Scout, Juggle, and Ignore Technology to Out-Innovate the Competition: Lessons from CSAA. Retrieved from https://outthinker.com/2018/05/01/scout-juggle-ignore-technology-innovation/

Ovans, A. (2015). What we know, now, about the internet's disruptive power. *Harvard Business Review*.

Parth, S. C. (2020). Disruptive marketing strategy. *Iconic Research and Engineering Journals, 3*(10), 85–88.

Rambe, P. (2012). Constructive disruptions for effective collaborative learning: Navigating the affordances of social media for meaningful engagement. *Electronic Journal of e-Learning, 10*(1), 132–146.

Riemer, K., & Johnston, R. B. (2019). Disruption as worldview change: A Kuhnian analysis of the digital music revolution. *Journal of Information Technology, 34*(4), 350–370.

Schiavi, G. S., & Behr, A. (2018). Emerging technologies and new business models: A review on disruptive business models. *Innovation & Management Review, 15*(4), 338–355.

Sheppard, J. (2017). Business disruption: Technological advancements and their appeal to consumer preferences.

Sheriff, M. K. (2018). Big data revolution: Is it a business disruption?. In *Emerging Challenges in Business, Optimization, Technology, and Industry: Proceedings of the Third International Conference on Business Management and Technology, Vancouver, BC, Canada 2017* (pp. 79–91). Springer International Publishing.

Skog, D. A., Wimelius, H., & Sandberg, J. (2018). Digital disruption. *Business & Information Systems Engineering, 60*, 431–437.

Sousa, M. J., & Rocha, Á. (2019). Skills for disruptive digital business. *Journal of Business Research, 94*, 257–263.

Thakur, R., & AlSaleh, D. (2021). Drivers of managers' affect (emotions) and corporate website usage: A comparative analysis between a developed and developing country. *Journal of Business & Industrial Marketing, 36*(6), 962–976.

Van Wyk, H., Cruz-Antonio, O., Quintero-Perez, D., Garcia, S. D., Davidson, R., Kendra, J., & Starbird, K. (2023). Searching for signal and borrowing wi-fi: Understanding disaster-related adaptations to telecommunications disruptions through social media. *International Journal of Disaster Risk Reduction, 86*, 103548.

Walters, C. (2023). Disruptive marketing: What is it? *Copypress.*

Watters, A. (2014). Texting in the classroom: Not just a distraction. Edutopia.

Wysseier, J. (2019). *Disruptive marketing: What It is and why you need it.* Linkedin.

Zhang, F., & Zhu, L. (2021). Social media strategic capability, organizational unlearning, and disruptive innovation of SMEs: The moderating roles of TMT heterogeneity and environmental dynamism. *Journal of Business Research, 133*, 183–193.

The Best Change Models for Asian Business and Management

Ayşe Meriç Yazıcı

Abstract Change is an inevitable but difficult aspect of a growing business. Change management models are concepts, theories, methodologies, and strategies that provide an in-depth approach to organizational change. Change management strategies in Asia must take into account the unique cultural, economic, and political factors that exist in the region. Asia is a diverse region with many different cultures, languages, and traditions. It is important to understand these cultural differences in order to develop effective change management strategies. Understanding the basic principles of Asian change management models and frameworks enables organizations to draw on best practices, tactics, and strategies that they can rely on when facilitating change projects. Relying on the foundations of these change models allows organizations to develop more effective, strategic, and contextual change initiatives. There are a variety of established models available today. The challenge is to find the most appropriate change model for the organization. In this study, Lewin's change management model, the McKinsey 7-S model, ADKAR change management model, the Kubler-Ross change curve, Kotter's 8-step theory, and Deming Cycle (PDCA) change models are designed to serve as compasses to ensure adoption of new processes and maximize return on investment for business process changes.

Keywords Change · Change management models · Asian business

Introduction

When societies are analyzed through historical processes, they have been in change and development in social, cultural, political, and economic dimensions (Strangleman, 2016). Every change, no matter for what reason it is triggered, causes a disruption of balance in the area where it takes place. This means the deterioration of the relationships that people, organizations, and the environment develop with

---

A. M. Yazıcı (✉)
Department of International Trade and Business Administration, Istanbul Gelisim University, Istanbul, Turkey
e-mail: ayazici@gelisim.edu.tr

© The Author(s), under exclusive license to Springer Nature Singapore Pte Ltd. 2024
T. Endress and Y. F. Badir (eds.), *Business and Management in Asia: Disruption and Change*, https://doi.org/10.1007/978-981-99-9371-0_2

each other. For the disrupted relations, the parties try to adapt to the new situation and re-establish a balance by redeveloping their relations with each other. Achieving balance means the realization of change (Rüsen, 2012).

Asia is a continent with many countries and different cultures. Therefore, perspectives on change management may differ across the region. Asian cultures often prioritize stability, tradition, and harmony. As a result, there may be a greater emphasis on maintaining the status quo and being cautious about change (Garcia et al., 2014). Asian cultures often have a long-term orientation and focus on sustainable growth and stability rather than immediate results. This perspective can influence change management approaches by emphasizing gradual and incremental change rather than sudden, disruptive change (Whitley, 1990). Asian societies often value collective identity and group cohesion. This can influence change management efforts by emphasizing the collective benefit of changes rather than individual interests. Collaborative decision-making involving key stakeholders and encouraging the participation of employees or community members is often seen as crucial for successful change implementation (Guan et al., 2005). Business and management in Asia have experienced significant disruption and change in recent decades. Several factors are contributing to this transformative landscape, including technological advances (Gomber et al., 2018), changing demographics (Chatterjee & Ghosal, 2014), evolving consumer behavior (Kim et al., 2002; Kundu, 2009) and geopolitical developments (Kim, 2019; Krishna, 2018).

To navigate the disruptions and changes in Asia, businesses and executives need to adopt a forward-thinking approach. Embracing digital transformation, staying abreast of emerging technologies, understanding local consumer preferences, and building agile and flexible organizations are key factors for success in the dynamic Asian market. It is important to note that these observations are generalized and may not apply equally to all Asian countries or organizations. Each country and organization in Asia may have its unique perspective on change management, influenced by factors such as cultural diversity, economic development, and historical context. Change and change management in organizations may seem interchangeable, but there are important differences between the two, and in the absence of a clear boundary, people may lack clarity about what is required to drive a change initiative forward. In this context, this study addresses change management models that can help improve the deterioration of business and management in Asia.

The Concept of Change

The concept of change refers to the process or act of moving from one state, condition, or form to another (Iverson, 1996). Change is a natural part of life and is observed in various aspects of human existence, including personal, social, cultural, organizational, and natural phenomena. Change can occur at different scales, ranging from individual transformations to broader societal changes (Yazıcı, 2022). The change covers a wide range of dimensions, including physical, emotional, psychological, social, economic, political, and environmental aspects. Change can be driven by various factors such as technological advances, cultural changes, economic trends, scientific discoveries, political developments, or personal experiences (Jansen, 2000).

Understanding and managing change effectively is a critical skill in a variety of fields, including leadership, management, psychology, sociology, and organizational development. It involves recognizing the need for change, analyzing the current situation and desired outcomes, planning and implementing strategies, monitoring progress, and adapting as necessary. Change management frameworks and methodologies have been developed to guide individuals and organizations through the complexity of change, promote successful transitions, and minimize potential disruptions (Al-Haddad & Kotnour, 2015).

Change Management

Change management refers to the process of planning, implementing, and leading individuals, teams, and organizations through a significant transition or transformation. It involves understanding and addressing the human side of change to ensure its successful adoption and integration within an organization (Moran & Brightman, 2001). Effective change management helps organizations navigate through changes in strategy, technology, processes, structure, or culture. It involves managing resistance to change, communicating the need for change, and providing support to individuals and teams as they adapt to new ways of working (Stouten et al., 2018). Change management is a dynamic process that requires flexibility, adaptability, and continuous improvement. By following these principles and practices, organizations can increase the likelihood of successful change implementation and minimize resistance and disruption (Revenio & Jalagat, 2015).

Change management is the deviation of an organization from the status quo or uniform trends (Huber & Glick, 1993). Organizations should manage change to prevent change from being a problem. Change management is simply the art of managing change. In other words, change management is planning the change process in the organization, determining an appropriate strategy, and implementing the change around a systematic model. Therefore, the purpose of the change is to transform the organization into a more competitive, more effective, and higher-performing one (Gill, 2003). In this respect, change management is a discipline that enables businesses and employees to efficiently achieve performance goals such as creativity and market share. This process involves achieving and sustaining change objectives by developing the right change strategies, implementation models and processes, organizational structures, organizational culture, competencies, and employees (Worren & Moore, 1999).

Theories of Change Management

Change management is an important field of study to examine the application of existing innovators to a constantly changing world. Models and processes in change management contribute to success with new plans in a challenging environment. In this part of the study, some change models are proposed for disruption and change in Asian businesses and management.

Lewin's Change Management Model

Lewin (1958) approaches the nature of the change process in three basic steps. The first step involves resolving the current level of behavior. The second step is called movement and involves taking action to change the social system of the organization from the original level of behavior or operation to a new level. The third step is called refreezing. This involves establishing a process that ensures that new levels of behavior are relatively safe from returning to previous modes of operation (Siegal et al., 1996). Despite its apparent simplicity, it has also been argued that Lewin's theory focuses on the magnitude of change while ignoring the speed of change and is therefore not applicable to radical processes (Dickens & Watkins, 1999).

Lewin's change management model can be effective in raising awareness among Asian businesses and management of the need for change and preparing individuals and the organization for the transformation that is coming. In Asian cultures, where hierarchical structures and respect for authority are often prominent, it is important to gain support from employees and stakeholders, highlight the benefits of change and emphasize how it is aligned with the overall vision and values of the organization (Phau & Chan, 2003). Asian organizations can face unique challenges due to cultural factors such as the often close-knit and risk-averse nature of the organization. To overcome these challenges, it is crucial to involve employees at all levels in the change process (Rao, 2019). Asian cultures often value harmony and consensus, so encouraging a participatory and collaborative approach helps to overcome resistance. Providing training, support, and resources to employees can increase their readiness for change and facilitate a smoother transition (Alexa, 2022).

In Asian businesses, where loyalty and long-term relationships are highly valued, it is crucial to ensure that changes are embedded and sustainable over time. Recognizing and rewarding employees who embrace change and demonstrate desired behaviors can further entrench the new culture. Leadership must also play a vital role in role modeling and continually reinforcing desired changes. It is important to note that Asian cultures are diverse and there may be differences in the application of change management approaches between different countries and contexts. Cultural sensitivity and adaptability are required when applying any change management model to Asian businesses. Understanding local cultural nuances, values and communication styles will enhance the effectiveness of change initiatives in these contexts. Overall, Lewin's change management model can serve as a valuable framework for guiding and implementing change in Asian organizations. By focusing on unfreezing, changing, and refreezing phases, organizations can navigate cultural considerations and successfully drive change in their specific contexts.

McKinsey 7-S Model

The McKinsey 7-S model is a research tool that takes into account the multidimensionality of an organization, team, and individual level. McKinsey's 7-S model consists of strategy, structure, systems, skills, personnel, style, and shared values (Chmielewska et al., 2022).

The strategy involves the transformation of the organization from its current position to its new position as determined by the objectives. Structure defines and determines roles, responsibilities, and accountability relationships (Singh, 2013). Systems are the formal procedures of the organization or project team. They include management control systems, performance measurement/reward systems, planning, budgeting, resource allocation systems, and information systems. Systems influence behavior because they are the mechanisms that affect the resources available for a particular entity, as well as the mechanisms by which individuals are rewarded and groups are measured (Spaho, 2014). Skills are the actual skills and competencies of employees. Personnel refers to the number and type of staff within the organization. Style is how key managers behave in achieving the organization's goals. Common goals refer to the central beliefs and attitudes of an organization (Sumbane et al., 2023).

When applying the McKinsey 7-S model to Asian businesses, it is important to consider the cultural context and unique characteristics of the region. Asian businesses need to develop strategies that are aligned with their specific market dynamics, competitive environment, and cultural factors. Asian businesses may face unique challenges, such as diverse customer preferences, government regulations, or cultural norms. It is essential to adapt strategy to these factors. Asian businesses often have hierarchical structures with decision-making concentrated at the top (Fregidou-Malama et al., 2023). This can lead to slower decision-making processes and limited empowerment of lower-level employees. Implementing a structure that allows for greater agility, delegation of authority, and collaboration at different levels can improve organizational effectiveness. Systems in Asian businesses should support the organization's strategy and structure. This includes processes, procedures, and technology that facilitate efficient operations and communication. Asian businesses often prioritize relationships and face-to-face interactions, so finding ways to balance traditional practices with modern systems can be beneficial (Rundh, 2021).

Developing and nurturing the right skills and capabilities in employees is crucial for Asian businesses. Investing in training programs, talent development, and cross-functional collaboration can enhance an organization's ability to adapt to changing market conditions and drive innovation. Building a diverse and inclusive workforce is important for Asian businesses to benefit from different perspectives and expertise (Wei & Nguyen, 2020). Talent acquisition, retention, and development practices should focus on attracting and retaining the best talent, regardless of their cultural background or gender. Leadership styles in Asian organizations may vary across different countries and regions. Understanding and adapting to local leadership styles, as well as adopting more modern and inclusive leadership approaches, can improve employee engagement and organizational effectiveness (Li et al., 2019). Asian businesses often have different cultural values and philosophies that influence decision-making and organizational behavior. These values may include respect for authority, emphasis on relationships, long-term orientation, and hierarchical structures. Understanding and adapting to these shared values is crucial for success.

ADKAR Change Management Model

ADKAR model consists of five elements that define the basic building blocks for successful change. These five elements are awareness, willingness, knowledge, ability, and reinforcement (Ali et al., 2021). ADKAR change management model is a framework that helps organizations and individuals navigate through change. It provides a structured approach to effectively manage and guide individuals through change, helping them to be ready, willing, and able to adapt and embrace new behaviors or ways of working (Hiatt, 2006):

While ADKAR model is not specific to any region or culture, its principles can be applied to Asian businesses or any other region, taking into account some cultural considerations. ADKAR model can be applied to Asian business and management as follows.

In Asian cultures that value hierarchy and respect authority, it is crucial to involve leaders and senior management in communicating the reasons for change. They can use their influence and credibility to emphasize the importance of the change initiative and its impact on the future of the organization. Once awareness has been created, it is necessary to create a desire for change among employees. In Asian cultures, where loyalty and collective cohesion are highly valued, it is crucial to emphasize how the proposed change is aligned with the long-term goals of the organization and how it benefits employees personally (Sogancilar & Ors, 2018). Emphasizing the potential positive outcomes for both the individual and the organization can help to foster a desire for change.

Improving the ability to implement change involves providing employees with the necessary resources, support, and tools. In Asian cultures where teamwork and cooperation are valued, fostering a collaborative environment can improve employees' ability to adapt to change. Encouraging cross-functional teams, peer learning, and mentoring can contribute to the development of necessary skills and abilities (Sharifirad & Ataei, 2012). The final step is to reinforce change by recognizing and celebrating successes, providing ongoing support, and monitoring progress. In Asian cultures that value recognition and maintaining a good reputation, recognizing and rewarding individuals and teams for their efforts can reinforce change and motivate greater participation. Regular communication, feedback mechanisms, and local contextualization can also contribute to sustaining change in the long term (Franco et al., 2002).

Kubler-Ross Change Curve

The Kubler-Ross change curve consists of five stages: denial, anger, bargaining, depression, and acceptance (Kubler-Ross, 1969). The Kuler-Ross change curve is now widely used to manage dramatic change and perceived crises, particularly in large organizations where staff is often faced with sudden news associated with major reorganizations. By understanding both personal and staff reactions to change, understanding one's position on the change curve can help manage the situation by maintaining perspective and objectivity and ultimately enabling leaders and followers to transition to the new normal (Corr et al., 1999).

The Kubler-Ross change curve can be applied to Asian business and management as follows. Individuals may initially reject or reject the need for change. In some Asian cultures, there may be a strong emphasis on stability, hierarchy, and tradition. As a result, employees and leaders may initially resist or downplay the need for change because of concerns about disrupting the status quo or challenging authority. As the reality of change sets in, individuals may experience frustration, anger, or resistance (Hon et al., 2014). In a business context in Asia, it is crucial to address any concerns or complaints openly and respectfully. Maintaining harmony and saving face are important cultural values in many Asian cultures, so finding ways to address anger and defuse anger without causing public embarrassment is crucial. Individuals may try to negotiate or find ways to prevent change or delay change (Markus & Kitayama, 1991). In a business context in Asia, this may involve seeking compromises or alternative solutions that balance the need for change with the desire to maintain stability or preserve existing relationships. Building consensus and involving key stakeholders in decision-making can help to reduce resistance.

As the full impact of change unfolds, individuals may experience a sense of loss or sadness. In an Asian business context, it is crucial to provide support, reassurance, and open channels of communication to help employees cope with these feelings (Henderson, 2003). Offering counseling or mentoring programs can also be useful. Individuals face change and begin to adapt. In an Asian business context, fostering a culture of learning, providing training opportunities, and celebrating successes can facilitate acceptance (Dana, 2001). Recognizing and rewarding individuals and teams for their adaptability and resilience can further encourage a positive attitude toward change.

It is important to note that the Kubler-Ross change curve is a theoretical model and individuals may not necessarily linearly progress through the stages. In addition, the application of the model may vary depending on the specific cultural and organizational context in Asian businesses. It is recommended to consider cultural differences, consult local experts, and adapt change management approaches to the specific needs and values of the organization and its employees.

Kotter's 8-step Theory

Organizations can increase their chances of success by strengthening their ability to change. Based on his many years of work, Kotter has implemented an eight-step process for leading change that contributes to the success of organizations in an ever-changing world. Kotter's eight steps include creating a sense of urgency, building a guiding coalition, developing a vision and strategy, communicating the vision, empowering broad-based action, creating short-term gains, consolidating gains and generating further change, and linking new approaches to culture (Kotter, 1995).

Kotter's 8-step theory is a widely recognized framework for leading organizational change. Kotter's 8-step theory provides a systematic approach to effectively managing and implementing change. Although the principles of Kotter's theory can be applied to organizations worldwide, they are particularly applicable to Asian organizations as follows.

In the context of Asian businesses, creating a sense of urgency may involve emphasizing the competitive environment and the need to adapt to changing market conditions. For example, emphasizing the rapid growth of emerging markets in Asia and the need to be ahead of the curve can help create a sense of urgency among employees. Asian cultures often emphasize collective decision-making and consensus-building. In this step, it is important to involve key stakeholders and influential people from different levels and departments of the organization (Lee et al., 2012). It is crucial to build a strong guiding coalition that represents different perspectives and can drive change. Asian businesses may need to adapt their strategic vision to align with cultural values and aspirations. Integrating cultural elements and addressing specific regional challenges can help make the vision more relevant and inspiring for employees (Zhao et al., 2021). It is vital to ensure that the vision is communicated and translated into actionable initiatives.

Effective communication is crucial in Asian cultures, where hierarchy and respect for authority are often valued. Communicating the vision and change initiatives through multiple channels such as town hall meetings, newsletters, and digital platforms is essential. Including leaders as role models and utilizing local language and cultural nuances in communication can improve understanding and acceptance. Asian businesses may face hierarchical structures that can inhibit employee empowerment. To address this, it is important to promote a culture of open communication, cooperation, and participatory decision-making (Yang, 2006). Empowering employees through training, delegating responsibilities, and creating cross-functional teams can encourage broad-based action and ownership of the change process. Celebrating quick wins is crucial to sustain momentum and build trust in the change process (Horwitz et al., 2003). In an Asian business context, recognizing and rewarding individual and team achievements can be particularly effective in motivating employees. These short-term gains help to reinforce the belief that change is achievable and beneficial.

Building on the momentum of early successes, Asian businesses should focus on consolidating gains and further integrating desired changes into the corporate culture. This may involve revisiting policies, processes, and performance management systems to ensure alignment with the new vision. Consistent reinforcement of the change message and continuous improvement efforts are key to sustaining transformation. Finally, to ensure long-term success, Asian businesses need to anchor changes in their organizational culture. This involves aligning desired behaviors and values with organizational systems and structures. Leaders play a crucial role in modeling desired behaviors and ensuring that cultural changes are deeply embedded in the organization.

Deming Cycle (PDCA)

Deming opposed the idea that Taylor's scientific management system should transfer the responsibility of quality to managers by making sharp distinctions between management and employees, and considered this understanding as an understanding that emphasizes quantity by pushing quality to the background and argued that the management system should give importance to the human factor and motivation (Garvin, 1988). Deming focused managers to concentrate on the variability and causes of problems. He played an important role especially in the teaching of total quality to the Japanese and in the development of the Japanese manufacturing industry, as a result of which the Deming Award was started to be organized every year in Japan (Garvin, 1988). Deming, who played an important role in the development and spread of total quality management, based total quality management on 14 principles that bear his name. These 14 principles are listed below (Deming, 1960);

(a) To ensure continuity in objectives for the development of services and products,
(b) To adopt a new philosophy of quality and continuous improvement apart from traditional methods,
(c) Stop depending on inspection to achieve quality,
(d) To stop rewarding work done only with money,
(e) To continuously improve service and production systems,
(f) To provide continuous training for better performance of the profession,
(g) Establishing leadership,
(h) Overcoming fear,
(i) Removing barriers between departments,
(j) Avoiding slogans and lectures,
(k) To abolish labor quotas,
(l) Eliminating the factors that prevent employees from feeling proud of their achievements,

(m) To prepare a rich training and self-renewal program,
(n) To take measures to ensure change.

The Deming cycle is an activity that utilizes the management by objectives technique. These activities are shown in a circle for better understanding. It is a system that ensures a better quality of work at every turn of the circle. The basic approach to achieving the goal is the PDCA cycle, which is systematized as "Plan—Do—Check—Action". The explanation of these cycles is given below (Jagusiak-Kocik, 2017):

Plan: Determining the goal answers the questions of how by whom, or by whom this goal will be realized. A plan needs to be developed to identify and define the problem, set objectives, and address the problem. This involves collecting relevant data, analyzing the current situation, and identifying the root causes of the problem. The plan should be specific, measurable, achievable, relevant, and time-bound (SMART).

Do: It is the implementation phase of the plan. This phase involves implementing changes, conducting experiments, and collecting data to test the effectiveness of the planned actions. It is important to document the process and the changes made during this phase.

Check: It is the stage of determining whether the changes in the implementation phase have achieved the desired result. It helps to determine whether the implemented changes resulted in improvement and, if not, to identify deviations or gaps. Statistical analysis and other quality tools can be used to evaluate the data.

Action: It means identifying and revising what is missing or incorrectly done. At this stage, appropriate measures are taken based on the findings. If the results are positive and the objectives have been achieved, the improved process or solution is standardized. If the results are not satisfactory, it is necessary to identify the reasons and modify the plan accordingly. This phase emphasizes learning from the results and continuously improving the process.

Asian businesses and managers can use the PDCA cycle as follows. Organizations set their goals, objectives, and strategies. They define what needs to be achieved and develop a plan to achieve it. For Asian businesses, the planning phase may involve setting specific goals and aligning them with region-specific cultural and market dynamics. In the "do" phase, the plan is executed. Asian businesses will implement the planned actions, allocate resources, and carry out the necessary activities (Andersson et al., 2014). This may involve training employees, utilizing technology, or changing processes to achieve the desired results. The "check" phase involves evaluating the results against the objectives set in the planning phase. Asian businesses will evaluate their performance, collect data, and analyze it to determine whether they are on the right track or if any adjustments are needed (Dahlgaard et al., 2013). This may involve monitoring key performance indicators (KPIs), conducting audits, or obtaining feedback from customers and stakeholders. In the final stage, "Action", Asian businesses take appropriate action based on the results and analyses conducted in the previous stages. If the desired objectives have been achieved, they can standardize and implement successful practices. If the results are not satisfactory, adjustments and improvements are made and the cycle starts again. This stage emphasizes the importance of continuous learning and adapting to changing conditions (Lee, 2002).

Asian businesses often place great emphasis on long-term planning, relationship building, and maintaining harmony within the organization and the wider community. The PDCA cycle aligns well with these cultural values by encouraging continuous improvement and a systematic approach to problem-solving. In addition, Asian businesses can benefit from the iterative nature of the PDCA cycle as it allows flexibility and adaptability in a dynamic and rapidly evolving business environment. The cycle enables businesses to continuously improve their processes, products, and services by encouraging feedback, collaboration, and learning from both successes and failures. In conclusion, the Deming Cycle (PDCA) is a valuable framework for Asian businesses as it facilitates continuous improvement, aligns with cultural values, and supports their long-term planning and relationship-orientated approach. By applying the PDCA cycle, Asian businesses can increase their competitiveness, operational efficiency, and customer satisfaction while adapting to changing market conditions.

Conclusion and Future Recommendation

Change management is a crucial process for organizations worldwide, including those in Asia. Below (Table 1) is a table to present a comparative analysis of Lewin's Change Management Model, McKinsey 7-S Model, ADKAR Change Management Model, Kubler-Ross Change Curve, Kotter's 8 Step Theory, and Deming Cycle (PDCA) models. This table will help to compare the characteristics, applicability, advantages, and disadvantages of change management models.

While there is no one-size-fits-all advice for change management, there are some considerations that may be particularly applicable to organizations and management in Asia. Here are some suggestions to help guide change management efforts in the Asian context:

1. Understand cultural nuances: Asia is a diverse continent with a wide range of cultures, traditions, and values. It is essential to recognize and respect these cultural nuances when implementing change. It is necessary to take time to understand local culture, norms, and communication styles to ensure that change initiatives are compatible with the cultural context. Understanding cultural nuances and aligning change management efforts with these nuances is critical for businesses in Asia. In this context, it is important to understand communication styles, respect for cooperation and community values, understanding leadership styles, training and training materials, patience and flexibility, soliciting local views and feedback, and respect for cultural celebrations and holidays. It should be remembered that each country and even each region in Asia has its own cultural

Table 1 Comparative analysis of change management models

Model	Basic principles	Applicability	Advantages	Disadvantages
Lewin's change management model	Unfreeze Change Refreeze	It has a simple and understandable structure	It offers a focussed change process	May proceed slowly and encounter resistance
McKinsey 7-S model	Strategy Structure Systems Skills Personnel Style Shared values	Suitable for large-scale organizations	It addresses all aspects of the organization	Can be complex and time consuming
ADKAR change management model	Awareness Willingness Knowledge Ability Reinforcement	Focuses on individual change and offers an approach tailored to personal goals	Provides a personalized and concrete roadmap	May be incomplete in addressing organization-wide changes
Kubler-Ross change curve	Denial Anger Bargaining Depression Acceptance	Focuses on individual emotional responses	Helps to understand emotional reactions	May not fit all change processes
Kotter's 8-step theory	Urgency Coalition Vision Communication Empower Short-term wins Consolidation Anchor	Suitable for complex changes in large organizations	Focuses on all layers of the organization	May require time and resources to implement
Deming cycle (PDCA)	Plan Do Check Act	Suitable for continuous improvement and quality control processes	It makes the improvement process cyclical	Can be complex in large organizations

Source: (Lewin, 1947; Kubler-Ross, 1969; Kotter, 1996; Deming, 2000; Alam, 2017)

differences, so it is important to customize your change management approach according to the region and local conditions. Close cooperation with local leaders and employees can ensure a successful change management process.
2. Encourage open communication: Establishing open and transparent channels of communication is vital for successful change management in Asian businesses. It is necessary to encourage open dialogue and create platforms for employees to share their thoughts and concerns. Cultural preferences for indirect communication or hierarchical structures that may affect the flow of information need to be considered. Understanding cultural differences, collaborating with employees,

training and effective communication, local leadership and mentoring, social responsibility and social sensitivity, using communication technologies, and evaluating and adapting feedback are important in this section. Every organization is different and change management strategies should be tailored to the culture and needs of the organization. These recommendations can be a starting point to support the change management efforts of businesses in Asia.
3. Involving key stakeholders: Hierarchical structures and respect for authority play important roles in Asian cultures. It is necessary to involve key stakeholders, such as senior managers and influential people, in the early stages of the change process. Their support and involvement can help increase acceptance and facilitate a smoother transition. Cultural sensitivity, persuasion and solidarity, persuasive communication, role and responsibility definitions, training and support, cooperation and participation, feedback mechanisms, patience and flexibility, celebrating successes, and long-term thinking can be effective in this section. Change management processes can be complex, but effective involvement of key stakeholders can be the key to a successful transformation. These recommendations can help you to navigate change management more effectively in the Asian context. However, the needs of each business are different, so it is important to develop a customized approach.
4. Build trust and manage relationships: Trust is a crucial element in Asian business cultures. In particular, developing relationships with employees and stakeholders based on trust and respect is key. It can be helpful to focus on building strong interpersonal connections and show empathy to gain support and cooperation during the change process. Cultural sensitivity, cooperation and participation, clarity and continuous communication, balance of traditional and modern approaches, long-term thinking, leadership by example, training and support, and feedback and improvement are important. These suggestions can help to guide change management processes more successfully for businesses in Asia, but it is important to pay attention to specific requirements and cultural differences.
5. Provide clear direction and purpose: It is necessary to clearly communicate the rationale, objectives, and benefits of the change initiative to employees. In Asian cultures, where a sense of purpose and collective identity is often valued, it is important to emphasize how the change aligns with the organization's mission and contributes to the greater good. Cultural sensitivity, community engagement and relationships, internal communication, training and skills development, leadership role, feedback and monitoring, sustainability and long-term thinking, dealing with change resistance, and celebrating success are important. These suggestions can help support change management efforts for businesses in Asia.
6. Offer support and training: Asian employees may need additional support and training to adapt to change, especially if it involves new technologies or processes. Examples include providing comprehensive training programs, coaching, and mentoring to help employees develop the skills and competencies necessary for change. Conduct needs analysis, develop training programmes, provide coaching and mentoring, provide role models, provide community involvement, consider

language and cultural factors, provide interim feedback, show patience, reward change, and design the change management plan with these contexts in mind.
7. Manage resistance sensitively: Resistance to change is a common challenge in any organization. In Asian cultures, where maintaining harmony and appearance is highly valued, resistance may be expressed indirectly. It is important to be sensitive to this and address concerns respectfully and constructively, focusing on collaboration and finding win–win solutions. Understanding and respecting cultural differences, open communication, leadership and role model behavior, training and skills development, making change simple and gradual, feedback and improvement, patience and flexibility. Change management can be challenging for businesses in Asia, but with cultural sensitivity and effective communication, it is possible to make the process more successful. Every business is different, so it is important to adapt these recommendations to suit the specific requirements of the organization.
8. Adapt to local regulations and practices: Different Asian countries have different legal and regulatory frameworks. It is necessary to ensure that your change management efforts comply with local laws and regulations. Adapting to local practices and customs can also increase acceptance and minimize cultural friction. Adapting to local regulations and practices is a critical part of being successful in change management processes for businesses in Asia. In this context, it is important to collaborate with local legal advisors, communicate with local business partners, cultural sensitivity training, collaborate with local business people, focus on sustainable business practices, local language and communication, flexibility and adaptability, and collaborate with local communities. Adapting to local regulations and practices in the change management process is an important step on the road to success. These recommendations will help support the organization's change management efforts in Asia. However, every situation is different and it is always best to develop a customized approach taking into account local conditions.
9. Celebrate successes and milestones: Achievements in the change journey should be recognized and celebrated. In Asian cultures, collective celebrations and acknowledgment of progress can foster motivation, morale, and a sense of achievement among employees. Rituals and celebrations, seminars and training, recognition and reward, open communication, community involvement, fun and rest time, and customization are important in this context. Celebrating successes in the change management process can increase employee motivation and promote a positive outlook on change. However, when implementing these suggestions, it is important to take into account the specific cultural dynamics of the organization and the expectations of its employees.

It should be noted that these recommendations are general in nature and may need to be adapted to specific countries, cultures, and organizations in Asia. Flexibility and an open mindset are essential to successfully manage change in diverse business environments.

Change management is constantly evolving as a field that aims to keep pace with the rapid changes and transformations in the business world. Apart from the models mentioned in this study, there are some recent trends in the field of change management.

Digital Transformation and Technology-Driven Change: Technological developments are rapidly changing business processes and ways of doing business. Businesses need to continuously use and update technology to stay competitive by adopting digital transformation. Change management now focuses more on digitalization (Kraus et al., 2021).

Flexible Working Models: The COVID-19 pandemic has shown how important remote working and flexible working patterns are. Change management requires adopting these flexible working models and taking into account the needs of employees (Chen, 2021).

Data-Driven Decisions: Change management is moving toward adopting more data-driven approaches to decision-making using tools such as data analytics and artificial intelligence. Data-driven decisions can increase the effectiveness of change processes (Sarker, 2021).

Sustainability and ESG (Environmental, Social and Governance) Principle: Businesses are focusing more on sustainability and social responsibility principles. Change management plays an important role in integrating these values into the organization and driving changes for a sustainable future (Aldowaish et al., 2022).

Global and Multicultural Working Environments: Organizations pay more attention to multicultural work environments when operating at a global level. Change management provides guidance on adapting and encouraging cooperation in such environments (Morris, 2023).

Human-Centered Design: Change management emphasizes adopting a human-centered approach when designing and implementing changes. It is important to understand the needs and emotional reactions of employees and integrate this information into change processes (Nguyen Ngoc et al., 2022).

These trends reflect the efforts of businesses to adapt to changing conditions and achieve sustainable success. Change management can help organizations successfully navigate change by closely following these trends.

References

Aldowaish, A., Kokuryo, J., Almazyad, O., & Goi, H. C. (2022). Environmental, social, and governance integration into the business model: Literature review and research agenda. *Sustainability, 14*(5), 2959.

Alam, P. A. (2017). Measuring Organizational effectiveness through performance management systems and Mckinsey's 7S model. *Asian Journal Management, 8*(4), 1280–1286. https://doi.org/10.5958/2321-5763.2017.001949

Alexa, O. A. (2022). Intercultural communication within the global economy. A look at Asia, *Journal of Public Administration, Finance and Law*, Issue 25.

Al-Haddad, S., & Kotnour, T. (2015). Integrating the organizational change literature: A model for successful change. *Journal of Organizational Change Management, 28*(2), 234–262. https://doi.org/10.1108/JOCM-11-2013-0215

Ali, M. A., Mahmood, A., Zafar, U., & Nazim, M. (2021). The power of ADKAR change model in innovative technology acceptance under the moderating effect of culture and open innovation. *LogForum, 17*(4), 485–502. https://doi.org/10.17270/J.LOG.2021.623

Andersson, R., Hilletofth, P., Manfredsson, P., & Hilmola, O.-P. (2014). Lean Six Sigma strategy in telecom manufacturing. *Industrial Management & Data Systems, 114*(6), 904–921. https://doi.org/10.1108/IMDS-02-2014-0069

Chatterjee, D., & Ghosal, I. (2014). E-commerce in India: Future and Its Perspective: A Study. *International Journal of Scientific Research and Egineering Studies, 1*(4).

Chen, Z. (2021). Influence of working from home during the COVID-19 crisis and HR practitioner response. *Frontiers in Psychology, 12*, 4177.

Chmielewska, M., Stokwiszewski, J., Markowska, J., & Hermanowski, T. (2022). Evaluating organizational performance of public hospitals using the McKinsey 7-S framework. *BMC Health Services Research, 22*, 7. https://doi.org/10.1186/s12913-021-07402-3

Corr, C. A., Doka, A. J., & Kastenbaum, R. (1999). Dying and its interpreters: A review of selected literature and some comments on the state of the field. *OMEGA- Journal of Death and Dying, 39*, 239–259.

Dahlgaard, J. J., Chen, C.-K., Jang, J.-Y., Banegas, L. A., & Dahlgaard-Park, S. M. (2013). Business excellence models: Limitations, reflections and further development. *Total Quality Management & Business Excellence, 24*(5–6), 519–538. https://doi.org/10.1080/14783363.2012.756745

Dana, L. P. (2001). The education and training of entrepreneurs in Asia. *Education + Training, 43*(8/9), 405–415.

Deming, W. E. (1960). *Deming, sample design in business research*. A Wiley Interscience Publication.

Deming, W. E. (2000). *Out of the crisis*. The MIT Press.

Dickens, L., & Watkins, K. (1999). Action research: Rethinking Lewin. *Management Learning, 30*(2), 127–140. https://doi.org/10.1177/1350507699302002

Franco, L. M., Bennett, S., & Kanfer, R. (2002). Health sector reform and public sector health worker motivation: A conceptual framework. *Social Science & Medicine, 54*, 1255–1266.

Fregidou-Malama, M., Chowdhury, E. H., & Hyder, A. S. (2023). International marking strategy of emerging market firms: The case of Bangladesh. *Journal of Asia Business Studies, 17*(4), 804–823. https://doi.org/10.1108/JABS-12-2021-0504

Garcia, F., Mendez, D., Ellis, C., & Gautney, C. (2014). Cross-cultural, values and ethics differences and similarities between the US and Asian countries. *Journal of Technology Management in China, 9*(3), 303–322. https://doi.org/10.1108/JTMC-05-2014-0025

Garvin, D. A. (1988). *Managing quality*. Edge The Free Press Adivision Of Macmillan Inc.

Gill, R. (2003). Change management-or change leadership? *Journal of Change Management, 3*(4), 307–318.

Gomber, P., Kauffman, R. J., Parker, C., & Weber, B. W. (2018). On the fintech revolution: Interpreting the forces of innovation, disruption, and transformation in financial sevices. *Journal of Management Information Systems, 35*(1), 220–265. https://doi.org/10.1080/07421222.2018.1440766

Guan, L., Pourjalali, H., Sengupta, P., & Teruya, J. (2005). Effect of cultural environment on earnings manipulatin: A five Asia-pacific country analysis. *Multinational Business Review, 13*(2), 23–41. https://doi.org/10.1108/1525383X200500007

Henderson, J. (2003). Communication in a crisis: Flight AQ 006. *Tourism Management, 24*, 279–287.

Hiatt, J. (2006). *ADKAR: A model for change in business, Government, and our community*. Colorado: Prosci Research.

Hon, A. H. Y., Bloom, M., & Crant, J. M. (2014). Overcoming resistance to change and enhancing creative performance. *Journal of Management, 40*(3), 919–941.

Horwitz, F. M., Heng, C. T., & Quazi, H. A. (2003). Finders? Keepers? Attracting, motivating and retaining knowledge workers. *Human Resource Management Journal, 13*(4), 23–44. https://doi.org/10.1111/j.1748-8583.2003.tb00103.x

Huber, G. P., & Glick, W. H. (1993). *Organizational change and redesign: Ideas and insights for improving performance.* Oxford University Press on Demand.

Iverson, R. D. (1996). Employee acceptance of organizational change: The role of organizational commitment. *International Journal of Human Resource Management, 7*, 122–149.

Jagusiak-Kocik, M. (2017). PDCA cycle as a part of continuous improvement in the production company- a case study. *Production Engineering Archives, 14*, 19–22.

Jansen, K. J. (2000). The emerging dynamics of change: Resistance, readiness, and momentum. *People and Strategy, 23*(2).

Kim, J.-O., Forsythe, S., Gu, Q., & Moon, S. J. (2002). Cross-cultural consumer values, needs and purchase behavior. *Journal of Consumer Marketing, 19*(6), 481–502. https://doi.org/10.1108/07363760210444869

Kim, M.-H. (2019). A real driver of US-China trade conflict, The Sino-US competiton for global hegemony and its implicaitons fort he future. *International Trade, Politics and Development, 3*(1), 30–40. https://doi.org/10.1108/ITPD-02-2019-003

Kotter, J. P. (1995). Change: Why transformation efforts fail. *Harvard Business Review*, March-April, 59–67.

Kotter, J. P. (1996). *Leading change.* Harvard Business School Press.

Kundu, A. (2009). Urbanisation and migration: An analysis of trends, patterns and policies in Asia. *United Nations Development Programme Human Development Reports Research Paper, 2009/16.*

Kubler-Ross, E. (1969). *On death and dying.* Simon & Schuster Inc.

Kraus, S., Jones, P., Kailer, N., Weinmann, A., Chaparro-Banegas, N., & Roig-Tierno, N. (2021). Digital transformation: An overview of the current state of the art of research. *SAGE Open, 11*(3), 21582440211047576.

Krishna, H. S. (2018). Evolution of high-tech start-up ecosystem policy in India and China: A comparative perspective. *Asian Journal of Innovation and Policy, 7*(3), 511–533. https://doi.org/10.7545/ajip.2018.7.3.511

Lee, P. (2002). Sustaining business excellence through a framework of best practices in TQM. *The TQM Magazine, 14*(3), 142–149. https://doi.org/10.1108/09544780210425883

Lee, S. M., Olson, D. L., & Trimi, S. (2012). Co-innovation: Convergenomics, collaboration, and co-creation for organizational values. *Management Decision, 50*(5), 817–831. https://doi.org/10.1108/00251741211227528

Lewin, K. (1947). Frontiers in group dynamics. *Human Relations, 1*, 5–41. https://doi.org/10.1177/001872674700100103

Lewin, K. (1958). *Group decision and social change.* In E. E. Maccoby, T. M. Newcomb, & E. L. Hartley (Eds), *Readings in Social Psychology*, (pp.197–211) Holt, Rinehart & Winston, New York, NY.

Li, J., Mehdiabadi, A., Choi, J., Wu, F., & Bell, A. (2019). Operationalizing talent management in Asia: A multi-case study of multinational corporations. *European Journal of Training and Development, 42*(7/8), 499–516.

Markus, H. R., & Kitayama, S. (1991). Culture and the self: Implications for cognition, emotion, and motivation. *Psychological Review, 98*(2), 224–253. https://doi.org/10.1037/0033-295X.98.2.224

Moran, J. W., & Brightman, B. K. (2001). Leading organizational change. *Career Development International, 6*(2), 111–118.

Morris, S. N. (2023). Cultural diversity in workplace and the role of management. *American Journal of Industrial and Business Management, 13*(5), 380–393.

Nguyen Ngoc, H., Lasa, G., & Iriarte, I. (2022). Human-centred design in industry 4.0: Case study review and opportunities for future research. *Journal of Intelligent Manufacturing, 33*(1), 35–76.

Phau, I., & Chan, K.-W. (2003). Targeting East Asian markets: A comparative study on national identity, Journal of Targeting. *Measurement and Analysis for Marketing, 12*(2), 157–172.

Rao, I. (2019). Competing values in Asian business: Evidence from India and Dubai. *Journal of Asia Business Studies, 13*(1), 93–103. https://doi.org/10.1108/JABS-09-2017-0164

Revenio, C., & Jalagat, J. (2015). The impact of change and change management in achieving corporate goals and objectives: Organizational perspective. *International Journal of Science and Research, 5*(11).

Rundh, B. (2021). International expansion or stagnation: Market development for mature products. *Asia-Pasific Journal of Business.* https://doi.org/10.1108/APJBA-11-2021-0560

Rüsen, J. (2012). Tradition: A principle of historical sense-generation and its logic and effect in historical culture. *History & Theory Studies in the Philosophy of History, 51*(4), 45–59. https://doi.org/10.1111/j.1468.2303.2012.00646.x

Sarker, I. H. (2021). Data science and analytics: An overview from data-driven smart computing, decision-making and applications perspective. *SN Computer Science, 2*(5), 377.

Sharifirad, M. S., & Ataei, V. (2012). Organizational culture and innovation culture: Exploring the relationships between constructs. *Leadership & Organization Development Journal, 33*(5), 494–517. https://doi.org/10.1108/01437731211241274

Siegal, W., Church, A. H., Javitch, M., Waclawski, J., Burd, S., Bazigos, M., Yang, T.-F., Anderson-Rudolph, K., & Burke, W. W. (1996). Understanding the management of change an overview of managers perspective and assumptions in the 1990s. *Journal of Organizational Change Management, 9*(6), 54–80. https://doi.org/10.1108/09534819610150521

Singh, A. (2013). A study of role of McKinsey's 7S framework for achieving organizational excellence. *Organization Development Journal, 31*(3), 39–50.

Sogancilar, N., & Ors, H. (2018). Understanding the challenges of multicultural team management. *Journal of Business, Economics and Finance, 7*(3). https://doi.org/10.17261/Pressacademia.2018.954

Spaho, K. (2014). 7S Model as a framework for project management. *8th International Scientific Conference on Economic and Social Development*, 450–464.

Sumbane, G. O., Mothiba, T. M., Modula, M. J., Mutshatshi, T. E., & Manamela, L. E. (2023). The McKinsey's 7-S model framework for a assessment of challenges faced by teachers of children with autism spectrum disorders in the Limpopo province. *South Africa, South Arfican Journal of Childhood Education, 13*(1), a1129. https://doi.org/10.4102/sajce.v13:1.1129

Strangleman, T. (2016). Deindustrialisation and the historical sociological imagination: Making sense of work and industrial. *British Sociological Association, 51*(2). https://doi.org/10.1177/0038038515622906

Stouten, J., Rousseau, D. M., & Cremer, D. D. (2018). Successful organizational change: Integrating the management practice and scholarly literatures. *Academy of Management Annals, 12*(2), 752–788. https://doi.org/10.5465/annals.2016.0095

Wei, Z., & Nguyen, Q. T. K. (2020). Local responsiveness strategy of foreign subsidiaries of Chinese multinationals: The impact of relational-assets, market-seeking FDI, and host country institutional environmentals. *Asia Pacific Journal of Management, 37*, 661–692. https://doi.org/10.1007/s10490-019-096-66-3

Whitley, R. D. (1990). Eastern Asian enterprise structures and the comparative analysis of forms of business organizations. *Organization Studies, 11*(1). https://doi.org/10.1177/017084069001100105

Worren, N., & Moore, K. (1999). From organizational development to change managementthe emergence of a new profession. *The Journal of Applied Behavioral Science, 35*(3), 273–286.

Yang, I. (2006). Jeong exchange and collective leadership in Korean organizaitons. *Asia Pacific Journal of Management, 23*, 283–298.

Yazıcı, A. M. (2022). Holographic organizations: Thinking organizations like a brain. *International Journal of Business and Economic Studies, 4*(2), 102–111. https://doi.org/10.54821/uiecd.1202495

Zhao, C., Cooke, F. L., & Wang, Z. (2021). Human resource management in China: What are the key issues confronting organizations and how can research help? *Asia Pacific Journal of Human Resources, 59*(3), 357–373. https://doi.org/10.1111/1744-7941.12295

Ayşe Meriç YAZICI (Ph.D.) is from Istanbul Gelisim University, Istanbul, Turkey. She received her bachelor's degree in Public Administration and received her master's degree in Business Administration. She holds a Ph.D. in Business Administration and received her post-doctoral in Space Humanities research platform at Lund University, Sweden. She is also part of a group at the Blue Marble Space Institute of Science in Seattle, Washington, U.S.A. analyzing approaches to sovereignty in the space settlement of Mars. Her research interests comprise networks and partnerships in diverse disciplines. She has been working on biomimicry, business management, and space technology. She published many articles and book chapters both in Turkish and English. In addition, she is also editor-in-chief of the Scientific Journal of Space Management and Space Economics and on the editorial board of Studia Humana.

Driving Success in Asia: The Essential Role of Disruption

David Galipeau

Abstract Asia is primed for digital disruption to achieve inclusive growth and shared prosperity. This chapter argues disruption is imperative, going beyond change to transform systems. Asia's dichotomy of advanced and developing digital economies presents opportunities for disruptive solutions to bridge divides. The cultural diversity necessitates localized innovations catering to distinct user needs. Rapid technological advances also require embracing disruption to tap into emerging technologies. Digital disruption can unlock immense potential by triggering innovation, efficiency, and new business models. Case studies like Grab and Paytm demonstrate this impact. Pioneering entrepreneurs must lead disruption with tech and business models meeting evolving consumer needs. Digital literacy and skills initiatives are vital to empower citizens. Governments play a crucial role through policies and leadership to optimize disruption while ensuring inclusivity. AI and automation will be profoundly disruptive but their impact can be managed strategically. Disruption is key for Asia to fulfill its vast potential.

Keywords Digital disruption · Asia · Innovation · Digital divide · Digital literacy · AI · Automation

Introduction

Asia, characterized by its cultural diversity and vibrant socio-economic landscape, is positioned at the brink of a transformative digital revolution. Such a revolution transcends mere change, embodying Richard Branson's notion of metamorphic transformation penetrating societal structures and processes (Branson, 2022). In this context, disruption emerges as a catalyst for progress, dismantling antiquated practices and introducing innovative, efficiency-enhancing solutions, promising unparalleled growth and prosperity.

D. Galipeau (✉)
Asian Institute of Technology (AIT), Bangkok, Thailand
e-mail: david@galipeau.com

© The Author(s), under exclusive license to Springer Nature Singapore Pte Ltd. 2024
T. Endress and Y. F. Badir (eds.), *Business and Management in Asia: Disruption and Change*, https://doi.org/10.1007/978-981-99-9371-0_3

Christensen (2015) defined that disruptive innovation involves novel entrants targeting overlooked, underserved sectors, often at the market's base. While existing entities focus on incremental improvements for their higher-end customers, disruptive innovators establish a foothold in newer, lower-end markets. They offer affordable, user-friendly functionality, transforming business models and value networks. Over time, these innovative models are widely adopted by incumbents, triggering disruption. Thus, disruptive innovation, characterized by its accessibility, basic features, and affordability, is a powerful engine for positive change.

With over half of the world's population, much of it young, tech-savvy individuals primed for a digital future, Asia provides fertile ground for such disruption (World Population Review, 2022). This demographic advantage and rapid economic growth set the stage for technological adoption and proliferation.

Asia's cultural richness presents abundant opportunities for localized solutions. Digital technologies enable tailored solutions catering to the unique needs of diverse communities, fostering inclusivity and improving user experiences (Ramani et al., 2023).

Branson's (2022) perspective on disruption, viewed as a deep-seated change, aptly reflects the ongoing shift in Asia's core sectors. From manufacturing and agriculture to services and technology, digital disruption is reinventing the modus operandi of businesses, governmental operations, and individual lifestyles. Asia's journey toward a digitally driven future promises a landscape of opportunity and growth and is a testament to positive disruption's power.

For example, the following two case studies exemplify the potential for positive disruption in Asia:

1. Grab (Chalermpong et al., 2023): Grab, initially a ride-hailing service in Malaysia, has evolved into Southeast Asia's premier super app, offering extensive services from food delivery to digital payments. Its transformation, fueled by insight into local needs and a dedication to using technology to address them, represents positive disruption. Today, Grab is a transformative force in the region's digital economy, enhancing the lives of millions.
2. Paytm (Tikku & Singh, 2023): Paytm started as a prepaid mobile recharge website in India and has grown into the country's most significant digital goods and mobile commerce platform. It has disrupted the financial sector by providing a digital wallet service, enabling millions of Indians to make cashless transactions in a country where cash has traditionally been king. Paytm's success demonstrates how digital disruption can drive financial inclusion and transform the economic landscape.

The Imperative for Disruption: Asia's Unique Context

As we examine the globe, Asia is a region that stands out with its distinctive socio-economic composition, cultural diversity, and an accelerated pace of technological advancements (Nandkishore & Chandra, 2023). With this unique blend, Asia presents a compelling, intriguing canvas ripe for disruption (Boyer et al., 2023). However, this impending disruption is not just a beneficial occurrence that can be passively observed from the sidelines. In our rapidly evolving world, the most significant risk lies in not taking any risk, a philosophy echoed by Facebook's founder, Mark Zuckerberg (Zuckerberg, 2022).

This perspective is crucial to unlocking the immense potential in Asia, a region marked by its vibrant socio-economic contrasts. It houses economic giants like Japan, South Korea, and Singapore, lauded for their extensive tech adoption underpinned by robust digital infrastructure.

In stark contrast, it also includes developing economies like India, Indonesia, Cambodia, Lao PDR, Myanmar, and Bangladesh. Embracing this dichotomy and harnessing the opportunities it presents is an absolute necessity in the pursuit of progressive digital disruption (Ha & Chuah, 2023). These countries have a significant population still striving to overcome the hurdles to access essential digital services.

Although stark, this dichotomy reveals a unique opportunity for disruption, where trailblazing solutions can serve as the bridge to close the gaping digital divide (Boyer et al., 2023). Consequently, such innovative endeavors can catalyze and promote inclusive growth across these diverse economies.

In the case of Asia, the region's rich cultural diversity further amplifies the call for disruption (Ramani et al., 2023). With a plethora of languages, traditions, societal norms, and perspectives, a blanket, one-size-fits-all approach to technology adoption is unlikely to succeed or yield optimal results. Instead, there is a compulsory requirement for localized, custom-made solutions that cater to each distinct community's unique needs and preferences (Ramani et al., 2023). It challenges the status quo, spurs innovation, and carves solutions explicitly tailored to Asia's diverse cultural milieu.

Adding another layer to this complex scenario is the breakneck speed of technological advancements that Asia is currently witnessing (Oliver, 2023). Asia is leading advancements in mobile connectivity, e-commerce, AI, and blockchain. These technologies are disrupting traditional business models, requiring new paradigms of operation. To tap their potential, willingness to embrace risk, change, and disruption is key. Courage to explore the uncharted and experiment with avant-garde ideas is vital in this rapidly evolving landscape.

To repeat Zuckerberg's (2022) assertion that the most significant risk lies in avoiding risk altogether assumes relevance in this context. Clinging tenaciously to obsolete practices and outdated technologies is the quickest path to irrelevance and obsolescence. Instead, businesses, governments, and individuals must willingly venture outside their comfort zones, embrace and experiment with new concepts, and adapt promptly to rapidly shifting circumstances.

This open-mindedness and receptivity to change form the very heart of disruption. It is the critical catalyst required to break free from the inertia of complacency and push the boundaries of innovation. With this disruptive mindset, Asia's tremendous potential can be unlocked, propelling the region toward unprecedented growth and development and setting a remarkable example for the rest of the world.

The imperative for disruption in Asia's unique context is clear. The region's socio-economic makeup, cultural diversity, and the speed of its technological advancements make disruption not just beneficial but crucial. By embracing risk and change, Asia can unlock its vast potential and chart a path toward a prosperous digital future.

Digital Disruption: The Key to Unlocking Potential

Digital disruption, characterized by integrating digital technologies into various areas of business and society, holds the potential to catalyze a series of positive changes across Asia (Ince, 2023). This transformative force can spur innovation, enhance efficiency, and create new, more efficient business models, unlocking the region's immense potential.

The power of digital disruption lies in its ability to redefine how we live, work, and interact. Breaking down traditional barriers democratizes access to goods, services, and information, making them available to a broader audience. This democratization, in turn, fosters inclusivity, equality, and empowerment, driving social and economic progress (Matsushita et al., 2023).

Innovation is a crucial outcome of digital disruption. Challenging the status quo encourages creative thinking and problem-solving, leading to the development of novel products, services, and solutions (Armstrong, 2023). These innovations meet existing needs more effectively and efficiently and anticipate and respond to emerging needs, ensuring that businesses and societies remain relevant and competitive in a rapidly evolving digital landscape.

Efficiency is another critical benefit of digital disruption (Ha & Chuah, 2023). Digital technologies can significantly enhance productivity and reduce costs by automating routine tasks and streamlining complex processes. This increased efficiency boosts profitability and frees up resources that can be redirected toward more strategic, value-adding activities.

The emergence of new, more sustainable business models is a further testament to the transformative power of digital disruption (Armstrong, 2023). By reimagining how value is created, delivered, and captured, these models disrupt established industries and create new markets, driving economic growth and prosperity.

The rise of Low-Cost Carriers (LCCs) in the aviation industry is a prime example of this positive disruption (Bowen & Burns, 2023). By leveraging digital technologies to optimize operations and reduce costs, LCCs have made air travel affordable for millions who previously could not afford it. This has democratized air travel and stimulated demand, contributing to a staggering increase in air travel in Asia.

Case studies that illustrate the potential of digital disruption in Asia are:

1. AirAsia (Endress, 2023; Tao, 2021): The leading LCC in Asia has disrupted the aviation industry by using digital technologies to offer low-cost flights to a broad cut of the population. Its innovative business model, which includes online ticketing, no-frills services, and efficient operations, has made air travel

accessible to millions of people, contributing to a significant increase in air travel in the region.
2. Shopee (Jaipong, 2022): This e-commerce platform has disrupted the retail industry by supplying a platform for buyers and sellers to transact online. Its user-friendly interface, secure payment system, and efficient logistics have made online shopping convenient and reliable for millions of consumers. A valuable resource during the Covid pandemic.

As the rise of LCCs in the aviation industry demonstrates, the impact of this disruption can be profound, transforming industries and improving lives. As Asia navigates its digital transformation journey, embracing and harnessing digital disruption will be crucial to its success.

Shopee exemplifies technology's potential for positive disruption by transforming online shopping and enabling entrepreneurship. It democratizes e-commerce for SMEs and individuals by providing easy store creation and vast customer access without major investment. This promotes economic inclusion. Shopee also enhances customer experiences through features like integrated payments, reviews, and live chat. During COVID-19, it served as an essential platform for constrained businesses.

Shopee promotes digital literacy and skills development for sellers. Its innovations and infrastructure investments contribute to the digital ecosystem. In essence, Shopee's disruptive impact benefits businesses, consumers, and the economy, demonstrating technology's power to drive progress.

Entrepreneurs and Businesses: Pioneering Change in Asia

In the era of digitization that is now reshaping the world's operations, Asian entrepreneurs and businesses find themselves strategically poised at the forefront of this sweeping revolution. Rather than simply adapting to the transformation around them, these leaders are active agents of change (Abduvakhobov, 2023). They are not only shaping this change in basic assumptions, but they are also the engine that propels it forward. These trailblazing pioneers drive growth and steer their industries into uncharted territories by embracing innovative methodologies and cutting-edge technologies. They echo Steve Jobs' profound perspective that innovation distinguishes leaders from followers (Jobs, 2022).

Today, innovation is not merely a desirable trait. It is the lifeblood pumping through the arteries of any enterprise, the cardinal force stimulating growth, fostering competitiveness, and ensuring long-term success. It acts as the kinetic energy that fuels the dynamics of a digital economy and the catalyst that transmutes raw potential into tangible progress. Entrepreneurs in Asia understand this vital imperative and strategically align their business strategies to tap into the transformative power of digital technologies (Vaidya, 2019).

Asian entrepreneurs are using advanced digital tech to create groundbreaking products, services, and business models that cater to evolving customer needs and enhance experiences. They employ data strategically to gain insights, make informed decisions, and offer compelling personalized experiences. These businesses are also leveraging digital opportunities around connectivity and scalability to expand into new markets, grow their customer base, and boost revenue.

In this case, the concept of innovation transcends beyond the realm of technology. It is a mindset, a culture that incubates creativity, encourages risk-taking, and embraces change. Asian entrepreneurs exemplify this ethos, showing an unwavering resolve to explore the uncharted and disrupt established norms (Luu, 2023).

They are also instrumental in cultivating a culture of innovation within their organizations. They are grooming a new generation of thinkers and innovators by fostering an environment that values creativity, experimentation, and continuous learning. They invest in their people, arming them with the skills and tools necessary to thrive in this digital era. They are champions of a knowledge-based economy where human capital and technology synergistically fuel the process of innovation.

These groundbreaking endeavors by Asian entrepreneurs and businesses have not escaped global attention. They have successfully attracted investments from around the globe, cementing Asia's position as a worldwide hub of innovation and entrepreneurship. Their inspiring journey and successes ignite a spark among a new generation of innovators, leading to a domino effect accelerating the pace of digital transformation across the entire region (Ray, 2023).

Asian entrepreneurs and businesses are seizing the digital revolution as an excellent opportunity for unprecedented growth and development. They are stretching the boundaries of what is possible, showcasing their innovative prowess, and establishing Asia as a formidable player in the global digital economy.

In recent years, many innovative businesses such as Grab (ridesharing, payments), Garena (gaming), Lazada (marketplace), and Razer (gaming hardware) have grown up in the start-up-friendly economy of Singapore.

They truly personify the essence of Steve Jobs' insightful words, distinguishing themselves as leaders in a world swiftly embracing digital transformation. Their journey is a testament to the incredible power of innovation and the transformative potential it holds for businesses, societies, and economies. In this context, these entrepreneurs and businesses are the architects of 'positive disruptions,' using the power of innovation to inspire change and drive progress.

Case studies that exemplify the role of entrepreneurs and businesses in pioneering change in Asia are:

1. **Razer** (Lin, 2020): Founded by Min-Liang Tan and Robert Krakoff, Razer is a world-leading lifestyle brand for gamers. The company's triple-headed snake trademark is one of the most recognized logos in the global gaming and esports communities. Razer has disrupted the gaming industry with its cutting-edge technology and innovative products, demonstrating the power of entrepreneurship and innovation. In early 2020, Razer announced that it would be converting some of its manufacturing lines in China to produce surgical masks. The first batch of face masks shipped within two weeks. To boost supply and avoid supply chain

disruptions, Razer announced that it had set up Singapore's first fully automated mask production and packing line, completed in just 24 days.
2. **Tokopedia** (Ray, 2023)**:** Tokopedia, an Indonesian technology company with a mission to democratize commerce through technology, is a prime example of a business driving change. Founded by William Tanuwijaya and Leontinus Alpha Edison, Tokopedia has transformed how Indonesians shop and sell online, making it easier for anyone anywhere in Indonesia to start and grow their business.

Asian entrepreneurs are spearheading the digital revolution, harnessing technology to innovate and expand. They are pioneers, not followers, displaying courage and a spirit of innovation. As Asia undergoes digital transformation, these leaders will be critical in shaping the future of business and the region.

Empowering Citizens: Digital Literacy and Upskilling

The wave of digital transformation sweeping across the globe significantly surpasses corporate entities' boundaries, permeating ordinary citizens' daily lives. This transformation is a potent catalyst capable of empowering individuals, communities, and societies on a vast scale. It nurtures inclusivity, equality, and progress, uplifting human experience in myriad ways. Digital literacy and upskilling stand as two pillars central to this empowerment process, equipping the population with the essential tools to navigate and flourish within a digital future. Furthermore, digitalization democratizes opportunities, extending them to an increasingly diverse audience across various regions (Saputra & Siddiq, 2020).

Digital proficiency, defined as the capacity to utilize digital technologies adeptly and responsibly, has emerged as a pivotal aspect of today's digital age. What was once viewed as a mere advantage has become an essential requirement for active social engagement. By enabling individuals to access, comprehend, and utilize digital information and services, digital literacy considerably enhances personal and professional spheres of life (Saputra & Siddiq, 2020). It promotes proactive involvement in the digital economy, revealing fresh avenues for job opportunities, entrepreneurial pursuits, and educational advancements. Furthermore, it endows individuals with the necessary understanding to traverse the digital terrain safely and responsibly, ensuring their privacy is protected and strengthening security protocols.

Simultaneously, upskilling, denoting acquiring new skills or enhancing existing ones, holds equal significance in digital transformation. As digital technologies continue to evolve, disrupting traditional sectors, the demand for digital skills escalates (Li, 2022). Employment roles are evolving, growing more technologically reliant, and requiring a heightened level of digital acumen. The process of enhancing one's skills allows individuals to stay relevant and competitive within this ever-changing employment landscape.

Digitalization promotes career growth, lifelong learning, and expanded opportunities by increasing access to goods, services, and information. This enables innovation, entrepreneurship, and economic prosperity. Realizing a digital society necessitates widespread digital literacy and upskilling initiatives through collaboration on digital education and vocational training. Affordable, reliable internet access is also crucial. Furthermore, policies and frameworks that protect digital rights and ensure online safety are vital. Digital literacy should encompass ethical, responsible use of technology, privacy, security, and avoiding online scams (Saputra & Siddiq, 2020).

The global digital economy is also fostering a shift toward lifelong learning. The skills needed to navigate the digital landscape continuously evolve as new technologies emerge. Lifelong learning, enabled by digital technologies, allows individuals to adapt to these changes and remain competitive (Li, 2022). Digital platforms offer a surplus of learning resources, from online courses to webinars and podcasts, making continuous learning accessible and affordable.

Digitalization creates opportunities that must be inclusive. Divides based on age, gender, income, and geography should be bridged through user-friendly interfaces, affordable services, and rural internet access. As digital transformation accelerates, digital literacy and upskilling are critical for economic success, empowerment, inclusivity, and progress. We must strive for a digitally inclusive society where everyone has the skills and opportunities to thrive.

One notable example of a digital literacy improvement program in Asia is the "Pradhan Mantri Gramin Digital Saksharta Abhiyan (PMGDISHA)" initiative launched by the government of India in 2017. This initiative aims to enhance digital literacy in rural areas of India, targeting to train over 60 million people (Wankhede et al., 2022).

The PMGDISHA program is part of the Indian government's broader Digital India initiative and is operated under the Ministry of Electronics and Information Technology. The program's primary goal is to digitally literate one person in every family. The curriculum includes digital devices, the internet, browsing government websites, sending emails, searching the web, digital payment methods, and more (Wankhede et al., 2022).

The PMGDISHA program has shown remarkable results. By 2020, over 40 million individuals had been registered under the program, with many of them having completed the course and become digitally literate. The program mainly focused on marginalized communities, helping to bridge the digital divide and ensure inclusivity in India's digital transformation (Wankhede et al., 2022).

A large-scale initiative like PMGDISHA highlights the importance of government-led programs in improving digital literacy. Ensuring that a large segment of the population can navigate digital technologies effectively helps empower individuals, creating new opportunities for personal and professional growth. It also fosters a digitally enabled economy and society where citizens can participate fully in digital life, maximizing the benefits of digital transformation.

Digital transformation affects both businesses and citizens. Digital literacy and upskilling are key to equipping people for the digital future, empower participation in the digital economy and promote safe, responsible tech use. Digitalization also increases access to opportunities regionally. As Asia undergoes digital change, citizen empowerment is crucial. People drive digital progress not just as end-users but as agents of change.

Governments and Policies: Leveraging Disruption to Steer the Digital Revolution

Strong leadership and comprehensive policy guidelines are crucial to directing the trajectory of the digital revolution, optimizing its advantages, and alleviating associated threats. With Asia positioned at the forefront of this digital revolution, the governments in the region bear a significant role in shaping an inclusive and advantageous digital future (Hicks, 2017).

Government bodies in Asia bear the responsibility for providing a favorable ecosystem that encourages creativity while simultaneously safeguarding the rights and concerns of its citizens. These authorities can guide the digital revolution's direction through various tactics.

Regulatory structures, for example, function as essential instruments in molding the digital environment. They have the power to promote fair competition, uphold consumer rights, and advocate for ethical conduct in the digital space. This can ensure an equal-opportunity platform where innovative ideas flourish and consumer interests are protected (Meltzer & Lovelock, 2018).

In our ever-evolving digital landscape, where information is considered a highly valuable commodity, government institutions can implement stringent data privacy and security standards. By safeguarding citizens' personal information, they can instill confidence in the digital ecosystem and ensure the ethical use of data (Meltzer & Lovelock, 2018).

Governments play a key role in regulating emerging tech and fiscal policies that encourage innovation and catalyze the digital economy. Investing in digital infrastructure promotes universal access and bridges divides. Digital literacy and upskilling initiatives are critical to equip citizens with digital skills. Governments should lead by digitizing operations to enhance public services, transparency, and engagement. Adopting best data and cybersecurity practices sets standards. Governments can demonstrate the transformative potential of digital tech to improve processes and service delivery. They can also support digital inclusivity by ensuring accessible, user-friendly, and culturally aware digital public services (Chang & Das, 2020).

Governments also have a duty to protect citizens from the potential risks and harms of the digital world. This includes online fraud, cyberbullying, misinformation, and digital addiction. Governments can create a safer and healthier digital environment by designing clear policies and guidelines, providing low-cost education and support, and enforcing strict penalties for violations.

International collaboration is vital to the digital revolution's success. Governments can work together to harmonize regulations, share best practices, and address global challenges like cybercrime. They can also partner to advance cross-border research and innovation. Asian governments play a key role in steering the regional digital transformation through regulation, influence, and leadership. Effective governance and policies can shape an inclusive, equitable digital future.

By doing so, they can ensure that the digital revolution, far from being a disruptive force, becomes a powerful tool for progress and prosperity.

Case studies that illustrate the role of governments in steering the digital revolution in Asia are:

1. Digital India (Goswami, 2016): Digital India is a flagship program of the Government of India with a vision to transform India into a digitally empowered society and knowledge economy. The program includes initiatives to improve digital infrastructure, deliver government services digitally, and promote digital literacy.
2. Smart Nation Singapore (Chang & Das, 2020): Smart Nation is a Singaporean initiative to harness digital technologies to build a future of better living, stronger communities, and more opportunities for all. The initiative includes projects in areas such as digital identity, smart mobility, and smart urban habitats.

Effective governance and policies are crucial in steering the digital revolution. Asian governments can play a vital role in shaping a digital future that is inclusive, fair, and beneficial to all citizens. By regulating, stimulating, and leading the digital revolution, they can ensure that it serves the public interest, fosters innovation, and promotes social and economic progress.

As Asia continues to navigate its digital transformation journey, the role of governments will be more critical than ever. They are not just observers of the digital revolution; they are its architects.

The Future is Digital: Embracing Disruption in Asia

The future of Asia is undeniably digital. As the region stands on the brink of a digital revolution, embracing disruption and strategically harnessing digital transformation is essential for a prosperous future. This transformation is not merely about adopting new technologies; it is about reimagining how we live, work, and interact in a digital world. It is about creating a future that is inclusive, sustainable, and beneficial to all.

The digital transformation sweeping across Asia is poised to bring about significant disruptions, the most notable of which is the rapid rise of artificial intelligence (AI) and automation technologies. These technologies are not just emerging trends; they are powerful forces that are revolutionizing sectors across the board, from manufacturing to service industries, and are set to redefine the future of Asia (Norman, 2017).

AI and automation profoundly alter traditional business models and job markets (Neary et al., 2018). They are automating routine tasks, freeing human resources to focus on more complex and creative tasks. This shift enhances productivity and enables new forms of innovation as businesses leverage these technologies to streamline operations, improve customer service, and create new products and services.

For instance, in manufacturing, AI and automation optimize production processes, reduce waste, and improve quality control. They are transforming customer service in the service sector, with AI-powered chatbots managing customer inquiries and automation streamlining administrative tasks. In the financial industry, AI is used for risk assessment, fraud detection, and personalized financial advice, transforming how businesses operate and compete.

On the one hand, AI and automation can potentially increase productivity, efficiency, and profitability for businesses. By automating routine tasks, companies can reduce operational costs and improve efficiency. By using AI for data analysis and decision-making, they can make more informed decisions, improve customer service, and identify new growth opportunities. This can increase profitability and economic growth, contributing to Asia's prosperity. On the other hand, the rise of AI and automation also presents significant challenges.

One of the main concerns is job displacement (Neary et al., 2018). As machines can perform tasks previously done by humans, many traditional jobs may become obsolete. This is particularly true in sectors heavily reliant on manual labor, such as manufacturing and transportation.

Job displacement could lead to increased unemployment and social and economic disparity. Workers who lack the skills needed in a digital economy could find themselves left behind, widening the gap between the digital haves and have-nots. This could lead to social unrest and economic instability, undermining the benefits of digital transformation.

It is important to note that while AI and automation may displace some jobs, they will also create new ones. Jobs that involve complex problem-solving, creativity, and human interaction are less likely to be automated and could see increased demand (Mindell & Reynolds, 2022). Furthermore, the rise of AI and automation could spur the creation of new industries and jobs that we cannot even imagine today (Mindell & Reynolds, 2022).

Therefore, the challenge for Asia is to refrain from resisting AI and automation but to manage their impact. This requires proactive adaptation and strategic planning. Governments, businesses, and educational institutions must work together to equip the workforce with the skills needed in a digital economy (Mindell & Reynolds, 2022). This includes technical skills, such as coding and data analysis, and soft skills, such as problem-solving, creativity, and emotional intelligence.

Policymaking should also focus on ensuring a fair transition for displaced workers. This could include social security measures, such as unemployment benefits and retraining programs, as well as policies to encourage the creation of new jobs and industries (Mindell & Reynolds, 2022).

In summary, the rapid rise of AI and automation is one of the most significant disruptions poised to impact Asia. These technologies present opportunities and challenges, and how Asia navigates this disruption will shape its future. By embracing AI and automation and managing their impact through proactive adaptation and strategic planning, Asia can turn this disruption into a stepping stone toward a prosperous digital future.

In the private sector, businesses need to embrace AI and automation as tools for innovation rather than mere cost-cutting measures. By embracing these technologies to create new products, services, and business models, companies can drive economic growth and job creation, turning disruption into a stepping stone toward a prosperous future for Asia (Sayyadi & Collina, 2023).

Case studies that illustrate the potential of AI and automation in Asia include:

1. Alibaba's AI-powered Customer Service (Sayyadi & Collina, 2023): China's leading e-commerce company uses AI to handle customer inquiries. The AI system can understand and respond to customer queries, improving efficiency and customer satisfaction.
2. Smart Cities in India (IoT) (Wankhede et al., 2022): The Indian government launched the Smart Cities Mission to develop sustainable and inclusive cities that enhance the quality of life of its citizens. IoT plays a crucial role in this initiative, with sensors and connected devices used to improve infrastructure, manage traffic, conserve energy, and provide high-quality public services. For instance, in Surat, a city in Gujarat State, IoT devices monitor air and water quality, while in Pune, another smart city, sensors are used for intelligent traffic management and waste disposal.
3. Ping An's AI in Healthcare (AI) (Leavy, 2023): Ping An, one of the largest insurance companies in China, is leveraging AI to revolutionize healthcare. Its "AskBob" AI doctor supplies personalized healthcare advice to doctors, helping them make more accurate diagnoses. The AI system uses machine learning algorithms to analyze medical data and recommend treatment recommendations. This improves healthcare quality and makes it more accessible, particularly in remote areas with scarce medical resources.

Conclusion

This chapter shows disruption is critical for Asia to fully harness its potential in the digital age. Disruption goes beyond change to transform systems with innovative solutions. In Asia's diverse landscape, disruption can bridge digital divides and cater to localized needs. With rapid technological advances, embracing disruption is key to tapping into emerging tech.

Digital disruption promotes innovation, efficiency, and new business models to reshape industries for inclusivity. By democratizing access, it empowers society. Grab and Paytm illustrate disruption improving transportation, payments, and financial inclusion.

Pioneering entrepreneurs must lead disruption, using tech and business models to meet evolving consumer needs. This establishes Asia as an innovation hub. Disruption also benefits society via digital literacy and upskilling.

Governments play a crucial role through regulation, policies, and leadership to optimize disruption while mitigating risks. Supporting digital infrastructure and education enables inclusive digital transformation.

The rise of AI and automation will be profoundly disruptive. Their transformative potential can be harnessed strategically. Digital disruption is vital for Asia to achieve its vast potential and shared prosperity.

References

Abduvakhobov, A. (2023). Role and effects of entrepreneurs on economic development in Central Asia countries [Master's thesis, Torino University].

Armstrong, P. (2023). *Disruptive technologies: A framework to understand, evaluate and respond to digital disruption*. Kogan Page Publishers.

Boyer, S., Gudauskas, J., & Hamel, M. (2023). *Powering social enterprise with profit and purpose: The tandem hybrid*. Taylor & Francis.

Bowen, J., & Burns, P. (2023). "We make people fly": Low-cost carriers, economic development, and sustainability in Asia. In *Airlines and developing countries* (Vol. 10, pp. 111–136). Emerald Publishing Limited.

Branson, R. (2022). *The power of disruption: How to start a business revolution*. Virgin Books.

Chalermpong, S., Kato, H., Thaithatkul, P., Ratanawaraha, A., Fillone, A., Hoang-Tung, N., & Jittrapirom, P. (2023). Ride-hailing applications in Southeast Asia: A literature review. *International Journal of Sustainable Transportation, 17*(3), 298–318.

Chang, F., & Das, D. (2020). Smart nation Singapore: Developing policies for a citizen-oriented smart city initiative. *Developing national urban policies: Ways forward to green and smart cities*, 425–440.

Christensen, C. M. (2015). *The innovator's dilemma: When new technologies cause great firms to fail*. Harvard Business Review Press.

Endress, T. (2023). Open innovation ecosystem in Asia. In T. Endress & Y. F. Badir (Eds.), *Business and Management in Asia: Digital Innovation and Sustainability* (pp. 35–48). Springer Nature. https://doi.org/10.1007/978-981-19-6418-3_3

Goswami, H. (2016). Opportunities and challenges of digital India programme. *International Education and Research Journal, 2*(11), 78–79.

Ha, H., & Chuah, C. P. (2023). Digital economy in Southeast Asia: challenges, opportunities and future development. *Southeast Asia: A Multidisciplinary Journal*.

Hicks, J. (2017). Digital disruption in Asia: Power, technology, and society. *Asiascape: Digital Asia, 4*(1–2), 5–12.

Ince, F. (2023). The digital edge for entrepreneurship. In *Digital natives as a disruptive force in Asian businesses and societies* (pp. 1–21). IGI Global.

Jaipong, P. (2022). Business expansion: A case study of Shopee Company in Thailand. *Advance Knowledge for Executives, 1*(2), 1–18.

Jobs, S. (2022). *The power of innovation*. Simon and Schuster.

Leavy, B. (2023). Integrating AI into business processes and corporate strategies to enhance customer value. *Strategy & Leadership, 51*(2), 3–9.

Li, L. (2022). Reskilling and upskilling the future-ready workforce for industry 4.0 and beyond. *Information Systems Frontiers*, 1–16.

Lin, C. (2020). COVID-19: Gaming firm Razer to give out about 5 million free masks to Singapore residents. Channel News Asia.

Luu, T. D. (2023). Foreign direct investment and domestic entrepreneurship: Insights from Asia. *International Journal of Development Issues, 22*(1), 38–56.

Matsushita, K., Snower, D., Yamaguchi, S. Y., Elder, M., Tsudaka, M., Takemoto, A., ... & Okitasari, M. (2023). Integrated approach for well-being, environmental sustainability, and just transition.

Meltzer, J. P., & Lovelock, P. (2018). Regulating for a digital economy-Understanding the importance of cross-border data flows in Asia (p. 113). SSRN.

Mindell, D. A., & Reynolds, E. (2022). *The work of the future: Building better jobs in an age of intelligent machines.* MIT Press.

Nandkishore, N., & Chandra, N. (2023). *Dance of disruption and creation: Epochal change and the opportunity for enterprise.* Taylor & Francis.

Neary, B., Horák, J., Kovacova, M., & Valaskova, K. (2018). The future of work: Disruptive business practices, technology-driven economic growth, and computer-induced job displacement. *Journal of Self-Governance and Management Economics, 6*(4), 19–24.

Norman, D. (2017). Design, business models, and human-technology teamwork: As automation and artificial intelligence technologies develop, we need to think less about human-machine interfaces and more about human-machine teamwork. *Research-Technology Management, 60*(1), 26–30.

Oliver, D. (2023). *Economic impact of the digital revolution on the Asian economy.*

Prof. Megha Wankhede, Komal Kumbhar, Amogh Biniwale, NCRD's Technical Review: e-Journal, Volume 7, Issue 1 (Jan-Dec 2022) ISSN: 2455–166X.

Ramani, S. V., Athreye, S., Bruder, M., & Sengupta, A. (2023). Inclusive innovation for the BoP: It's a matter of survival! *Technological Forecasting and Social Change, 194*, 122666.

Ray, S. (2023). Can change management be disrupted through leadership strategies?: Evidence from start-up firms in Asia. In *Change management during unprecedented times* (pp. 100–127). IGI Global.

Saputra, M., & Al Siddiq, I. H. (2020). Social media and digital citizenship: The urgency of digital literacy in the middle of a disrupted society Era. *International Journal of Emerging Technologies in Learning (online), 15*(7), 156.

Sayyadi, M., & Collina, L. (2023). How to adapt to AI in strategic management. *California Management Review Insights.*

Tao, C. C. (2021). Good practices of AirAsia's preparedness entering endemic phase in business process management's context. *Journal of Strategic Digital Transformation in Society, 1*(1).

Tikku, S. R., & Singh, A. K. (2023). Financial disruption and microentrepreneurs: Empirical study on adoption of e-wallet among micro-entrepreneurs in India. *International Journal of e-Collaboration (IJeC), 19*(1), 1–14.

Vaidya, H. I. (2019). Social entrepreneurs: Innovative change makers in emerging economies of Asia. Emerging trends in global management and information technology, 255.

World Population Review. (2022). Asia population 2022. https://worldpopulationreview.com/continents/asia-population

Zuckerberg, M. (2022). *Great by choice: Uncertainty, Chaos, and Luck—why some thrive despite them all.* Harper Collins.

David Galipeau is a 35-year veteran of a hybrid career within finance, publishing, digital technology, and social development and has worked in Canada, Europe, and Asia as a corporate executive, dot-com entrepreneur, and social innovator. After completing his graduate education in the USA, Mr. Galipeau became a start-up entrepreneur during the dot-com era in the late 1990s. After two successful exits, Mr. Galipeau joined the United Nations in 2005, leading several cutting-edge innovation initiatives in Europe, Africa, and Asia-Pacific. Mr. Galipeau left the United Nations in 2019 and co-founded SDGx, an impact investment and advanced technology research organization based in Singapore, Australia, and Germany. Mr. Galipeau also lectures at several universities, including the United Nations System Staff College (UNSSC) and the Asian Institute of Technology (AIT).

Frontier Technologies Supporting Sustainable Development in Business

Anjali Malik, Deepika Dhingra, and Seema Sharma

Abstract Sustainable technologies encompass innovative solutions that consider the utilization of natural resources and foster economic and social advancement. These technologies aim to substantially reduce environmental and ecological risks while creating sustainable products. The primary aim of this chapter is to acquaint readers with cutting-edge technological advancements applied across different sectors and industries to effectively attain sustainability objectives. Sustainability has become a mainstream issue, and there is mounting pressure from regulators and policymakers to adopt more sustainability-related practices in all business processes. Technological innovations and advancements can significantly help businesses achieve this goal. This chapter presents examples of real-life organizations that depict how technology has integrated into their business strategy and processes & enabled them to achieve the objective of sustainability as well as other economic goals. The chapter highlights the application of technology by citing cases of frontier technologies were being adopted by companies businesses in various sectors such as agriculture, packaging services, manufacturing, construction, and logistics, achieve operational efficiencies and contributed positively to sustainability goals. It illustrates how businesses can derive tangible benefits from the adoption of newer technology which involves artificial intelligence and machine learning. The chapter serves as a source of inspiration for businesses of all sizes to implement these technologies in their operations. The goal is to achieve the Sustainable Development Goals (SDGs) and promote sustainability at the company, business, national, and global levels.

A. Malik
Institute of Management Technology, Ghaziabad, India
e-mail: malik.anjali21@gmail.com

D. Dhingra · S. Sharma (✉)
School of Management, BML Munjal University, Gurugram, India
e-mail: seema.smm@gmail.com

D. Dhingra
e-mail: mithudhingra@gmail.com

Keywords Sustainability · Disruptive technologies · Cloud computing · 3D printing · Enterprise resource planning · Internet of things · Artificial intelligence · Sustainable business

Introduction

The exploitation and consumption of earth's resources at the current levels is unsustainable. On one hand, it has depleted the earth's natural resources at a fast pace while on the other hand, it has resulted in polluting air, water, and soil resources at an alarming level. Analysis of data by World Bank has reported that intensive material consumption has resulted in more than 100 billion tons of raw material entering the system each year, which would eventually lead to an increase in global waste from 2.24 billion tonnes in 2020 to nearly 3.88 billion tonnes by 2050 (Report & Bank, n.d.). Another recent report by The World Bank titled "More Growth, Less Garbage" provides insights into potential waste generation under a business-as-usual scenario and suggests how countries can opt for sustainable practices to reduce waste. The World Bank's "What a Waste 2.0: A Global Snapshot of Solid Waste Management to 2050" report warns that without immediate measures, global waste could surge by 70% by 2050 as compared to current levels (Kaza et al., 2020). Environmental pollution from businesses and other human activities has grown into a global transboundary problem affecting air, water, and soil ecosystems and directly impacting human health and well-being (European Environment Agency, 2015). According to the report, there is a clear association between rising pollution levels and three primary human activities. These activities include the combustion of fossil fuels, predominantly carried out by the industrial and transportation sectors, as well as the utilization of synthetic fertilizers and pesticides in agricultural practices.

Furthermore, the report highlights the escalating utilization and intricacy of chemicals as another contributing factor to pollution. Thus, global efforts must focus on reduction in levels of activities related to all three major sources of pollution. In this context, it is needed that integrated comprehensive measures emphasizing on reduction in consumption of natural resources as well as using more sustainable agricultural and industrial practices to overall reduce the emission of harmful pollutants in air, water, and soil are designed. In the past decade, various global and local entities have collaborated to suggest and enforce policies and recommendations centered on pollution management, sustainable farming practices, and the exploration of efficient and sustainable energy solutions. In anticipation of emerging guidelines and stricter regulations for businesses to adopt more sustainable practices, businesses are focusing their efforts on adopting technological interventions that can help them align with the emerging need for compliance with those new regulations. Let us first look at the definition of sustainability and its interpretation for businesses.

In 1987, the *United Nations Brundtland Commission* defined sustainability as "meeting the needs of the present without compromising the ability of future generations to meet their own needs." (Nations, 2007). Later, in 1992 International Institute for Sustainable Development published a business variation of the above definition which states that implementing business tactics and operations that address the current requirements of the organization and its stakeholders, while concurrently safeguarding and augmenting the human and environmental resources essential for future endeavours. Based on the book "Business Strategy for Sustainable Development: Leadership and Accountability for the 90s," published in 1992 by the International Institute for Sustainable Development in collaboration with Deloitte & Touche and the World Business Council for Sustainable Development, formal recommendations can be derived regarding business strategies for sustainable development on the topics of demonstrating leadership, engaging stakeholders, environmental management, social responsibility, integrating sustainability, collaboration & partnership (Business Council for Sustainable Development Deloitte & Touche & International Institute for Sustainable Development) (1992). This definition urges businesses to adopt more environmentally and socially responsible business practices to reduce adverse impacts on society, while businesses must at the same time safeguard their economic development as well. To an extent, it appears that organizations are at a crossroads such that even though they realize the pertinent need to fit sustainable business practices into current business strategy, they feel this can compromise the objective of achieving greater economic development for the business. Evolving advancements in technology offer promising potential to help today's businesses achieve the dual objective of sustainability and economic development. Thus, the sustainability agenda within businesses today is furthered through the adoption of new technologies and innovations.

New technologies are supporting businesses to derive benefits not only in terms of being more environmentally and socially conscious but also bringing in operational efficiency, thus making economic sense as well. Innovations in digital technologies are helping businesses transform their activities, processes, and competencies leading to the evolution of new business models. Some of the recent advancements include technologies related to cloud computing, mobile computing, big-data analytics, data science, artificial intelligence, Internet of Things (IoT), cyber-physical systems, blockchain, machine learning, etc. Technologies are getting integrated at various levels of business strategy. The focus of integration is not only to improve the efficiency of the operations but also to adapt to the current environment and societal needs of sustainability. In this chapter, we discuss some of the recent technological advancements and their impact on business processes to help achieve the overall goal of sustainable growth.

Frontier Technologies Supporting Sustainability Goals of Businesses

Sustainable Enterprise Resource Planning

Enterprise Resource Planning (ERP) systems have firmly established themselves as indispensable to modern business management. The evolution of ERP from 1960s to the present day is marked by transitions from MRP to MRP II and then to comprehensive ERP systems mirroring the interplay between evolving business needs and technological advancements. Constant innovation by ERP vendors and technological breakthroughs has kept these systems in step with the dynamic needs of contemporary businesses. The successful adoption of ERP system by business organizations has not only led to enhanced operational efficiencies but also contributed to sustainability development goals by being able to reduce intensity of material use, reduce waste generation, and increase energy efficiency. **As an illustration**, ERP systems curtail paper consumption by seamlessly integrating information and communication across the organization. Additionally, they lead to a substantial reduction in fuel usage for logistics through efficient fleet management systems. ERP systems gradually evolved into Cloud-based ERP systems further cutting down on the requirement of space and energy.

Since sustainability has emerged as a non-negotiable business tenet in the current global milieu. Researchers eloquently drive home the necessity for businesses to weave sustainability into their core practices (Chofreh et al., 2014). The modern vision of ERP must surpass the traditional boundaries of operational efficiency. ERP systems must metamorphose to encompass environmentally sound, socially responsible, and economically feasible practices. Businesses need to embed sustainability in their core practices. In one of the research projects, a proposed sustainable ERP framework integrates supply chain management and uses Information Technology (IT) to monitor sustainability metrics, emphasizing technology's role in promoting sustainable ERP practices resulting in the continual evolution of ERP systems (Chofreh et al., 2018). The integration of Industry 4.0 technologies into manufacturing processes including sensors and control systems, enables the collection and processing of manufacturing data. Architecture and the application of the Dynamic Life Cycle Assessment (LCA) system, Enterprise ERP system with a LCA tool through a Business Intelligence (BI) software was applied in a case in a study. This not only enhances production monitoring and improvement but also has the potential to expedite the Life Cycle Inventory (LCI) phase of LCA. The case study involves an Italian ceramic tile manufacturer where the implementation of a Dynamic LCA system was highlighted. This system fits in ERP with a customized LCA device through BI software. Rigorous validation processes confirm the system's functionality and its accuracy in assessing environmental impacts, both statically and dynamically caused due to business operations. Overall, the Dynamic LCA system proves to be a valuable tool for evaluating and monitoring environmental impacts in the production process, aligning with sustainability goals (Ferrari et al., 2021).

Cloud Computing Technology (CCT) for Sustainable Development

Cloud computing evolved as a model that enabled users from different locations to access IT resources without having the need to set up a fundamental infrastructure. CCT is a game-changer for Small and Medium-sized Businesses. It allows them to access powerful computing resources without hefty infrastructure investments, benefiting sustainability goals (Kumar & Vidhyalakshmi, 2012). CCT transforms high capital expenses into predictable operational ones, promoting cost efficiency and reducing physical resource use. This flexibility also ensures cost-effectiveness and reduction in use of resources. Another benefit is accessibility and collaboration among teams in different geographical boundaries as they can seamlessly access data and collaborate, ensuring business continuity, even amidst disruptions.

Agriculture, a crucial sector in densely populated countries like India and China, has also embraced these technologies, ushering in the era of Smart Agriculture. The implementation of IoT and Cloud Computing in agriculture holds the promise of improving crop production, cost control, performance monitoring, and maintenance, ultimately benefiting both farmers and the nation. A research paper introduces the concept of a Smart Drone for crop management, where real-time drone data, combined with IoT and Cloud Computing technologies, plays a pivotal role in establishing sustainable Smart Agriculture practices. Integrating cloud computing technology can enhance project efficiency, streamline planning, and improve team communication. It also holds the potential to boost financial efficiency and output quality, while reducing project issues. By implementing the identified critical success factors, stakeholders in Malaysia's construction industry can achieve their project goals and foster smart development (Waqar et al., 2023).

One of the concepts that the pandemic Covid-19 taught us is smart classrooms. The integration of IoT and Cloud technologies in education facilitated to create smart and sustainable campuses. It emphasizes how these technologies enhance learning, and provide intelligence, security, and unified services, enabling remote access to assignments and lectures, and transforming traditional education for efficiency and sustainability. IoT-enabled Radio Frequency Identification (RFID) tags help locate lost items, and visitor ID cards equipped with Global Positioning System (GPS) modules allow tracking within the campus, managed by an integrated system with various data sources (Faritha Banu et al., 2020). Facial recognition via open-source OpenCV is employed to automatically update student attendance, comparing captured faces with a cloud database, enabling faculty to track and notify absences. The system simplifies attendance, homework, and assignment management, allowing faculty to post assignments, send notifications, and automatically track on-time submissions. IoT enables automatic control of classroom lights, fans, and electrical appliances based on student movement, optimizing energy usage and efficiency. Thus, it can be summarized that Cloud computing promotes sustainability by minimizing physical data centres, reducing carbon footprints, and aligning businesses with eco-friendly practices.

Digital Fabrication Technology -Three-Dimensional Printing (3D)

3D printing also known as digital fabrication technology, is a part of additive manufacturing that can create a physical object from geometrical representation by successive addition of material (Shahrubudin et al., 2019). This frontier brings potential to revolutionize the production lines in manufacturing sector by increasing speed and at the same reducing costs. 3D technology-based manufacturing systems can be situated near to customer locations minimizing the overall transportation costs. Launch of this technology has far-reaching implications for sustainability in manufacturing sector by reducing material inputs, reduction in use of energy, carbon emissions as well as reduction in waste generation. Other sectors use this technology are sustainable construction and agriculture. Both sectors are rapidly advancing, motivated by environmental consciousness and resource efficiency. In sustainable construction, the confluence of cloud manufacturing, IoT, and 3D printing is revolutionizing processes. 3D printing emerged as the game-changer in construction industry. While it is renowned for intricate custom designs, its real potential lies in revolutionizing infrastructure creation. It promotes sustainable manufacturing by minimizing material waste, energy use, and carbon emissions and has applications in sustainable manufacturing, air quality, water treatment, and alternative energy sources (Nadagouda et al., 2019).

Rapid population growth necessitates 10–30 million new homes annually and extensive infrastructure development. Concrete, the construction industry's primary material, depletes natural resources and contributes to 8–9% of global CO_2 emissions. Conventional construction generates significant waste from formwork, exacerbated by urbanization and industrialization, posing environmental risks. Improper disposal of such waste in landfills can contaminate groundwater with toxic heavy metals.

A study explores the potential of industrial wastes in 3D printed concrete, aiming to reduce waste and enhance material properties for printability, and explains how 3D concrete printing offers rapid construction solutions, aligning with Sustainable Development Goals (SDGs) concerning industrial innovation and sustainable urban living. The review article is valuable for academia and industry, focusing on cleaner production of 3D printed structures with industrial wastes. It may also serve as a reference for policymakers striving to achieve UN SDGs (Dey et al., 2022). Combining innovative technologies with sustainable practices shapes a progressive and practical future. Amid environmental challenges, this union provides hopeful, efficient, and planet-friendly solutions.

The Internet of Things (IoT) and Sustainable Businesses

IoT refers to a network that links various devices to the internet using specified protocols that facilitate data exchange and communication, enabling intelligent identification, location tracking, monitoring, and management. IoT has various fields of application including healthcare, agriculture, manufacturing, resource planning, and asset management to name a few. One of the studies presents a framework illustrating how businesses can leverage IoT and blockchain to foster invention and prospects aligned with the UN SDGs. These technological advancements are reshaping established business models, spurring start-up innovation, and giving rise to social enterprises with a pronounced social mission (de Villiers et al., 2021). Literature documents IoT connections in three categories, people to people, people to machine/things, things/machines to people all interacting through internet. This interconnectedness will help improve organizational efficiencies through optimization of resources, energy savings, and bringing quality efficiency and speed to the operations. In one of the studies, a framework was designed to address specific issues, leading to the creation of a Mixed-Integer Non-Linear Programming (MINLP) optimization model that minimized the overall rate of the virtual supply chain network. This model effectively addressed challenges in order packaging, handling, and transporting textile products from manufacturers to wholesalers (Prajapati et al., 2022).

Information and Communication Technologies (ICT) and the Internet of Things (IoT) play pivotal roles in the realization of Smart Homes (SHs) and Smart Cities (SCs). The incorporation of ICTs in Smart Homes and Smart Cities offers substantial societal and environmental advantages. These encompass heightened efficiency, decreased energy inefficiencies, reduced utility costs, heightened safety and security, improved mobility choices, and the creation of a sustainable urban environment through Vehicle-to-Grid (V2G) technology. Additionally, the integration of technologies like IoT and data-driven solutions can yield improved decision-making processes, more agile public services, and increased citizen involvement.

In the realm of Smart Homes, ICT and IoT enable:

(i) Home Automation: IoT devices, such as smart thermostats, lighting systems, and security cameras, are interconnected through ICT networks which can be remotely controlled to monitor these devices via smartphone apps, enhancing convenience, security, and energy efficiency.
(ii) Energy Management: ICT systems gather data from IoT sensors to optimize energy consumption allowing homeowners to make informed decisions about energy-efficient practices.
(iii) Healthcare: IoT-enabled health monitoring devices can transmit vital health data to healthcare providers, allowing for remote patient monitoring and early intervention.
(iv) Security: ICT networks enable the integration of IoT-based security systems, including smart locks, alarms, and surveillance cameras, enhancing home security, and providing real-time alerts.
(v) Voice assistants, such as Amazon Alexa or Google Assistant, allow for hands-free control of home devices and systems. Users can use voice commands to

manage lighting, play music, set timers, and control other connected smart devices (Abdussalam Ali Ahmed et al., 2023).

AI and IoT-Supported Precision Farming

Agriculture, an age-old practice, is transitioning towards a modern paradigm driven by the pressing need to nourish an expanding global population, while also addressing pressing ecological challenges. The intersection of emerging technologies such as AI, innovative irrigation methods, and sustainable farming techniques is a promising future for agriculture, as substantiated by a collection of seminal papers. IoT is crucial in real-time data monitoring, especially in intelligent watering systems. Leveraging advanced technology and automation can address water crises by efficiently using available freshwater. The technologies like IoT, Wireless Communications, Machine Learning, Artificial Intelligence, and Deep Learning can address agricultural challenges including crop diseases, storage management, pesticide control, weed management, and irrigation issues, offering solutions to enhance the agriculture field (Jha et al., 2019). Further, the incorporation of solar PV energy emphasizes the fusion of energy independence with environmentally sound farming practices.

Studies on drip irrigation—regarded as the epitome of precision agriculture—showcase the enhancements AI can bring. By processing complex datasets, AI refines drip irrigation strategies. This not only guarantees appropriate crop hydration but also prioritizes sustainable water consumption, which is a necessity in areas facing water shortages (Tymoshenko, 2017). Another study integrates Analytic Hierarchy Process (AHP), Multiple-Criteria Decision Analysis (MCDA), with Geographic Information Systems (GIS) tools to model site suitability for wheat, maize, and broad bean cultivation using modern irrigation. Applied in the West Nile Delta, Egypt, the aim was to choose the best crop and identify constraints for sustainable land-use planning (Abuzaid & El-Husseiny, 2022).

Nanotechnology, AI, and drones are revolutionizing agriculture. Precise sensors, coupled with AI, optimize irrigation, and predict weather. Drones with advanced imaging monitor crop health, soil conditions, and hydration, aiding in early threat detection. This integration of technology fosters precision agriculture, ensuring sustainable food production and optimal yields while minimizing threats and wastage. Using emerging models to address food security and promote SDG2 can offer crucial insights and strategies for sustainable agriculture and improved nutrition (Zhang et al., 2021). These advancements reflect the agricultural sector's evolution from conventional methods to precision farming, blending technology with best practices.

Take a reference of an intelligent farming system model that aims to support by offering greenhouse management using an Internet of Things (IoT) powered precision farming system. This framework enables agriculturists to remotely monitor and control various greenhouse essentials, such as soil moisture, CO_2 levels, light intensity, and temperature. Based on soil moisture values, the system can also issue commands to roll up or down the greenhouse doors or windows. Research portrays the architecture that consists of four layers: cloud, fog, edge, and sensor/device where each layer plays a crucial role in the system's functioning. The brief overview of the proposed model is as follows:

Sensor Layer: This layer comprises various sensors and actuators that are deployed in the field environment.

Edge Layer: The edge layer functions in such a way that connects the sensor layer and the fog layer. It incorporates a controller unit responsible for interacting with various sensors and actuators to gather data. Subsequently, this collected data is transmitted to the fog layer for additional processing.

Fog Layer: The main goal of the fog layer is to create analytical insights and decision-making models using the data obtained from the edge layer. It also provides control indications to the edge layer for governing the actuators.

Cloud Layer: The cloud layer displays a data depiction of sensors and actuators in the form of a user interface (UI) dashboard. Literature contributes to emerging precision agriculture (PA) research areas. These studies highlight that we are on the brink of a smarter agriculture era (Rokade et al., 2022).

A Glimpse of the Frontier Technologies and its Applications in Various Sectors

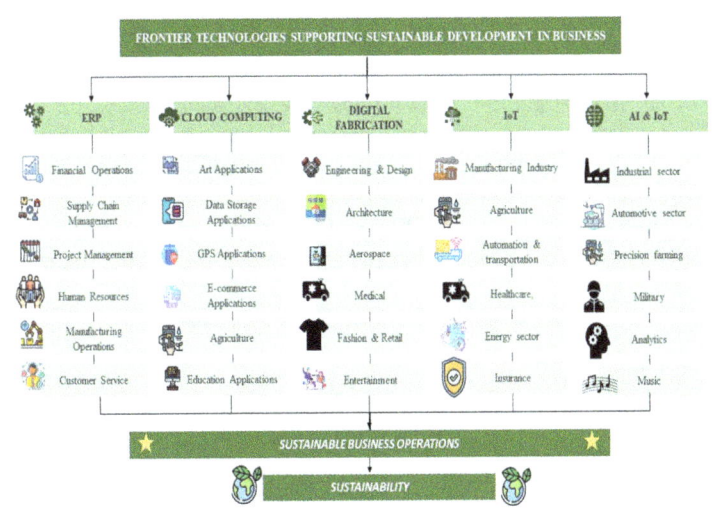

An overview of the applications of the frontier technologies discussed. *Source* Author's contribution

Case Studies

ICT-IoT Integration Smart Waste Management System in Indonesia

The current waste management system lacks detailed insights into municipal waste specifics, hindering efficient treatment. A holistic approach, involving stakeholders, is essential to address these challenges. Leveraging ICT and the IoT provides a modern solution, using local sensing, data analytics, and actionable intelligence to enhance waste management in developed countries.

The smart waste management system boosts decision-making and policy, promoting sustainable development goals (SDGs). It optimizes resource recovery, reduces virgin material and energy use, minimizes environmental harm, and upholds social values by employing skilled workers.

Jakarta's waste management system, overseen by the Provincial Environmental Service Agency, relies heavily on landfilling. The city's landfill, "Pyramid," employs basic water treatment and methane-to-electricity conversion. With over 10 million tons of waste produced annually, 74% being organic, Jakarta was anticipated to surpass its waste management capacity by 2019. Most waste originates from households and traditional markets. To address this, Jakarta's government is promoting eco-technologies, including composting, waste banks, and intermediate waste facilities.

Jakarta's sustainability goals in waste management include landfill water treatment, energy conservation, composting, and waste to Energy Project. These goals are directed toward efficiently managing the rapidly increasing waste, reducing environmental degradation, and ensuring long-term sustainability in Jakarta. Initiatives were taken by Jakarta government to improve waste management by using a 3R approach. Two waste management facilities were built in the form of temporary disposal centre (TPST) with transfer station and final disposal centre (TPA) along with other intermediate waste facilities. TPST has transfer station in which waste is separated into recycled waste (TPST 3R) and non-recycled waste with an aim to promote waste reduction, recycling, and efficient waste management practices (Fatimah et al., 2020).

Senior Aerospace Formerly Baxter Woodhouse and Taylor (BWT) takes Fused Deposition Modeling (FDM) Additive Manufacturing to the Skies

3D printing, or additive manufacturing, has heralded significant sustainability benefits for the aerospace industry which include material efficiency, reduced Supply Chain Footprint, Energy efficiency, and reduced overproduction. Situated in Greater

Manchester, UK, Senior Aerospace BWT, a subsidiary of Senior plc, is a distinguished AS/EN/JISQ 9100:2016 certified manufacturer known globally for its advanced ultra-lightweight, low-pressure air distribution system tailored for the aerospace sector. They cater to a diverse clientele that spans regional airlines, military aircraft, private jets, and rotorcrafts; this company boasts decade-long expertise in additive manufacturing.

Senior Aerospace BWT collaborated with Tri-Tech 3D which holds a prominent authority on 3D printing in the United Kingdom. Tri-Tech 3D integrated Stratasys FDM® 3D printing into their manufacturing process for aircraft interior components, replacing some aluminum parts. This shift resulted in notable benefits including reduced weight, cost, and production time, with potential cost savings of up to 75%. The technology facilitated production of flight-ready components with intricate geometries, revolutionizing aerospace manufacturing. It also allowed for lean inventory management, and customizing production quantities. The weight and cost savings achieved through FDM additive manufacturing have set a precedent for sustainable manufacturing. This innovation not only minimizes waste but also offers diversification possibilities into areas like automotive, indicating a sustainable and green future for aerospace production (Butterworth, 2018).

Maersk Collaborates with Tata Consultancy Services (TCS) to provide a Comprehensive IoT-Based Solution for Monitoring Refrigerated Containers (Reefer Containers)

TCS, as a leading global IT service, consulting, and business solutions organization, plays a significant role in streamlining and digitizing container shipping processes for many global clients.

Maersk, a global leader in ocean carrier and integrated logistics, recognized the critical need to enhance its monitoring of temperature-sensitive cargo like fruits, vegetables, and pharmaceuticals. Traditionally, the company relied on manual methods and third parties for detecting and resolving issues in their (reefers), leading to delays and higher costs. Recognizing the need for automation and real-time monitoring, Maersk collaborated with TCS to implement an IoT-based monitoring solution. TCS, with its profound expertise in container shipping processes, played a pivotal role in collaborating with Maersk to design a modular, tailor-made digital architecture.

TCS' solution combines real-time data from reefers with Maersk's enterprise system, facilitating rapid decision-making and implementing predictive algorithms for early issue detection. Using Microsoft's cloud IoT platform, the solution now oversees more than 385,000 reefers and 450 vessels, drastically reducing response times to potential issues.

From a sustainability standpoint, this digital transformation has profound implications. The new system reduces the risk of food wastage and ensures the safe transportation of crucial cargo like medicines. By maintaining precise ambient conditions inside containers, Maersk not only boosts its customer service but also promotes more sustainable and responsible business operations. By providing real-time insights into container conditions, Maersk can guarantee the integrity of perishable goods, reducing waste and supporting sustainable supply chain solutions. The contribution of TCS resulted in attaining SDGs in digital transformation, supply chain optimization, reducing operational costs, improving overall efficiency, and reducing their carbon footprint and waste ("Automation in shipping: Maersk sets benchmarks in reefer monitoring," n.d.).

International Business Machines (IBM) Cloud Case Studies: UBank

IBM's cloud computing facilitates scalable, efficient, and flexible digital solutions. It reduces infrastructure cost, streamlines operation, and supports rapid innovation, enabling businesses to adapt to changing needs while minimizing their environmental footprint. By offering robust and secure platforms, IBM's cloud empower organizations to operate more sustainably and efficiently.

UBank, an Australian direct bank subsidiary of the National Australia Bank, has revolutionized the banking industry by offering an online platform for savings and home loan applications. This innovation challenges traditional banking methods, providing customers the convenience of applying for loans anytime, anywhere. By transitioning to the IBM Cloud, UBank streamlined its digital operations, reducing the need for physical infrastructure, thus decreasing its carbon footprint. Following consultations with IBM's Watson and Cloud Adoption Leadership team, UBank introduced new projects within an IBM Cloud platform development environment. This includes the implementation of RoboChat, a virtual agent utilizing IBM Watson conversation technology to assist customers in applying for home loans. This minimizes the environmental impact associated with traditional banking—from paper waste to energy consumption. IBM's cloud solution ensures efficient use of resources, allowing UBank to scale its services without a proportional increase in energy or resource consumption. Additionally, cloud-based platforms offer enhanced longevity and adaptability, reducing the constant need for new hardware and the associated electronic waste. In the broader picture, by promoting digital banking and diminishing the necessity for in-person transactions, UBank, with IBM's assistance, indirectly reduces transportation emission for its customers. Through this strategic alliance, UBank not only enhances its customer service and operational efficiency but also significantly contributes to creating a more sustainable and eco-friendly banking environment. IBM's cloud computing significantly advanced UBank's pursuit of sustainability goals. While promoting digital innovation, this collaboration emphasized the significance of secure cloud-based solutions in handling sensitive customer data, highlighting IBM Cloud's capacity to drive innovation and operational efficiency in the banking sector. UBank. (n.d.)

A Glimpse of the Frontier Technologies with the Usefulness and Indicative Assessment Indicators of each

See Table 1.

Conclusion

During the past few decades, the world has faced a lot of uncertainty, ambiguity, and complexity in the context of climate change and the continuous depletion of world resources. Major technological innovations today are considered critical for managing sustainable business practices to address global issues such as climate change, depletion of natural resources, pollution, income equality, etc. In the recent past, we have observed very rapid development of technological interventions as a potential solution to the imminent threat of disasters due to climate change. This chapter reveals how some frontier technological innovations are acting as a driving force and a precursor to future sustainability. Technology has permeated every facet of both industrial processes and individuals' daily lives, playing a foundational role that intersects with all these domains. Technological innovations that have emerged have a potential to optimize processes and foster societal progress, thus it is essential to recognize technology as a catalyst for enabling sustainability.

In order to thrive amidst the digital revolution, agriculture, manufacturing, as well as service firms must enhance their digital capabilities being mindful of the economic, environmental, and social impacts. This process will ensure a balance between an industry's economic growth, environmental stewardship, and the well-being of the society into which it is integrated.

The initiation of a completely new business value proposition necessitates a genuine commitment to long-term viability. This commitment is primarily achieved through regulatory requirements; however, they must also overcome financial and knowledge constraints and convert their business models into green business models. As a result, AI, IoT, cloud computing, and other technologies can help to innovate business models and impact society's long-term development. Furthermore, policy-makers should also work to create incentives for a smooth and comprehensive digital conversion. This transformation necessitates changes to the strategy as well as the business model. The adoption of sustainable and digital practices at a firm level requires acknowledging the existing challenges that need to be addressed through structural reforms. Additionally, it is important to identify the specific benefits unique

Table 1 Innovations supporting sustainable development and measures of eco-efficiency

S no	Technological innovation	Definition	Usefulness in business process	Indicative assessment indicators	References
1	Sustainable Enterprise Resource Planning (ERP) Systems	S-ERP consists of both sustainability and decisional paradigms including environmental, social as well as economic indicators	Reduction in use of mineral and material intensity such as raw material, water, paper, fuel Reduction in use of energy intensity Reduction in waste generation	Environmental sustainability indicators such as carbon footprint, raw material use intensity, water use intensity, improved life cycle of the product Social indicators including health and safety of employees, labor welfare, etc Economic indicators such as financial performance, quality, costs	Chofreh et al. (2014) Chofreh et al. (2018) Ferrari et al. (2021)
2	Cloud Computing	Cloud computing is a model that enables shared pool of computing resources without investing in physical infrastructure	Resources sharing reduced material use Scalability of operations to a very wide network Reduces energy use as no in-house data centres Big data analytics to bring supply chain efficiencies, energy use efficiencies	Material use intensity Energy use intensity Data analytics for supply chain efficiency, waste reduction, etc. Economic efficiency	Kumar and Vidhyalakshmi (2012) Faritha Banu et al. (2020) Waqar et al. (2023)

(continued)

Table 1 (continued)

S no	Technological innovation	Definition	Usefulness in business process	Indicative assessment indicators	References
3	Three/Four-dimensional printing (3DP)	3D/4D printing is a method of additive manufacturing that incorporates intelligent materials from the onset, creating 3D printed structures and components	Reduction in use of material intensity, energy requirement, Carbon emissions Better monitoring of work, reduction in building time Increase in safety features during manufacturing process Reduced waste generation, possibilities of recycling and reusing the printed materials Reduction in cost involved	Raw material use intensity Energy use intensity Carbon emissions score Biodegradability of 3D printing filament Economic efficiency	Shahrubudin et al. (2019) Nadagouda et al. (2019) Dey et al. (2022)
4	Internet of Things	A system of partially autonomous devices that can interact and communicate amongst themselves in a manner that enhances resource utilization and improves the user experience through the efficient exchange of information	Equipment management performance Water management performance Reduces intensity of material use Reduces logistics cost by monitoring and optimization Effectively monitor recycling and energy management	Energy use intensity Water use intensity Material use intensity Economic efficiency	de Villiers et al. (2021) Prajapati et al. (2022) Abdussalam Ali Ahmed et al. (2023)

(continued)

Table 1 (continued)

S no	Technological innovation	Definition	Usefulness in business process	Indicative assessment indicators	References
5	Information and Communication Technology (ICT) and the Internet of Things (IoT) integration	A unified system model that utilizes IoT-enabled bins for efficient waste collection, aiming to decrease the operational expenses of the current municipal system	Reduction in cost of waste management and service Low-cost resource consumption Low carbon emission of waste management process Employing the right technology to convert urban waste into valuable resources or energy	Carbon emissions score Environmental impact, water pollution reduction Cost efficiency Economic efficiency through recycling and reuse	Fatimah et al. (2020)
6	AI and IoT supported technological innovations	Precision agriculture encompasses techniques for livestock management in addition to site-specific field practices using satellite GPS further supported by latest technologies such as AI and IoT	Appropriate crop hydration through drip and micro irrigation Use of nano sensors, IoT devices for water dispersion, weather deviation, soil mineral conditions	Water use intensity Minerals use intensity Reduction in losses due to early detection of diseases Early detection of change in weather conditions	Jha et al. (2019) Tymoshenko (2017) Abuzaid and El-Husseiny (2022) Zhang et al. (2021) Rokade et al. (2022) Fatimah et al. (2020)

Source Author's contribution

to the company that can arise from these changes, benefiting both the firm and its value chain. Integrating sustainability and digitalization into a company's strategy necessitates significant changes at the organizational level, accompanied by a transformation in the company's mission and obligations.

Summary

The chapter discusses the adoption of frontier technologies into business strategy such that it promotes environmentally friendly and socially responsible operations. These practices aim to minimize negative impacts on the environment, conserve resources, support social well-being, and ensure long-term economic viability. Information and communication technologies (ICTs) have the potential to expedite advancements in all 17 United Nations Sustainable Development Goals (SDGs). A portion of the chapter substantially talks about the digital technologies that have the potential to contribute to the fulfillment of SDGs. By minimizing environmental impacts, enhancing social well-being, and managing resources responsibly, companies can gain a competitive edge, improve brand reputation, attract environmentally and socially conscious customers, and contribute to a more sustainable future.

References

Abdussalam Ali Ahmed, Belrzaeg, M., Nassar, Y., El-Khozondar, H. J., Khaleel, M., & Alsharif, A. (2023). A comprehensive review towards smart homes and cities considering sustainability developments, concepts, and future trends. *World Journal of Advanced Research and Reviews*, *19*(1), 1482–1489. https://doi.org/10.30574/wjarr.2023.19.1.1530

Abuzaid, A. S., & El-Husseiny, A. M. (2022). Modeling crop suitability under micro irrigation using a hybrid AHP-GIS approach. *Arabian Journal of Geosciences*, *15*(13). https://doi.org/10.1007/s12517-022-10486-8

Automation in shipping: Maersk sets benchmarks in reefer monitoring. (n.d.). Tata Consultancy Services: Driving Innovation and Building on Belief. https://www.tcs.com/what-we-do/industries/travel-and-logistics/case-study/maersk-cloud-iot-platform-automate-reefer-monitoring-system

Butterworth, D. (2018). Aerospace takes FDM additive manufacturing to the skies. *Stratasys*.

Chofreh, A. G., Goni, F. A., & Klemeš, J. J. (2018). Sustainable enterprise resource planning systems implementation: A framework development. *Journal of Cleaner Production, 198*, 1345–1354. https://doi.org/10.1016/j.jclepro.2018.07.096

Chofreh, A. G., Goni, F. A., Shaharoun, A. M., Ismail, S., & Klemeš, J. J. (2014). Sustainable enterprise resource planning: Imperatives and research directions. *Journal of Cleaner Production, 71*, 139–147. https://doi.org/10.1016/j.jclepro.2014.01.010

Dey, D., Srinivas, D., Panda, B., Suraneni, P., & Sitharam, T. (2022). Use of industrial waste materials for 3D printing of sustainable concrete: A review. *Journal of Cleaner Production, 340*, 130749. https://doi.org/10.1016/j.jclepro.2022.130749

de Villiers, C., Kuruppu, S., & Dissanayake, D. (2021). A (new) role for business—Promoting the United Nations' Sustainable Development Goals through the internet-of-things and blockchain technology. *Journal of Business Research, 131*, 598–609. https://doi.org/10.1016/j.jbusres.2020.11.066

European Environment Agency. (2015). Increasing Environmental Pollution (GMT 10). *Environmental Information Systems, Gmt 10*, 8–11. http://www.eea.europa.eu/soer-2015/global/pollution/#additional-information

Faritha Banu, J., Revathi, R., Suganya, M., & Gladiss Merlin, N. R. (2020). IoT based Cloud integrated smart classroom for smart and a sustainable campus. *Procedia Computer Science, 172*(2019), 77–81. https://doi.org/10.1016/j.procs.2020.05.012

Fatimah, Y. A., Govindan, K., Murniningsih, R., & Setiawan, A. (2020). Industry 4.0 based sustainable circular economy approach for smart waste management system to achieve sustainable development goals: A case study of Indonesia. *Journal of Cleaner Production, 269*, 122263. https://doi.org/10.1016/j.jclepro.2020.122263

Ferrari, A. M., Volpi, L., Settembre-Blundo, D., & García-Muiña, F. E. (2021). Dynamic life cycle assessment (LCA) integrating life cycle inventory (LCI) and Enterprise resource planning (ERP) in an industry 4.0 environment. *Journal of Cleaner Production, 286*(Lci), 125314. https://doi.org/10.1016/j.jclepro.2020.125314

International Institute for Sustainable Development, Touche, D. &., & Business Council for Sustainable Development. (1992). Business strategy for sustainable development: Leadership and accountability for the '90s.

Jha, K., Doshi, A., Patel, P., & Shah, M. (2019). A comprehensive review on automation in agriculture using artificial intelligence. *Artificial Intelligence in Agriculture, 2*, 1–12. https://doi.org/10.1016/j.aiia.2019.05.004

Kaza, S., Yao, L. C., Bhada-Tata, P., & Van Woerden, F. (2020). What a waste 2.0: a global snapshot of solid waste management to 2050. *What a Waste 2.0: A Global Snapshot of Solid Waste Management to 2050*. https://doi.org/10.1596/978-1-4648-1329-0

Kumar, V., & Vidhyalakshmi, P. (2012). Cloud computing for business sustainability. *Asia-Pacific Journal of Management Research and Innovation, 8*(4), 461–474. https://doi.org/10.1177/2319510x13481905

Nadagouda, M. N., & Megan Ginn, V. R. (2019). A review of 3D printing techniques for environmental applications. *Advances in Ecological Research, 60*(218), 1–24. https://doi.org/10.1016/j.coche.2020.08.002.A

Nations, U. (2007). Framing sustainable development. The Brundtland Report—20 Years On. *Sustainable Development in Action*.

Prajapati, D., Chan, F. T. S., Chelladurai, H., Lakshay, L., & Pratap, S. (2022). An Internet of Things Embedded Sustainable Supply Chain Management of B2B E-Commerce. *Sustainability (Switzerland), 14*(9). https://doi.org/10.3390/su14095066

Report, L. G., & Bank, W. (n.d.). *Understanding Poverty PUBLICATION*.

Rokade, A., Singh, M., Malik, P. K., Singh, R., & Alsuwian, T. (2022). Intelligent data analytics framework for precision farming using IoT and regressor machine learning algorithms. *Applied Sciences (Switzerland), 12*(19). https://doi.org/10.3390/app12199992

Shahrubudin, N., Lee, T. C., & Ramlan, R. (2019). An overview on 3D printing technology: Technological, materials, and applications. *Procedia Manufacturing, 35*(August), 1286–1296. https://doi.org/10.1016/j.promfg.2019.06.089

Tymoshenko, D. K., & A. (2017). Studies in Computational Intelligence 912 Artificial Intelligence for Sustainable Development : Theory , Practice and Future Applications. In *Arabian Journal of Geosciences* (Vol. 10, Issue 17).

UBank. (n.d.). Retrieved April 3, 2021, from https://www.ibm.com/case-studies/ubank

Waqar, A., Skrzypkowski, K., Almujibah, H., Zagórski, K., Khan, M. B., Zagórska, A., & Benjeddou, O. (2023). Success of Implementing Cloud Computing for Smart Development in Small Construction Projects. *Applied Sciences (Switzerland), 13*(9). https://doi.org/10.3390/app13095713

Zhang, P., Guo, Z., Ullah, S., Melagraki, G., Afantitis, A., & Lynch, I. (2021). Nanotechnology and artificial intelligence to enable sustainable and precision agriculture. *Nature Plants, 7*(7), 864–876. https://doi.org/10.1038/s41477-021-00946-6

Prof. Anjali Malik is associated with the Institute of Management Technology, Ghaziabad, India as Associate Dean (Academic Operations). Her previous affiliations include Professor of Marketing with School of Management, Bennett University, Greater Noida, S. P. Jain Institute of Management and Research, Mumbai and Lal Bahadur Shastri Institute of Management, Delhi. She completed her Doctoral Degree from University Business School (UBS), Chandigarh in the year 2005. She has more than twenty-three years of teaching, training, research, and industry experience. Knowledge and practical expertise extend across the fields of marketing management, customer relationship management, and consumer behavior. Her research interests include consumer insights, consumer adoption process, sustainable consumption, etc.

Dr. Deepika Dhingra is an Academician, Researcher and a Finance professional with Ph.D. from Faculty of Management Studies, Delhi University. Currently working as an Associate Professor in Finance with BML Munjal University. She has over 15 years of experience across academia and industry. Dr. Deepika is skilled in Mergers and Acquisitions, Investments and Portfolio Management, and Financial Innovation. She has presented her research work at conferences organized by IITs, IIMs and her scholarly work has been published in various ABDC and Scopus indexed journals.

Seema Sharma is a full-time research scholar pursuing a Ph.D. in Finance at BML Munjal University, Gurugram, India. She holds a B.Com. (Hons.) and an M.Com. (Finance) from the University of Calcutta, an LL.B., and a B.Ed. from Rajasthan University. Her research focuses on valuing distressed companies within the Insolvency and Bankruptcy Code framework. Prior to her research journey, she has a teaching experience of more than eight years in middle school. Her research interest area includes valuation methodology, valuation of companies, bankruptcy prediction, financial distress, corporate governance, and financial distress.

Cultural Change at a Shipbuilding Joint Venture in Vietnam: Hard or Soft Value for Partnership?

Que N. Tran, Chuyen T. Nguyen, and Cat-My Dang

Abstract International joint ventures include two or more parties with different cultures and this joint venture practice has been employed in many international shipbuilding enterprises. Cultural differences may bolster the management and leadership to creative solutions to share knowledge and engage employees to drive attitude and behavior changes at organizational and individual levels. Change management is a pressing challenge in the intercontinental shipbuilding industry. Shipbuilding production has shifted significantly to Asian countries over the last four decades. This chapter illustrates how Dutch and Vietnamese managers have changed in three cultural dimensions of power distance, individualism and collectivism, and uncertainty avoidance in a shipbuilding joint venture in Vietnam. A culture change framework is developed to illustrate these changes over nine years of operation. This chapter recommends open communication in the organizational culture to foster employee engagement toward joint venture sustainability, technology usage to provide continuous trainings at home and host cultures for the competitive advantages, and the development of penalty-free policies as well as a low-risk-taking organizational culture with accountable autonomy for other joint ventures.

Keywords Joint venture · Culture change · Shipbuilding · Power distance · Uncertainty avoidance · Individualism · Collectivism

---

Q. N. Tran (✉) · C. T. Nguyen · C.-M. Dang
Department of Management RMIT, Ho Chi Minh, Vietnam
e-mail: que.tran@rmit.edu.vn

C. T. Nguyen
e-mail: chuyen.nguyen2@rmit.edu.vn

C.-M. Dang
e-mail: my.dang11@rmit.edu.vn

Introduction

Joint venture business is an international practice in the globalization that generates changes in management and organizational culture between involved parties. There is a call for more attention to understand organizational culture and organizational climate in shipbuilding industry that directly relate to various stakeholders such as employees and customers besides financial and technical performance (Gebhardt & Zilbershtein, 2006). The shipbuilding business is also facing rapid changes due to global competition and technological advancement. This chapter provides a case study of an international joint venture in shipbuilding industry between Dutch and Vietnamese partners that is of limited studies in relation to culture change in Asia to show what hard and soft values are gained at managerial level. The chapter contributes to extending the understanding of joint venture leadership, management, and human resource-related practices to leverage the organizational culture in this oligopoly industry.

There are many joint ventures in shipbuilding industry around the world such as Hyundai and local partners in Saudi Arabia—International Maritime Industries (IMI), Zvezda-Hyundai in Russia, Hyundai Vietnam, a joint venture between China Shipbuilding, Mitsubishi (Japan) and Wartsila (Finland) (Hwang, 2022; Thomson, 2007). Barkema et al. found "international joint venture longevity decreased with the cultural distance between a Dutch investor and a host country" based on Hofstede's dimensions of culture (Barkema et al., 1997, p. 437). The DMSY joint venture in this chapter is a case study that has shifted the management and leadership to reduce the power distance, change individualistic and collective approach among Dutch and Vietnamese managers, and foster efficiency when both parties collectively engage with the uncertainty avoidance. The results of the joint venture partnership over the past nine years have set foundations and accelerated cooperative development of the joint venture in the next four decades (VIR, 2022). This case study illustrates that organizations must manage the change well to flourish in a competitive business environment.

The following sections demonstrate a contemporary view of the Asian shipbuilding industry; external and internal factors that influence on shipbuilding enterprises; cultural change at international joint venture in Vietnam; and presents cultural change in the DMSY joint venture case. Recommendations for joint venture businesses and summary conclude the chapter.

A Contemporary View of the Asian Shipbuilding Industry and Vietnam Context

The world's top three shipbuilding nations in 2022 are China, South Korea, and Japan (Statista, 2023a). The global shipbuilding market is projected to increase by 3.2% annually between 2020 and 2030, while the market size was US$ 152bn in 2022 and predicted to reach US$195bn by 2030 (Statista, 2023b). China accounted for 49% of the shipbuilding orders in 2021 whereas South Korea received 39% market share (Statista, 2022). On the other hand, the shipbuilding demolition activity such as ocean-going dismantled vessels centered in Asia with 76% of the global ship scrapping activity in Bangladesh, India, and Pakistan (Statista, 2022).

At regional level, the maritime and shipbuilding industries have been prioritized in ASEAN members' national economic strategies such as Indonesia, the Philippines, Malaysia, and Vietnam (SmartComp, 2013). Indonesia government has envisioned to be a Global Maritime Axis in 2014 to collaborate in strategic diplomacy with China whose ambition is Maritime Silk Road since 2013 (Sd et al., 2018). ASEAN is an important hub of the world economy where the ASEAN's inward foreign direct investment stock accounts for 18% in manufacturing, 73% in services, and 9% in mining, oil, and agriculture (ASEAN, 2017; SmartComp, 2013). The shipbuilding cooperation between ASEAN member countries and European member states, United Kingdom, China, or within ASEAN members such as Indonesia and Singapore has emerged. The Philippines has become the world's fourth largest shipbuilder thanks to the international cooperation with Japan, South Korea, and Singapore (Negara, 2017).

Vietnam's shipbuilding is the world's fifth largest shipbuilding nation and shipbuilding is a major industry in Vietnam's economic development strategy up to 2030, with orientations toward 2045 (Negara, 2017; Vietnam Ministry of Finance, 2019). Vietnam has three ports, respectively ranked #26, 33, 50, among the world's top 50 container ports (World Shipping Council, 2023). Vietnam's shipyard has performed well during the last five years while ship production from other Asian members including the Philippines, Malaysia, Taiwan, and Indonesia declined (Laurent & Lee, 2022). Laurent and Lee (2022) also reported Vietnam has received new orders of shipbuilding from 25 countries during 2018–2021 and 49% of the contracts are from ship owners in Greece, Japan, South Korea, and the UK. Joint venture business in the shipbuilding industry is one of three categories of Vietnam's shipyards, besides subsidiaries of the Shipbuilding Industry Cooperation (SBIC) and other state-owned enterprises (Laurent & Lee, 2022). There are 20 state-owned shipyards and eight foreign shipyards active in Vietnam (Vietnam marine & offshore expo, 2023).

The next section illustrates external and internal factors influencing contemporary shipbuilding enterprises. The external factors include global competition and technological advancement for the shipbuilding industry. The internal factors position enterprise management challenge and cultural role in the joint venture. The following sections present DMSY joint venture case, and three dimensions of Hofstede's framework employed to reflect the DMSY case.

External Factors Influence on Shipbuilding Enterprises

The global competition in the shipbuilding industry has dramatically changed over the last four decades. The Toyota Production System was launched during the twentieth century to change the quality culture of the shipbuilding industry that directly competes with companies in Europe and the United States (Gebhardt & Zilbershtein, 2006). In the early twenty-first century, the shipbuilding capacity has expanded significantly to meet the sustained global economic growth. However, capacity-demand imbalance and low prices have pushed severely the shipbuilding enterprises' competition, especially in the financial crisis of 2008 despite the fact that Cournot oligopoly model is dominant in the shipbuilding industry (Shin & Lim, 2014). The recent global pandemic Covid-19 also affected how the shipbuilding industry adapted to continuously improve resilience using the Lean Six Sigma framework (Praharsi et al., 2021). Japan, Korea, and China have emerged to occupy a larger proportion of the global market and contribute an important role in each national economy (Statista, 2023a, 2023b).

Technology advancement such as virtual reality, 3D printing, autonomation, and green technologies is another external factor that has strong impacts on the shipbuilding industry in recent years and drives further this industry's competition. Jha (2016) reported technology impacts on refit and repairs, retrofits, and logistic chain improvements. Technology facilitates cost and time reduction with 3D printing for spare parts, automation applies artificial intelligence and robotics that will remarkably change the industry as a disruptive ship design and operations, and green technologies comply with the international regulations such as the International Convention for the Prevention of Pollution from Ships (Jha, 2016). Moreover, virtual reality applications in the shipbuilding industry are in a wide range from the ship design stage, commercial uses, shipyard management, to ship-owner management and naval shipbuilding management (Fernández & Alonso, 2015). Both global competition and technology advancement have impacts on shipbuilding firms' organizational culture that influence daily practice such as internal knowledge sharing and purchasing performance (Kvalsvik, 2012), accounting management (Johnson et al., 2009), concurrent engineering, design for safety, and product safety performance (Zhu et al, 2016).

Internal Factors Influence on Shipbuilding Enterprises

The overcapacity–demand uncertainty illustrated in the external factors requires building enterprises to develop a demand forecasting model for efficiency (Wada et al., 2021). International joint ventures (IJVs) have received attention from scholars because of their significant role in facilitating global business expansions (Mesquita, 2016) that shipbuilding enterprises can actively control to include in their demand modeling. However, this chapter focuses on cultural dimensions in the shipbuilding enterprise, particularly between the Dutch and Vietnamese partners in the Vietnam context.

An IJV involves the collaboration of partners from different cultural backgrounds to establish a new entity separate from, but owned by, the parent firms (Kobernyuk et al., 2014). IJVs also involve diverse ownership and shared control, in which partners contribute their distinct responsibilities to collectively pursue shared objectives (Li et al., 2009). IJVs present an ideal context for examining cultures because two (or more for some IJVs) partners from different national origins are in close juxtaposition, with the potential for conflict greater than for homogeneous cultural settings (Kogut & Singh, 1988; Shenkar, 2012). Reported survival rates for IJV business forms vary between 40–70% due partly to cultural conflict between partners (Yang, 2011). Cultural homogeneities may help IJVs to avoid issues and foster cooperation and trust between partners but cultural dissimilarities can lead to misunderstandings and conflicts, which can impede effective collaboration and damage relationships (Sirmon & Lane, 2004).

Cultural Change at International Joint Ventures in Vietnam

Vietnam's economic policy known as *doi moi* since 1986 (Harvie & Tran, 1997) resulted in a general growth in FDI. In 2020, Vietnam for the first time was named among the top 20 FDI destinations with an inflow of USD$16bn (Vietnamplus, 2021). Researchers have started to study Vietnamese work culture to understand its impact on international business as Vietnam was notably absent from famous studies on cultural dimensions such as Hofstede (1991), Trompenaars and Hampden-Turner (1998), GLOBE (House et al., 2004), or Schwartz et al. (2001). Accordingly, some researchers have characterized Vietnamese culture as collectivism, moderate uncertainty avoidance, and high power distance (e.g. Quang & Vuong, 2002; Ralston et al., 1999; Truong et al., 2017). Other scholars identified a certain set of characteristics attributed to Vietnamese individuals, such as that they are likely to be indirect in their communication with others, or high context, to avoid losing face (e.g. Borton, 2000). In addition, Vietnam shares cultural aspects that can be seen in China, such as guanxi—social networks and related reciprocity (Thang et al., 2007). Another recent study sheds light on Vietnam being recognized as a culture influenced by Confucian principles, emphasizing harmony and stability within a society, but Confucianism is strongly associated with both hierarchical relationships and collectivism (Truong et al., 2017). Especially, famous studies on cultural dimensions, such as Hofstede (2023) started to include Vietnam and they became useful tools to basically understand national culture between countries.

Many studies employed Hofstede's cultural dimensions and a cross-cultural perspective to understand culture at IJVs in Vietnam such as impact of leadership (Quang et al., 1998), comparison of managerial work values in collectivism and individualism dimensions between Vietnamese and Chinese, U.S. managers (Ralston et al., 1999), IJVs' performance due to cultural discrepancy (Thuc Anh & Minh

Hang, 2009), Vietnamese mangers' risk adverse in the uncertainty avoidance dimension (Hofstede, 2023; Nguyen, 2021). There are change recognition at different levels within joint ventures due to the cultural dimensions and the following section illustrates changes at DMSY joint venture.

Joint venture is a pathway to achieve the maritime strategy development by 2030 of the Government of Vietnam to access the latest knowledge and technology, job generation, and productivity improvement. This case study illustrates DMSY joint venture ownership ratio of 70:30 between a Dutch family-owned partner and a Vietnamese state-owned partner respectively. The DMSY joint venture has approximately 750 employees, producing mainly tugs and workboats up to 40 workboats annually. The Dutch side holds the General Director in charge of business strategy, primarily controlled production and management, whereas the Vietnamese side holds the Deputy General Director in charge of government relationships, handled tasks related to Vietnamese land, Vietnam laws, and human resource management. The next section describes a cultural comparative view between Dutch vs. Vietnamese (Fig. 1) with three distinct cultural dimensions of Hofstede's framework (1991) including power distance, individualism and collectivism, and uncertainty avoidance. The fourth dimension of masculinity and femininity is under-investigated in the shipbuilding industry because only two percent of the world's maritime workforce is female (Michael Kyprianou & Co LLC, 2021).

To begin with, power distance refers to "… *extent to which less powerful members of organizations and institutions (like the family) accept and expect that power is distributed unequally*" (Hofstede & Bond, 1988, p. 10). Decision-making in high power distance cultures tends to be autocratic, with a small group at the top making decisions. Vietnam scores 70 out of 100, exhibiting a high level of power distance (Hofstede, 2023). This means that social status is determined by factors such as age,

Fig. 1 Comparison of the Dutch and Vietnamese three cultural dimensions. Adapted from Hofstede (2023)

social/political position, and educational degree (Van Bich, 2013). Respect is typically expected from younger or lower-status individuals toward their elders, indicating the presence of a hierarchical structure. In contrast, Dutch society is characterized by a low power distance. Dutch individuals uphold egalitarian values, considering everyone equally important with equal rights and opportunities in life (Vossestein, 2001). In organizations, Dutch people rarely seek permission from their superiors when making decisions as it may be perceived as a sign of incompetence (Ybema & Byun, 2009). Dutch managers encourage employees to demonstrate initiative and assertiveness, and hierarchies are based on functional and professional skills rather than external status or authority (van Marrewijk, 2010).

Second, individualism is defined as "... *stands for a society in which the ties between individuals are loose: Everyone is expected to look after her/his immediate family only*" (Hofstede, 2001, p. 225). Vietnam scored only 20 out of 100 on this dimension, indicating that harmony, in-group thinking, and group-oriented decision-making are emphasized in the society (Hofstede, 2023; Nguyen & Mujtaba, 2011). In contrast, Dutch culture is characterized as individualistic since the country scored 80 out of 100 (Hofstede, 1991, 2023). In organizational settings, Dutch individuals rarely seek permission from superiors, reflecting a focus on individual problem-solving abilities (Ybema & Byun, 2009).

The third dimension pertains to uncertainty avoidance which refers to individuals' discomfort with unstructured, unclear, or unpredictable situations and their tendency to avoid such circumstances by adopting rigid codes of behavior and unwavering beliefs in absolute truths (Zhang & Zhou, 2014). In cultures characterized by strong uncertainty avoidance, people are generally reluctant to engage in new intercultural relationships (Hofstede, 2001). Vietnam scored 30 out of 100, exhibiting a low level of uncertainty avoidance in terms of "adventurousness", which reflects a willingness to embrace new and diverse tasks and a keenness to pursue fresh opportunities (Hofstede, 2023; Nguyen & Aoyama, 2013). In contrast, the Netherlands scored 53 out of 100 on the uncertainty avoidance dimension, indicating a slight preference for avoiding uncertainty (Hofstede, 2023; Hofstede & Soeters, 2002). Societies with higher level of uncertainty avoidance tend to exhibit a lower capacity for risk-taking and avoiding ambiguous situations (Selvarajah et al., 2018).

The shipbuilding industry is one which is involved in designing, building and constructing, converting and upgrading vessels, as well as the manufacture of marine equipment (Caniëls et al., 2016). A shipbuilding company often uses different subcontractors and each of them is subject to different local rules and regulations, utilizes different production methods, and has different technologies (Caniëls et al., 2016; Pires & Lamb, 2008). Shipbuilding is considered one of the most dangerous industries in the world and thus requires continuous care of its workers, their training, ongoing safety education, and adequate infrastructure. The industry must maintain machinery and working equipment, and ensure that they have appropriate occupational risk mitigation standards in place (Para-González et al., 2020). It is thus fair to assume that participants' daily practices in shipbuilding companies could also be affected by the professional culture. Merritt (2000) replicated Hofstede's indexes of national culture for a commercial aviation, with 9,400 pilots in 19 countries, and this has resulted in changes in the dimensions' indices due to the different working environment. A recent study on a shipbuilding joint venture found Vietnamese managers and employees preferred risk adverse which contradicts to Hofstede's findings for Vietnamese managers (Hofstede, 2023; Nguyen, 2021). There are changes in recognition at different levels within joint ventures due to the cultural dimensions and the following section illustrates changes at DMSY joint venture.

What Leaders and Mid-Managers Have Changed at DMSY Joint Venture

Cultural changes of the Vietnamese and Dutch leaders and managers at DMSY joint venture over the last nine years of partnership come from a participatory approach that lowers the gap between superiors and subordinates, group tendency and experiences from mistakes among the Dutch managers while individual tendency, mistakes resistance and avoidance among the Vietnamese managers. The Dutch managers based in Vietnam indicated their lessons learnt in the host country benefit the joint venture's management.

Power Distance Perspective

The Dutch side displays a preference for a company structure that is relatively flat or one which has a low hierarchy from their family business-based culture, emphasizing equality among employees regardless of their positions or ranks. They embrace a culture where it is considered normal to engage in discussions with and even critique the ideas of superiors. To foster this work environment, they have implemented various methods. First, they adopt an open-door policy to create an inclusive atmosphere, encouraging participation in informal conversations and discussions. Second, they regularly encourage everyone, particularly those in lower positions, to actively discuss things in meetings and to share their opinions. Third, during casual events such as lunchtime, the Dutch managers often choose to sit with colleagues regardless of their hierarchical standing, aiming to diminish any perceived distance between individuals. These practices align with existing literature which highlighted the Dutch's inclination toward low power distance (Erwan, 2019; Hofstede, 2023). Prior studies have consistently portrayed the Dutch as strong proponents of egalitarianism where equal treatment and the right to voice one's opinions are valued (van den Berg, 2016; van Eijk, 2013; Vossestein, 2001).

Vietnamese managers admitted that the working environment in DMSY has changed the way they and other employees behave. They explained that in Vietnamese companies, bosses usually have absolute authority over lower ranked employees who are expected to strictly follow the guidelines without offering criticisms. However,

DMSY's organizational culture promotes a low hierarchy structure that led the Vietnamese managers and employees to adopt a more participatory approach, diminishing the emphasis on rank and authority. The Vietnamese managers felt comfortable to express ideas to senior managers and encouraged lower-ranked employees to participate in conversations, thereby bridging the gap between superiors and subordinates. This finding contradicted earlier studies that indicated Vietnamese culture exhibited hierarchical tendencies or power disparities based on individuals' positions (Hofstede, 2023; Quang & Vuong, 2002).

Individualism and Collectivism Perspective

Dutch managers exhibited a tendency to prioritize collective advantages for the whole company. They highlighted the company's motto ("we are one family") and emphasized that all decisions need to align with the company's objectives. The company offered managers opportunities to foster stronger connections among themselves through specially designed activities aimed at promoting cohesiveness. For example, the IJV arranged regular meetings to facilitate discussions and collaborative problem-solving among managers. These meetings occurred at different intervals, ranging from daily, weekly, bi-weekly, or monthly, and sometimes even unscheduled when urgent issues required immediate attention and resolution. Vietnamese managers acknowledged the importance of these meetings in improving communication transparency and enhancing working efficiency, and therefore, maximizing the benefits of the entire company. Furthermore, the Dutch managers promoted a sense of inclusiveness by encouraging all individuals and departments to be a part of a unified team working toward the company's collective goals. To facilitate interactions and foster teamwork, the company intentionally designed its office building with spacious rooms where teams could sit together. The finding contrasts previous research which suggested that the Dutch tend to be individualistic and prioritize their own personal benefits over being part of a larger group (Hofstede, 2023; van Marrewijk, 2010).

Vietnamese managers at DMSY displayed a tendency to prioritize individual benefits over the collective goals of the company. Their primary focus often revolved around personal reward and salary, rather than considering the overall benefit of the entire group. According to the Vietnamese managers, they deemed it unfair for everyone to receive equal salaries, as some individuals were significantly less efficient. Vietnamese managers frequently encountered challenges in reaching a consensus on issues within the IJV as they tended to complain about their own individual difficulties. Their lack of teamwork stemmed from a self-centered approach that disregarded the potential impact of their decisions on other groups or departments. This finding diverged from the existing studies on Vietnamese collectivism (Hofstede, 2023) which highlighted that Vietnamese cultural inclination toward valuing group goals and demonstrating loyalty to a collective over personal objective (Hofstede, 2023; Park et al., 2005).

Uncertainty Avoidance Perspective

Dutch managers perceived problems or mistakes as valuable opportunities for experiential learning and personal growth. They recognized that encountering challenges could enhance individuals' problem-solving abilities. Problem-solving was given priority by Dutch managers whenever errors or issues arose in their day-to-day activities. To foster an environment that encouraged everyone to develop their problem-solving and innovative skills, DMSY implemented a fine-free policy to eliminate any fear associated with making mistakes. The Dutch managers firmly believed that making mistakes is inevitable in everyday activities and individuals must extract valuable lessons from these experiences. This ethos was actively encouraged in the workplace and played a fundamental role in shaping the company's organizational culture. This finding challenged prior research on Dutch culture and indicated a general inclination among the Dutch to avoid uncertainty in which individuals tended to shy away from ambiguous changes in their work environment (Hofstede, 2023; Hofstede & Soeters, 2002).

While Dutch managers in DMSY encouraged everyone to embrace the idea of making new mistakes and learn from them, Vietnamese managers perceived mistakes as potential threats to be avoided. Instead of focusing on potential solutions, they allocated time to identify individuals responsible for the mistakes. Furthermore, they often denied or minimized the occurrence of mistakes due to the belief that such errors would lead to personal disgrace in front of their peers. Vietnamese managers admitted that many colleagues preferred to have someone else responsible for the final outcomes, even if they were competent and experienced employees. Consequently, when there were new tasks or company changes, Vietnamese managers would actively seek reasons to decline the assignment or resist change. This finding differs with the previous literatures that Vietnamese culture exhibits a low level of uncertainty avoidance (Hofstede, 2023). One factor that could influence this behavior is the shipbuilding culture. Considering shipbuilding's reputation as one of the most perilous sectors globally, it requires the consistent prioritization of worker well-being, continuous training and safety education, proper infrastructure, suitable machinery, and adherence to occupational risk prevention standards (Para-González et al., 2020). Given that Vietnamese middle managers in the IJV had direct involvement with high-value building materials, they displayed a tendency to be risk-averse as they were acutely aware that any errors or missteps could lead to substantial financial losses.

Recommendations for Joint Ventures

Given the DMSY joint venture and previous studies, the Dutch managers employ low power distance from their cultural originals to bring into an international joint venture, the cultural distance between Dutch and Vietnamese is decreased over time as a result. This suggests open communication at workplace in Vietnam since more and more FDI attraction to Vietnam. Open communication facilitates dialogues between foreigners and domestic counterparts at different levels and reduces power distance for the purpose of knowledge sharing and knowledge transfer, mutual understanding enhancement leading to sustainable business partnership (Joseph & Raghunath, 2017; Mizoabata et al., 2020). Moreover, the popular online channels such as Microsoft Teams and Zoom have become seamless and less hierarchical, particularly have saved costs and been more obliquitous to exchange ideas and enhance mutual understanding. Low power distance organizational culture via the internet communication can make ease and boost eagerness, reduce misunderstanding, and stronger employee engagement at firms. Future joint ventures in Vietnam benefit the openness of young Vietnamese generation who enter the labor workforce with better international communication skills (EF report, 2022a, b). Young generations in Vietnam also benefit international education offered in Vietnam or experienced overseas study, they are acquainted with open conversation in English language that allows them to express directly rather than high context in mother tongues, that means they expect low power distance like Western culture to communicate at workplace rather than hierarchical climate. Furthermore, leaders at the international joint ventures prioritize to develop organizational culture to support local employee engagement and enhance their willingness to participate in organizational culture for the purpose of successful partnership (Mizobata et al., 2020; Gebhardt et al., 2006; Dan & Canh, 2016; Huynh et al., 2020).

International joint ventures can develop an organizational culture with a global mindset that requires minor changes in different settings. Gen Y and gen Z tend to exhibit change-oriented culture because they are grown up with global intercultural connection such as Youtube, Google, and other social media platforms that provide them an extensive access to international views. Vietnamese youths are not exceptional in the modern fast technology changing society (Decision Lab report, 2023). Many international companies in Vietnam are investing in growth opportunities for young talents through internships, mentorship, future leader programs, and increasing localized leadership at Coca Cola, Unilever, Nestle, and L'Oreal (Decision Lab report, 2023), so young workforce can easily adapt and overcome cultural differences, and have global leadership competences.

Another recommendation for other joint ventures for sustainable business development and partnership is to offer training opportunities for the host partner. The trainings foster technical skills and advance knowledge that lead to positive engagement and create sustainable soft value in the partnership. With the rocketing technology development nowadays, continuous training is essential than ever to enhance employee's capacity. In the DMSY joint venture, the Dutch partner has made significant investments in training and sharing knowledge with the Vietnamese middle managers. Over 50 engineers were trained in the Dutch partner company in the home country and many of them had become middle managers. Furthermore, experiencing advanced career development increases employee retention which supports the joint venture's long-term competitive innovation and growth. For joint ventures with high demand of expensive equipment such as in shipbuilding industry and fast-changing technology today, we recommend providing trainings such as online learning hub or simulation to transfer procedure and skills as well as to empower managers in the host country with penalty-free policies, so they can practice in a low-risk-taking organizational culture and engage with accountable autonomy. This practice enables employees to learn more for cautious usage, minimize potential conflict of communication, increase creativity and innovativeness (Hong-Xoan & Earl, 2020).

Despite the substantial disparities in ownership, the influences exerted by foreign and local management and leadership do not align with these differences, but rather demonstrate reciprocal impacts. We recommend IJVs embrace a learning and adaptive approach to strike a suitable balance between the home and host cultures, thereby enhancing work efficiency. This chapter provides evidence on how the home partner has changed although their ownership accounts for more than double the host partner. While Dutch partners convey their objectives through the company's mission and framework, they also adapt a more supportive environment that encourages Vietnamese employees and managers' discussions and participation in the decision-making process.

We summarize the culture change framework of shipbuilding joint ventures in Fig. 2 between the Dutch and Vietnamese counterparts which illustrates what factors affect the industry and what change occurred at DMSY joint venture.

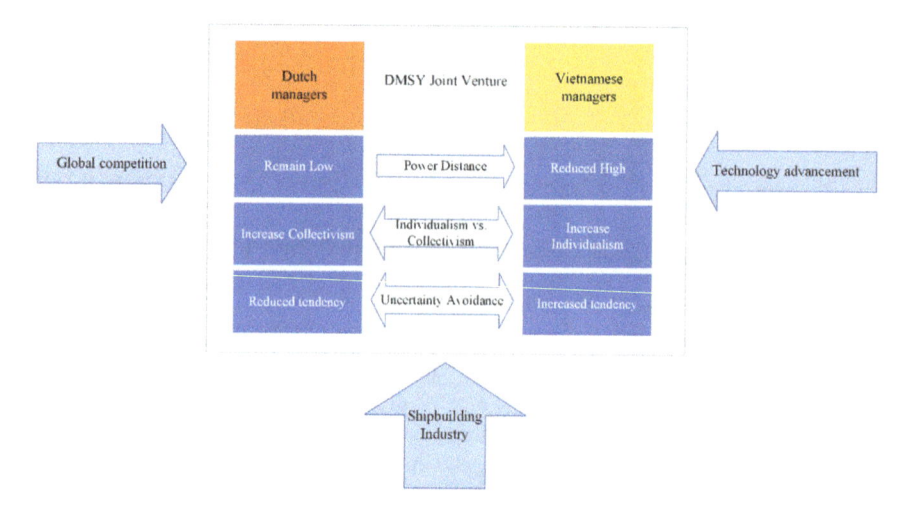

Fig. 2 Culture change framework at shipbuilding joint ventures

Summary

This chapter has several key limitations. Firstly, it solely considers the context of IJVs in the single case of Vietnamese and Dutch partnerships within the shipbuilding industry in Vietnam. Expanding our focus to include partnerships among similar cultural backgrounds, such as two Asian or Western partners, would enhance the comprehensiveness of our findings. Additionally, our concentration on this singular case underscores the need for future efforts encompassing multiple cases across diverse industries, which would provide a more robust foundation for drawing generalized conclusions and insights. Furthermore, it is essential to acknowledge that the chapter does not explore another dimension of Hofstede's cultural framework, "Masculinity and Femininity." This omission is due to the limited representation of females in leadership positions within the shipping industry. Recognizing this gap in our analysis is crucial, as it may impact the generalizability of our findings to industries with more gender-balanced leadership structures.

Despite these limitations, the chapter offers significant contributions. Notably, it provides valuable insights into the practical aspects of IJVs and their influence on corporate culture and individual behaviors within the shipbuilding industry. It outlines positive changes aimed at fostering mutual understanding, capacity development, and the nurturing of long-term partnerships. Additionally, the chapter offers recommendations for other joint ventures seeking successful operations in Vietnam. It highlights that international companies in Vietnam are investing in the development of young talents who own a change-oriented mindset, influenced by global intercultural connections through platforms like YouTube and Google. They expect open communication and a low-power-distance workplace culture. Moreover, offering training opportunities to host partners, promoting knowledge transfer, and developing learning organizational culture can enhance employee engagement, reciprocal impacts exist between foreign and local management, and foster long-term competitiveness in joint ventures despite ownership disparities in international joint ventures. Culture change takes place when leaders actively foster open dialogues, engage managerial risk-averse, and maintain a delicate equilibrium between individualistic and collectivistic values.

References

ASEAN.: (2017). *A historic milestone for FDI and MNEs in ASEAN*. Retrieved from Jakarta, Indonesia. https://asean.org/wp-content/uploads/2020/12/ASEAN-at-50-A-Historic-Milestone-for-FDI-and-MNEs-in-ASEAN.pdf

Barkema, H. G., Shenkar, O., Vermeulen, F., & Bell, J. H. J. (1997). Working abroad, working with others: how firms learn to operate international joint ventures. *The Academy of Management Journal, 40*(2), 426–442. https://doi.org/10.2307/256889

Borton, L. (2000). Working in a Vietnamese voice. *The Academy of Management Executive, 14*(4), 20–29.

Caniëls, M. C., Cleophas, E., & Semeijn, J. (2016). Implementing green supply chain practices: an empirical investigation in the shipbuilding industry. *Maritime Policy and Management, 43*(8), 1005–1020. https://doi.org/10.1080/03088839.2016.1182654

Dan, M. C. H., & Canh, L. Q. (2019). Impacts of organizational culture on employee engagement with organizations in Vietnamese enterprises. *Socio-Eonomic and Environmental issues in Development, 493*

Decision Lab Report. (2023). *Gen Z and the Workplace in Vietnam.* https://www.decisionlab.co/

EF. (2022a). *The world's largest ranking of countries and regions by English skills.* https://www.ef.com/wwen/epi/

EF Education First. (2022b). EF EPI 2022 Regional Fact Sheet. https://www.ef.com/assetscdn/WIBIwq6RdJvcD9bc8RMd/cefcom-epi-site/fact-sheets/2022/ef-epi-fact-sheet-vietnam-english.pdf

Erwan, H. (2019). *Business Cultures Across the World.* PUG.

Fernández, R. P., & Alonso, V. (2015). Virtual Reality in a shipbuilding environment. *Advances in Engineering Software, 81,* 30–40.

Gebhardt, L. P., & Zilbershtein, D. (2006). *Vision in a Knowledge Era: A New Look at the Culture, Price, Cost and Value of Quality in the US Shipbuilding Industry.*

Gebhardt, G. F., Carpenter, G. S., & Sherry Jr, J. F. (2006). Creating a market orientation: A longitudinal, multifirm, grounded analysis of cultural transformation. *Journal of marketing, 70*(4), 37–55. https://doi.org/10.1509/jmkg.70.4.037

Harvie, C., & Tran, V. H. (1997). *Vietnam's reforms and economic growth.* St. Martin's Press.

Hofstede, G. (1991). *Cultures and organizations: Software of the mind.* McGraw-Hill.

Hofstede, G. (2023). Coutry comparison tool: Netherlands and Vietnam. Retrieved from https://www.hofstede-insights.com/country-comparison-tool?countries=netherlands%2Cvietnam

Hofstede, G., & Bond, M. H. (1988). The Confucius connection: From cultural roots to economic growth. *Organizational Dynamics, 16*(4), 5–21. https://doi.org/10.1016/0090-2616(88)90009-5

Hofstede, G., & Soeters, J. (2002). Consensus societies with their own character: National cultures in Japan and the Netherlands. *Comparative Sociology, 1*(1), 1–16. https://doi.org/10.1163/156913202317346728

Hofstede, G. H. (2001). *Culture's consequences: Comparing values, behaviors, institutions, and organizations across nations* (2nd ed.). Sage Publications.

Hong-Xoan, N. T., & Earl, C. (2020). Camaraderie and conflict: Intercultural communication and workplace interactions in South Korean companies in Bình Dương province, Vietnam. *Journal of Asian and African Studies, 55*(6), 832–847.

House, R. J., Hanges, P. J., Javidan, M., Dorfman, P. W., & Gupta, V. (2004). *Culture, leadership, and organizations: The GLOBE study of 62 societies.* Sage.

Huynh, Q. L., Thi, T. T. N., Huynh, T. K., Thi, T. A. D., & Le Thi, T. L. (2020). The effects of organizational culture on human resources management: a study on Vietnamese publicly listed enterprises. *Asian Economic and Financial Review, 10*(7), 885.

Hwang, J.-H. (2022). Hyundai's first Saudi JV shipyard slated for 2023 completion. *The Korean Economic Daily.* Retrieved from https://www.kedglobal.com/shipping-shipbuilding/newsView/ked202203020011

Jha, S. K. (2016). Emerging technologies: Impact on shipbuilding. *Maritime Affairs: Journal of the National Maritime Foundation of India, 12*(2), 78–88.

Johnson, S. D., Koh, H. C., & Killough, L. N. (2009). Organizational and occupational culture and the perception of managerial accounting terms: an exploratory study using perceptual mapping techniques. *Contemporary Management Research, 5*(4).

Joseph, T., & Raghunath, S. (2017). International strategic alliances for innovation in the Indian biotechnology industry. *International Business Strategy: Perspectives on Implementation in Emerging Markets,* 175–190.

Kobernyuk, E., Stiles, D., & Ellson, T. (2014). International joint ventures in Russia: Cultures' influences on alliance success. *Journal of Business Research, 67*(4), 471–477. https://doi.org/10.1016/j.jbusres.2013.03.034

Kogut, B., & Singh, H. (1988). The effect of National culture on the choice of entry mode. *Journal of International Business Studies, 19*(3), 411–432. https://doi.org/10.1057/palgrave.jibs.8490394

Kvalsvik, L. K. (2012). *Intra-organizational information sharing for purchasing activities in shipbuilding* (Master's thesis, Høgskolen i Molde-Vitenskapelig høgskole i logistikk).

Laurent, D., & Lee, S. (2022). Shipbuilding policy and market developments in selected economies 2022. *IDEAS Working Paper Series from RePEc.* https://doi.org/10.1787/f3faeb3d-en

Li, J., Zhou, C., & Zajac, E. J. (2009). Control, collaboration, and productivity in international joint ventures: Theory and evidence. *Strategic Management Journal, 30*(8), 865–884. https://doi.org/10.1002/smj.771

Mesquita, L. F. (2016). Location and the global advantage of firms. *Global Strategy Journal, 6*(1), 3–12. https://doi.org/10.1002/gsj.1107

Michael Kyprianou & Co LLC. (2021). Empowering wome in the maritime industry. https://ocean.economist.com/innovation/articles/empowering-women-in-the-maritime-industry

Mizobata, S., Nguyen, T. N. A., & Pham, Q. T. (2020). The Impacts of organizational culture on knowledge transfer between Japanese managers and Vietnamese employees in Japanese Enterprises. *KIER Discussion Paper, 1030*, 1–22.

Negara, S. D. (2017). *Can the Decline of Batam's Shipbuilding Industry be Reversed?* Retrieved from Singapore https://www.iseas.edu.sg/wp-content/uploads/pdfs/ISEAS_Perspective_2017_10.pdf

Nguyen, N. T. D., & Aoyama, A. (2013). Exploring cultural differences in implementing international technology transfer in the case of Japanese manufacturing subsidiaries in Vietnam. *Contemporary Management Research, 9*(1), 013–034. https://doi.org/10.7903/cmr.10338

Nguyen, T. C. (2021). *Cultural influences on strategising in a Dutch-Vietnamese shipbuilding international joint venture.* (Doctoral thesis, University of Canterbury), Christchurch, New Zealand. https://go.exlibris.link/MGHTSTvD

Nguyen, L. D., & Mujtaba, B. G. (2011). Stress, task, and relationship orientations of Vietnamese: An examination of gender, age, and government work experience in the Asian culture. *Competition Forum, 9*(2). American Society for Competitiveness.

Para-González, L., Mascaraque-Ramírez, C., & Cubillas-Para, C. (2020). Maximizing performance through CSR: The mediator role of the CSR principles in the shipbuilding industry. *Corporate Social Responsibility and Environmental Management, 27*(6), 2804–2815. https://doi.org/10.1002/csr.2004

Park, H., Rehg, M. T., & Lee, D. (2005). The influence of Confucian ethics and collectivism on whistleblowing intentions: A study of South Korean public employees. *Journal of Business Ethics, 58*(4), 387–403. https://doi.org/10.1007/s10551-004-5366-0

Pires Jr, F. C., & Lamb, T. (2008). Establishing performance targets for shipbuilding policies. *Maritime Policy and Management, 35*(5), 491–502.https://doi.org/10.1080/03088830823 52129

Praharsi, Y., Jami'in, M. A., Suhardjito, G., & Wee, H. M. (2021). The application of Lean Six Sigma and supply chain resilience in maritime industry during the era of COVID-19. *International Journal of Lean Six Sigma, 12*(4), 800–834.

Quang, T., Swierczek, F. W., & Thi Kim Chi, D. (1998). Effective leadership in joint ventures in Vietnam: A cross-cultural perspective. *Journal of Organizational Change Management, 11*(4), 357–372. https://doi.org/10.1108/09534819810225904

Quang, T., & Vuong, N. T. (2002). Management styles and organisational effectiveness in Vietnam. *Research and Practice in Human Resource Management, 10*(2), 36–55.

Ralston, D. A., Thang, N. V., & Napier, N. K. (1999). A comparative study of the work values of North and South Vietnamese managers. *Journal of International Business Studies, 30*(4), 655–672. https://doi.org/10.1057/PALGRAVE.JIBS.8490889/METRICS

Schwartz, S. H., Melech, G., Lehmann, A., Burgess, S., Harris, M., & Owens, V. (2001). Extending the cross-cultural validity of the theory of basic human values with a different method of measurement. *Journal of Cross-Cultural Psychology, 32*(5), 519–542. https://doi.org/10.1177/002202 2101032005001

Sd, H. A., Sarifudin, M., & Rahayu, D. S. (2018). The strategic cooperation between Indonesia and China Under Jokowi's Foreign policy towards global maritime diplomacy. *Jurnal Hubungan Internasional Indonesia, 1*(1), 01–18.

Selvarajah, C., Meyer, D., Waal, A., & d. (2018). Dutch managerial leadership strategies: Managing uncertainty avoidance, feminine-related social roles, organisation prosperity focus, and work orientation within a Polder framework. *Contemporary Management Research, 14*(2), 087–120.

Shenkar, O. (2012). Cultural distance revisited: Towards a more rigorous conceptualization and measurement of cultural differences. *Journal of International Business Studies, 43*(1), 1–11. https://doi.org/10.1057/jibs.2011.40

Shin, J., & Lim, Y. M. (2014). An empirical model of changing global competition in the shipbuilding industry. *Maritime Policy and Management, 41*(6), 515–527.

Sirmon, D. G., & Lane, P. J. (2004). A model of cultural differences and international alliance performance. *Journal of International Business Studies, 35*(4), 306–319. https://doi.org/10.1057/palgrave.jibs.8400089

SmartComp. (2013). *Maritime sector developments in the global markets.* https://www.utu.fi/sites/default/files/media/PEI_SmartComp_ResearchReport3.pdf

Statista. (2022). Topic: Shipbuilding industry worldwide. *Statista.*

Statista. (2023a). Largest shipbuilding nations in 2022, based on deliveries.

Statista. (2023b). Size of the global shipbuilding market in 2020 and 2021, with a forecast through 2030. *Statista.*

Thang, L. C., Rowley, C., Quang, T., & Warner, M. (2007). To what extent can management practices be transferred between countries?: The case of human resource management in Vietnam. *Journal of World Business, 42*(1), 113–127. https://doi.org/10.1016/j.jwb.2006.11.005

Thomson, R. (2007). Commission approves joint venture between China Shipbuilding, Mitsubishi and Wartsila. *Practical Law.*

Thuc Anh, P. T., & Minh Hang, N. T. (2009). Culture and performance of international joint ventures in Vietnam. In H. Schamumburg-Müller & P. H. Chuong (Eds.), *The new Asian dragon: Internationalization of firms in Vietnam* (1st ed.). Copenhagen Business School Press.

Trompenaars, A., & Hampden-Turner, C. (1998). *Riding the waves of culture: Understanding diversity in global business.* McGraw Hill.

Truong, T. D., Hallinger, P., & Sanga, K. (2017). Confucian values and school leadership in Vietnam: Exploring the influence of culture on principal decision making. *Educational Management Administration and Leadership, 45*(1), 77–100. https://doi.org/10.1177/1741143215607877

Van Bich, P. (2013). *The Vietnamese family in change: The case of the Red River Delta.* Routledge.

van den Berg, M. (2016). Egalitarian paternalism: Interactional forms of negotiating equality and intervention in Dutch policy practices. *Citizenship Studies, 20*(3–4), 457–474. https://doi.org/10.1080/13621025.2015.1122740

van Eijk, G. (2013). Hostile to hierarchy? Individuality, equality and moral boundaries in Dutch class talk. *Sociology (oxford), 47*(3), 526–541. https://doi.org/10.1177/0038038512453788

van Marrewijk, A. (2010). Situational construction of Dutch-Indian cultural differences in global IT projects. *Scandinavian Journal of Management, 26*(4), 368–380. https://doi.org/10.1016/J.SCAMAN.2010.09.004

Vietnam marine and offshore expo. (2023). Vietnam Maritime, Offshore and Shipbuilding technology and equipment expo, Hanoi, naval expo, fpso exhibition, fishery, trawler, fishing vessels, coastguard technology, ports technology, ho chi minh, shipping expo.

Vietnam Ministry of Finance. (2019). Phát triển bền vững kinh tế biển Việt Nam. https://mof.gov.vn/webcenter/portal/ttpltc/pages_r/l/chi-tiet-tin-ttpltc?dDocName=MOFUCM154410

Vietnamplus. (2021). Vietnam named among world's top 20 host economies for FDI for first time. https://en.vietnamplus.vn/vietnam-named-among-worlds-top-20-host-economies-for-fdi-for-first-time/204861.vnp

VIR. (2022). Dutch firms plan to invest in shipbuilding and logistics projects. *Vietnam Investment Review—VIR.* https://vir.com.vn/dutch-firms-plan-to-invest-in-shipbuilding-and-logistics-projects-98478.html

Vossestein, J. (2001). *Dealing with the Dutch: The cultural context of business and work in the Netherlands in the early 21st century* (Rev). KIT.

Wada, Y., Hamada, K., & Hirata, N. (2021). Shipbuilding capacity optimization using shipbuilding demand forecasting model. *Journal of Marine Science and Technology*, 1–19.

World Shipping Council. (2023). *The Top 50 Container Ports*. https://www.worldshipping.org/top-50-ports

Yang, F. (2011). Toward understanding IJV control: Parent inside and outside control—An exploratory case study. *International Journal of Business and Management, 6*(4), 30. https://doi.org/10.5539/ijbm.v6n4p30

Ybema, S., & Byun, H. (2009). Cultivating cultural differences in asymmetric power relations. *International Journal of Cross Cultural Management, 9*(3), 339–358. https://doi.org/10.1177/1470595809346600

Zhang, X., & Zhou, J. (2014). Empowering leadership, uncertainty avoidance, trust, and employee creativity: Interaction effects and a mediating mechanism. *Organizational Behavior and Human Decision Processes, 124*(2), 150–164. https://doi.org/10.1016/j.obhdp.2014.02.002

Zhu, A. Y., Von Zedtwitz, M., Assimakopoulos, D., & Fernandes, K. (2016). The impact of organizational culture on concurrent engineering, design-for-safety, and product safety performance. *International Journal of Production Economics, 176*, 69–81.

Dr. Que N. Tran is a lecturer in People and Organization at RMIT Vietnam. She has lectured courses in marketing research, educational statistics, multicultural management, and human resource management. Dr Tran has more than 20 years of professional experience in various international and local organizations. Her research focuses on human capital, capacity building, innovation, and sustainable development. Dr. Tran holds a master's degree in Marketing at University College Dublin, Ireland, and a Ph.D. degree in Education at Montana State University, USA. She was a Hubert Humphrey Fellow at Pennsylvania State University.

Dr. Chuyen T. Nguyen is a lecturer in International Business at RMIT Vietnam. He has extensive experience living and working in various countries, including Taiwan and New Zealand. Prior to earning his Ph.D. in Management from the University of Canterbury in New Zealand, he worked for a sea transportation company and a Manpower Agency in Taiwan. Throughout his academic career, he has been involved in lecturing on a range of business-related courses such as global business, political economy of global business, and cross-cultural management. Dr. Nguyen's research interests revolve around culture and strategy-as-practice in cross-cultural organizations.

Dr. Cat-My Dang is a lecturer in International Business at RMIT Vietnam. Her academic background includes a Dr.rer.pol degree from the University of Bremen, Germany, and her doctoral thesis focused on the entrepreneurship of immigrants in Germany. She also has experience in supporting new startups in host countries through non-governmental organization activities. Dr. Dang's research interests are primarily centered on ethnic entrepreneurship, social entrepreneurship, and the contribution of entrepreneurship to both economic development and the integration process of ethnic groups.

Digital Transformation and Resilience: Navigating Disruptions in Asian Emerging Markets

Mohamad Zreik

Abstract The implications of digital disruption on Asia's developing economies are examined in depth in this chapter. These economies are being put to the test by the significant changes brought on by the Fourth Industrial Revolution (4IR). The chapter opens by discussing the historical background of these markets and the considerable influence of digital disruptions. The significance of digital technology in these developing economies is demonstrated by a comprehensive analysis of the relevant literature and by examples drawn from actual events. The next section breaks down what 4IR means for Asian developing economies, analyzing the positive and negative effects of technologies like automation, AI, the IoT, and blockchain. Potential resilience techniques and approaches are presented after the chapter acknowledges the obstacles to digital transformation, such as inadequate infrastructure, digital literacy gaps, and regulatory constraints. In order to better weather shocks, governments and businesses can utilize these strategies by investing in digital infrastructure and literacy and promoting policies that are conducive to digital change. The chapter concludes with case studies of effective digital transformation and resilience, each of which provides lessons learned and recommendations for future efforts. This chapter offers an in-depth exploration of digital disruption in developing Asian economies by seamlessly weaving theoretical frameworks with empirical evidence.

Keywords Digital disruption · Asian emerging markets · Fourth industrial revolution · Digital transformation · Resilience strategies · Digital literacy · Policy hurdles

---

M. Zreik (✉)
School of International Studies, Sun Yat-Sen University (Zhuhai), No. 2 Daxue Road, Xiangzhou District, Zhuhai 519082, China
e-mail: mohamadzreik1@gmail.com

© The Author(s), under exclusive license to Springer Nature Singapore Pte Ltd. 2024
T. Endress and Y. F. Badir (eds.), *Business and Management in Asia: Disruption and Change*, https://doi.org/10.1007/978-981-99-9371-0_6

Introduction

Disruption from digital technologies is having far-reaching effects on industries all across the world (Onyeaka et al., 2021). This phenomenon has already begun to transform the economic landscape of Asia's emerging nations, bringing with it both substantial potential and challenges. Accelerated digital growth is being seen in countries like China, India, Indonesia, Vietnam, and the Philippines as these nations use technology to boost their economies, alleviate poverty, and increase quality of life (World Bank Group, 2016).

Due to the specifics of their socioeconomic structure, these markets present a particularly challenging environment in which to implement digital disruption. A number of reasons are creating a favorable environment for technological advancements, including expanding urbanization, a rising middle class, rising consumer demands, and an influx of young, tech-savvy populace (Yeganeh, 2019). These economies are skipping development milestones and launching headfirst into the digital age, with mobile technology and internet adoption leading the way. Mobile commerce, online shopping, digital entertainment, and telemedicine have quickly become the rule rather than the exception (Lee & Lee, 2021).

These rising markets face substantial hurdles in addition to the opportunities. There is still a significant "digital divide" in many areas, meaning that not everyone has the same level of access to things like computers, the internet, and other digital services. The situation is further complicated by the lack of a robust digital infrastructure, low rates of digital literacy, and poor data protection regulations (Kitsara, 2022). Furthermore, governments and institutions have struggled to keep up with sufficient legislation and regulations due to the quick rate of digital change (Kwon & Kim, 2022).

Despite all of the difficulties, the Asian rising markets have proven their tenacity, adaptability, and creativity. To maintain a competitive edge, businesses have rushed to adopt new technologies and digitize their processes, while governments have increased spending on digital infrastructure and pushed for greater digital literacy (Sahay et al., 2020). These economies' responses to digital disruptors provide a case study of transformation under duress, exemplifying how to thrive by both adapting to the new and overcoming formidable obstacles. As these economies continue their transition to the digital age, the lessons they learn can be applied to other developing nations around the world.

Markets, organizations, and individuals need to be resilient in order to weather the disruptive waves of the digital revolution brought on by the Fourth Industrial Revolution. In this setting, resilience is being able to cope with and even thrive in the face of the rapid and, at times, unexpected changes that digital technologies inevitably bring. It demonstrates resilience in the face of adversity, the ability to bounce back swiftly, and the foresight to find opportunities in setbacks.

While digital transformation is a key factor in driving growth and new ideas, it also introduces volatility, uncertainty, complexity, and ambiguity (VUCA) factors

(Jengwa & Pellissier, 2022). Policy frameworks, business models, employee abilities, and mentalities, all need to be resilient in this constantly shifting environment.

Adaptability in the face of digital disruption requires a mindset that prioritizes learning and change. It necessitates that businesses have adaptive strategies, structures, and procedures that allow them to rapidly change course in response to shifting market conditions. To create a sustainable digital economy, nations must invest in high-quality digital infrastructure, supportive regulations, and widespread digital literacy.

This chapter takes a deep dive into the idea of resilience as a key strategy for meeting the threats posed by digital disruptions in Asia's developing economies. It looks at how these markets are preparing for the challenges of digital transformation through a series of case studies and established best practices.

The Role and Impact of Digital Technology in Asian Emerging Markets

The significance of digital technology in promoting economic growth, improving social welfare, and fostering creativity is becoming increasingly important in the Asian rising markets. Several case studies and real-world examples demonstrate the revolutionary potential of these technologies in molding Asia's emerging digital landscape.

E-commerce giants like Alibaba and JD.com are just two examples of how digital technology has disrupted the retail sector in China (Ma et al., 2022). The use of big data analytics and AI by these businesses to tailor offerings to individual consumers and streamline supply chains sparked a retail revolution. Alibaba's Singles' Day is an annual shopping event that constantly breaks sales records around the world, showcasing the strength of e-commerce in the largest online market (Zhao et al., 2019).

The Indian financial system has also been significantly altered by the advent of digital technologies. The advent of the real-time payment system Unified Payments Interface (UPI) paved the way for a dramatic transition to a digital economy. This innovation made it possible for customers of multiple banks to do transactions with their mobile devices in an effortless, 24/7 manner (Kumar, 2020). Because of this, the use of digital payment methods has exploded, helping to revitalize local economies and expand access to banking services in rural areas.

Companies like Gojek and Tokopedia have led the way in Indonesia's booming digital economy, which has changed the face of urban transportation and online shopping in the country (Adiningsih, 2019). Once only a ride-hailing business, Gojek has expanded to become a one-stop shop for everything from food delivery to digital payments to even healthcare. It has enhanced urban mobility and given millions of Indonesians new ways to make a living.

Access to education has greatly improved in Vietnam as a result of the widespread use of digital technologies. Kyna and Topica Edtech Group are two platforms that provide students in underserved areas and rural areas with access to online courses and vocational training, thereby removing physical barriers to education (Grau, 2020).

These cases show how digital technology is helping to expand opportunities for all people in Asia's developing economies. They demonstrate the promise of these technologies to spur innovation and raise living standards, while also stressing the importance of these markets being able to successfully handle digital changes.

Literature Review on the Subject Matter

Many different perspectives on the opportunities, difficulties, and countermeasures that can be taken in the face of disruptions are presented in the contemporary literature on digital transformation in Asian developing economies and the concept of resilience. From technical progress to the societal and economic effects of these shifts, the literature covers it all.

According to Foster and Azmeh (2020), the digital economy will have a major impact on the development of Asia's emerging markets. They claim that digital technologies are essential for promoting economic progress for all groups and stimulating new ideas. They also emphasize how the digital transformation has affected industries like finance, education, retail, and logistics, revealing the far-reaching and varied effects that these technologies will have on Asian economies.

Khanna et al. (2015) conducted research emphasizing the role of institutions in the digital transformation of developing economies. They point to "institutional voids," such as unreliable infrastructure, inadequate legal and regulatory systems, and a lack of market intermediaries, as reasons why digital technologies haven't been widely adopted.

The research of Vera et al. (2020) is important in the area of resiliency in the face of digital transformation. They argue that resilience encompasses not just surviving setbacks but also growing stronger and better in the face of uncertainty. To successfully manage the digital revolution, they stress the importance of flexibility and agility on a policy, organizational, and personal level.

In this regard, the concept of "digital resilience" put forth by Giustiniano et al. (2018) is quite pertinent. They argue that there is a connection between defensive and offensive strategies in digital resilience. Safeguarding against online dangers falls under the category of "protective resilience," while "proactive resilience" refers to making the most of online chances for growth and reinvention.

Unfortunately, there is a dearth of empirical studies that examine the precise measures used by businesses and governments in Asian emerging countries to fortify themselves against the effects of digital disruptions. In addition, further comparative evaluations that illuminate the differences in the digital transformation journey across different Asian markets would enrich the existing research. This chapter's goal is to fill in such blanks and add to the available literature.

Implications and Opportunities of 4IR in Asian Emerging Markets

The Fourth Industrial Revolution (4IR), driven by innovations like AI, IoT, robotics, and blockchain, will have far-reaching effects on Asia's developing economies. Increasing productivity and efficiency, encouraging creativity, and developing whole new business models are just a few of the many possible outcomes of 4IR (Manners-Bell & Lyon, 2019).

The possibility that 4IR may increase production and efficiency in many different industries is a major advantage of this technology. For instance, AI and IoT allow businesses to automate mundane operations, freeing up employees for higher value work. They also provide better resource management by optimizing processes in real time. In agriculture, for instance, IoT devices may track weather patterns and adjust the amount of water and fertilizer used to maximize crop production while decreasing wastage. Artificial intelligence (AI) can similarly increase efficiency, enhance quality control, and lessen downtime in the industrial sector (Mehla & Deora, 2022).

In addition to boosting productivity, 4IR technologies can also spur innovation and usher in fresh avenues for commercial expansion. Using these advances, businesses can create cutting-edge goods and services to meet the demands of new consumer markets. For instance, FinTech firms in these markets are utilizing blockchain technology to serve the underserved population that is largely unbanked. Telemedicine services, made possible by AI and the Internet of Things, are another way that HealthTech businesses are expanding access to medical treatment in underserved areas (Dash, 2020).

There is hope that 4IR can likewise improve government operations and public service delivery. Public service delivery in areas such as transportation, public safety, healthcare, and education can all be enhanced by using AI and big data analytics. By facilitating more effective monitoring and auditing procedures, these technologies can help increase government openness and accountability.

However, despite these possibilities, it is essential to remember that overcoming obstacles like inadequate infrastructure, a lack of qualified workers, and cumbersome regulations is necessary to reap the rewards. Therefore, to effectively capitalize on the opportunities presented by 4IR in Asia's emerging countries, a planned and concentrated effort on the part of all stakeholders—governments, corporations, and civil society—is required.

Examination of the Threats and Challenges Posed by 4IR

The Fourth Industrial Revolution offers promising prospects for Asia's developing economies, but it also poses a number of risks. Automation-related job loss, insufficient infrastructure, data privacy and security risks, and digital divide are all issues that need to be addressed.

The possible loss of jobs due to automation is one of the greatest dangers posed by 4IR. There is concern that manual and repetitive professions could be lost to automation due to the widespread adoption of artificial intelligence and robots across multiple industries. While it's true that new employment will be created as technology advances, the transition could be bumpy, and workers who lose their jobs to automation may not have the skills essential for the new roles that are created. This may make unemployment and wealth disparity worse in these economies.

Data privacy and security are also a major obstacle. The risk of data breaches and cyber-attacks is growing as businesses and governments rely more and more on digital technology and data. Concerns about privacy and the ethical use of data are also rising as firms acquire more information about consumers (La Torre et al., 2018). Significant difficulties exist for these developing economies in the form of enacting and enforcing effective data protection rules and cybersecurity safeguards.

The lack of adequate infrastructure in these markets is another obstacle to the widespread adoption of 4IR. There are still barriers to the broad use of 4IR technologies, including as slow internet speeds, insufficient power, and a dearth of supporting infrastructure. In addition, many of these markets lack the appropriate legal and regulatory structures to adequately deal with the effects of these innovations.

The issue of digital inequality is also quite important. Some people may not be able to access the advantages of modern technologies. Those who have access to digital technologies have a huge advantage over those who do not; this divide threatens to widen already existing socioeconomic gaps.

Finally, it's possible that the speed at which 4IR is developing will exceed the rate at which these markets can adjust to and regulate these technologies. It may be difficult for policymakers to keep up with technological developments, which could lead to a delay in policy and regulatory responses and reduce the technology's potential impact. To achieve broad and sustained benefits from these technologies, it is essential for Asian emerging markets to proactively address these issues and dangers brought about by 4IR.

Analysis of the Impact of Technologies Like Automation, AI, IoT, and Blockchain

Numerous industries across Asia's developing economies are being profoundly impacted by the 4IR technologies of automation, artificial intelligence, the Internet of Things, and blockchain.

Automation, or the use of machines to do previously manual tasks, is having a profound effect on the manufacturing and industrial sectors in these economies. Automation has improved operating efficiency, decreased error, and raised production everywhere from factory assembly lines to supply chain management. However, as regular operations that humans have historically performed become computerized, worries about job displacement have been raised (Cascio & Montealegre, 2016).

AI, another game-changing technology, has also made major gains in many industries. As an example, in healthcare, AI has been used to aid in diagnosis and patient care; in finance, AI has been used to aid in risk assessment and fraud detection; and so on. It has also been used to improve chatbots powered by artificial intelligence for use in customer support (Pallathadka et al., 2023). However, there are ethical, privacy, and the need for transparency and explainability in AI decision-making concerns that arise from AI use.

The term "Internet of Things" (IoT) is used to describe the growing trend of connecting various types of physical items to the internet so they may collect and share data. With the help of IoT-enabled sensors, farmers can track factors like soil moisture and temperature to ensure their crops thrive. Waste management, traffic management, and power consumption are all areas where smart cities can benefit from IoT (Da Xu et al., 2014). While the IoT has great promise for enhancing productivity and inspiring new ideas, it also raises concerns about privacy, data integrity, and the sheer volume of data that will need to be managed.

While Bitcoin and other cryptocurrencies are the most well-known applications of blockchain technology, the technology's potential applications extend far beyond money. It could be used in supply chain management to verify the authenticity and traceability of products, as well as in government services to increase transparency and decrease fraud, thanks to its capacity to establish safe, transparent, and tamper-proof records (Wang et al., 2019). However, there are still obstacles to be overcome in regard to the scalability, energy consumption, and regulatory status of blockchain technologies.

These 4IR technologies are having a profound impact on the growth, innovation, and enhanced service delivery in the rising Asian markets. In order for these markets to fulfill their full potential, however, they must first overcome the difficulties and dangers that they provide. It will be vital in determining the future of these markets to make use of these technologies while mitigating their possible dangers and disadvantages.

Challenges, Barriers, and Infrastructure Issues in Digital Transformation

The lack of adequate infrastructure has been a major obstacle for many developing economies in Asia on their path to digital transformation. The disparity between cities and rural communities is at the heart of the problem. In contrast to the relatively robust digital infrastructure found in most urban areas, those living in rural areas are frequently hampered by poor internet connectivity, inadequate telecommunications equipment, and a dearth of modern technology. This digital divide exacerbates the already existing economic and social imbalance between urban and rural areas, making it more difficult to implement digital transformation plans effectively (Wang et al., 2021).

A more specific barrier is the absence of constant, high-speed internet access. The success of any digital transformation effort hinges on the accessibility and consistency of online data sharing. Many digital technologies are unfeasible or inefficient because of the inconsistent or slow internet access that is common in many Asian emerging markets.

The lack of sufficient cloud and data center infrastructure is still another obstacle. The demand for safe, dependable, and fast data storage and processing centers is critical as organizations and governments rely more and more on information to inform their decisions. The problem is that these markets frequently lack the capital, technological know-how, and regulatory support necessary to build and maintain such facilities (Khanna & Palepu, 2010).

Last but not least, there is a problem with the lack of funding for digital transformation-related physical infrastructure, such as the computers, mobile phones, and other tools people require to really use digital technology (Brunetti et al., 2020). Limits in availability and affordability of necessary hardware often act as roadblocks to the widespread use of digital technology.

In order for digital transformation in Asia's developing markets to be a success, these infrastructure issues must be resolved. Even the most well-funded and carefully planned digital transformation initiatives may fail if an adequate digital infrastructure is not in place.

Digital Literacy and Its Importance in the Transformation Process

The term "digital literacy" refers to the proficiency with and knowledge of digital technology and its applications (Neumann et al., 2017). The significance of this cannot be understated in the context of Asian developing economies, where the level of digital literacy among the population varies greatly.

The capacity to utilize digital resources and environments is the foundation of digital literacy. This is the most obvious facet of digital literacy, and it covers things like knowing how to use a computer or smartphone, finding one's way through the internet, and figuring out how to make the most of digital applications. Having these fundamental abilities is necessary to take part in the digital economy as a consumer or a worker.

Understanding how digital technologies function and being able to engage with them successfully is certainly part of what we mean when we talk about "digital literacy," beyond just knowing how to use them. This necessitates familiarity with ideas like personal information security, cyber ethics, and data confidentiality. Employees' familiarity with these ideas is crucial to the success of companies undergoing digital transformation because it affects the way in which new technologies are adopted and employed.

The ability to critically assess digital information and apply digital technologies to solve problems is also an important part of digital literacy. These abilities are crucial for making smart decisions based on digital data in the era of big data and fake news. Employees with these abilities can use digital technologies to boost creativity and output for their companies (Falloon, 2020).

Digital literacy is important for more than just individuals. Transitions to digital economies are more likely to be successful in societies where people are highly literate in the use of digital technologies. Because it allows people of various socioeconomic backgrounds to take part in and benefit from the digital economy, digital literacy can also aid in closing the digital gap and fostering social inclusion in the digital age (Reisdorf & Rhinesmith, 2020).

Therefore, it is crucial for Asian developing economies to prioritize digital literacy as they begin their digital transition. These economies will have a better chance of surviving digital upheavals if they invest in digital education and training for their citizens and workers.

Policy and Regulatory Hurdles that These Markets Face

Despite the promise of digital revolution, Asian emerging markets face major governmental and regulatory impediments. If these problems aren't solved, these countries won't be able to become completely digitalized economies any time soon.

The absence of all-encompassing and future-oriented digital regulations is one of the biggest obstacles to regulatory success. These regulations are essential to creating an atmosphere supportive of digital change. They lay out the ground rules for the interaction between the government, corporations, and consumers. However, such policies are either nonexistent or ineffective in many of Asia's growing markets. The expansion of the digital economy may be stunted if crucial issues like data privacy and cybersecurity, e-commerce rules, and digital taxation are left unaddressed.

While digital policies may be in place, they may be difficult to put into practice due to inefficiencies in administration or a lack of funding. Ineffective policy outcomes are frequently the result of a large void between policy formulation and implementation. As a corollary, the rate at which technology evolves typically outstrips the rate at which policy evolves, leading to outmoded legislation that is ill-equipped to handle modern digital concerns (O'Donovan, 2020).

Another difficulty stems from the fact that these markets do not have uniform regulations. The lack of standardized standards, notwithstanding the global nature of digital activity, can impede the development of regional digital commerce by increasing the complexity of cross-border digital transactions. Regulatory arbitrage, in which companies take advantage of legal loopholes in one country in order to operate more freely in another, is another possible outcome (Patrikios, 2008).

Last, but not least, it's not uncommon for these markets to have trouble striking a balance between encouraging innovation and protecting shoppers' privacy and safety.

Under-regulation can lead to consumer abuse and increased cybersecurity threats, while over-regulation can discourage innovation and slow digital transformation.

The governments in these markets will need to take a proactive and coordinated strategy to navigate these regulatory challenges. This includes working toward regional regulatory harmonization, improving policy implementation processes, and updating digital policies to keep up with technological developments. More importantly, they need to encourage open communication between businesses, consumers, and technology specialists to find the optimal middle ground between encouraging innovation and guaranteeing digital safety and security.

Strategies and Approaches for Building Resilience to Navigate Digital Disruptions

A combination of initiatives emphasizing digital infrastructure strengthening, digital literacy promotion, and the creation of hospitable policy settings is necessary to build resilience to digital disruptions in Asian emerging markets.

Accepting digital infrastructure as essential is the first step. The foundation for digital transformation and protection against interruptions is a solid digital infrastructure. This involves making investments in data centers, cloud services, and cybersecurity to provide constant, high-speed internet connectivity (Petrenko, 2022). These investments would guarantee company continuity even in the face of interruptions, and they would also pave the way for the adoption of cutting-edge technologies like AI, the IoT, and blockchain. It also prepares the way for "smart city" efforts, which use digital technologies to boost quality of life and promote long-term prosperity.

Developing digital literacy is essential to creating resilience. Understanding the inner workings of digital technology and its effects on the workplace, daily life, and society at large are also crucial components of digital literacy. The goal of fostering digital literacy is to help individuals and organizations profit from, adapt to, and overcome the opportunities and threats presented by digital technologies. Schools, the current workforce, and the general public can all benefit from instructional initiatives and awareness drives to achieve this goal.

Finally, building resilience to digital disruptions requires policy settings that are both stable and flexible. The acts of policymakers have the potential to either promote or stymie digital change, making them pivotal players in the process (Wu et al., 2017). Governments should establish progressive digital regulations that not only outline acceptable conduct for online interactions, but also promote healthy competition and innovation. At the same time, these regulations need to safeguard both individuals and enterprises from the hazards of using digital tools. To keep up with the speed at which technology evolves, policymakers must be adaptable and open to revising existing regulations.

When put into practice together, these methods would offer Asian emerging markets a holistic method of bolstering resilience and making them more able to deal with digital upheavals.

Importance of Investing in Digital Infrastructure

For Asian developing economies to be resilient in the face of digital upheavals, investment in digital infrastructure is a cornerstone. For economies to reap the benefits of the 4IR, they need a solid digital infrastructure upon which to build.

First, many 4IR technologies, including AI, IoT, and blockchain, rely on a reliable digital infrastructure, which includes things like high-speed internet connectivity, data centers, and cloud services. In order to function properly, these technologies necessitate stable and rapid connectivity. The potential benefits these technologies could offer to businesses and economies would be much reduced without the requisite digital infrastructure being in place.

Second, addressing the digital gap, a serious problem in many developing economies, is facilitated by spending money on digital infrastructure. The term "digital divide" is used to describe the disparity between those who have and those who do not have access to various forms of digital technology (Van Dijk, 2006). Governments and businesses may do more to promote equality and social inclusion by investing in and expanding the digital infrastructure that allows more people to use digital tools.

Thirdly, in order to keep operations going no matter what happens, having a solid digital infrastructure is crucial. Having dependable digital infrastructure, for instance, enables firms to convert to remote work settings during crises like pandemics, ensuring operations continue without interruption. The growth of e-commerce, e-learning, and healthcare are just a few examples of the digital services that benefit from this (Zreik, 2023).

Finally, funding digital infrastructure development can help the economy expand and innovate. In addition to luring in new companies and capital, it also opens the door to the creation of novel digital services and products, which in turn promotes a more inventive and competitive business climate.

Role of Digital Literacy in Building Resilience

In the context of digital transformation, digital literacy is especially important in Asian emerging markets. Literacy in the digital age refers to one's facility with locating, analyzing, utilizing, sharing, and generating content online. Digital literacy promotes resilience in many ways because it provides individuals and groups with the tools they need to thrive in the modern digital world.

A person's ability to adapt to a dynamic labor market is directly correlated to their level of digital literacy. The Fourth Industrial Revolution has resulted in a change in the most in-demand talents. Even in industries that have not always relied largely on technology, workers are finding that digital literacy is a need (Spöttl & Windelband, 2021). The ability to adapt to new circumstances, grab new opportunities, and weather fluctuations in the job market all depend on a person's level of digital literacy.

Organizational digital literacy strengthens a company's ability to weather disruptions. Businesses that have staff who are comfortable with various forms of digital technology are better able to respond to market shifts and technological innovations. In addition, being tech-savvy encourages creativity, which is essential for thriving in today's ever-evolving digital world. Employees who are comfortable using digital tools are more inclined to do so, helping businesses innovate through the creation of novel solutions, processes, and business models.

Economic stability is bolstered on a societal scale when people are literate in digital technologies. To establish a digital economy, it is essential to have a populace with high levels of computer literacy. The demand for digital services and goods is boosted when a sizable section of the population is able to use and create digital information, which in turn encourages economic growth and innovation. Further, it contributes to a more equitable distribution of digital transformation advantages, which helps lessen societal inequities and conflicts.

Necessity of Conducive Policies for Facilitating Digital Transformation

It is impossible to overestimate the importance of supportive policies for enabling digital transformation, especially in the context of Asian emerging markets. Rapid expansion and evolution are common features of many markets, and digital transformation is a major factor in this dynamic. However, without the appropriate policies in place, these markets may become unstable due to issues like economic inequality and employment displacement. For digital transformation to result in long-term prosperity, policymakers must adopt measures that encourage it.

First, supportive policies can promote creativity and technological advancement. Business-friendly policies, such as those that safeguard intellectual property, encourage companies to spend money on R&D and embrace digital innovations. More companies will be able to join the digital economy if rules are put in place to encourage healthy competition and discourage monopolies (Rikap, 2021).

Second, supportive policies can aid in controlling the social effects of digital disruption. For instance, in an increasingly digital economy, it may be necessary to revise labor rules in order to adequately safeguard workers' rights. Policies addressing the "gig economy," telecommuting, and the loss of jobs to automation are all examples. In a similar vein, reducing economic inequality can be accomplished through educational policies that emphasize digital literacy and help more individuals acquire the skills necessary to thrive in a digital economy.

Last but not least, supportive policies can pave the way for the requisite technology to support the digital revolution. Broadband networks and other hard infrastructure are necessary, but 'soft' infrastructure, such as privacy regulations, is also essential (Jie et al., 2015). Building trust in digital services and encouraging their use requires policies that support the development of such infrastructure to ensure that digital services are available, dependable, and secure.

Best Practices and Successful Case Studies from Asian Emerging Markets

Several instructive case studies of competent handling of digital transformation may be found in the diverse setting of Asia's growing markets. These examples show how businesses and economies have used the benefits of digital technologies to pave the road for future success.

The dramatic increase in digital payment usage in India is one such example. The Unified Payments Interface (UPI) was introduced in 2016 by the National Payments Corporation of India, ushering in a new era in the country's monetary system (Gochhwal, 2017). This easy, mobile-first payment method allowed instantaneous transfer of payments between any two parties, decreasing dependency on cash and allowing even those without a bank account to participate in financial transactions. The widespread ecosystem of financial institutions, fintech startups, and regulators that the UPI system has fostered is largely responsible for its success.

Similar revolutionary consequences have been seen in China after the introduction of mega-apps like WeChat and Alipay. The features of these platforms span from instant messaging and social media to e-commerce and payment processing, and even further. This groundbreaking strategy has not only increased user participation, but also given millions of micro- and small-sized businesses access to a robust digital marketplace. To a large extent, this explosion of digital innovation can be attributed to government measures like the "Internet Plus" initiative (Su et al., 2021).

Meanwhile, the Philippines has made great progress in using digital technology to expand access to banking services. Digital wallet market leaders like GCash and PayMaya are empowering previously unbanked Filipinos to take part in the online economy. The digital transformation plan of the Bangko Sentral ng Pilipinas (BSP) has encouraged these efforts to make the Philippines' financial system more accessible and efficient for all its citizens (Nair, 2016).

Success in each of these examples can be traced back to the introduction of new digital technologies, the formation of strategic collaborations between different industries, and the existence of receptive policy frameworks. They underline the importance of both reactive and proactive initiatives to exploit digital technologies for economic growth and societal good as key components of digital resilience. Other developing economies can learn a lot from these experiences as they undertake their own digital transformation.

Discussion on the Best Practices Learned from These Case Studies

Several best practices and lessons learned can aid other markets who are embarking on similar journeys to the digital transformation seen in the Asian emerging markets. The UPI system in India is a shining example of the need to work together on digital transformation. Banks, non-banking financial institutions, and tech startups worked together to build a single, accessible financial system. This exemplifies the value of multi-sector partnerships in promoting innovation and enhancing service provision.

The rise of Chinese super-apps like WeChat and Alipay demonstrates the potential of digital platforms for driving economic expansion. The multi-service nature of these platforms has increased user engagement and provided a boost to many micro- and medium-sized businesses. This indicates that embracing and promoting cutting-edge digital solutions that meet a variety of consumer requirements in a unified setting is a key factor in fostering digital transformation.

The Philippines is a great example of how digital technology may be used to broaden access to financial services. The importance of digital solutions in achieving financial inclusion is highlighted by the fact that digital wallets like GCash and PayMaya have allowed the unbanked people to participate in the digital economy.

In each of these examples, digital transformation was aided by a policy climate that was both hospitable and encouraging. Policy plays a crucial role in creating a hospitable environment for digital transformation, as seen by government programs like India's push for a cashless economy, China's "Internet Plus" strategy, and the Philippines' digital transformation strategy.

One thing that all these achievements have in common is that they have guaranteed widespread and dependable access to digital technologies. In order to facilitate and maintain digital transformation, it is essential to invest in strong digital infrastructure, such as broadband connectivity and digital payment platforms.

Successfully navigating digital disruptions calls for a diverse strategy, which is highlighted by these best practices. The resilience of nations and their ability to reap the benefits of digital transformation can be strengthened by a concerted effort to innovate, collaborate, be inclusive, enact enabling legislation, and invest in necessary infrastructure.

Conclusion

The opportunities and threats that the Fourth Industrial Revolution (4IR) poses to Asia's rising markets are equal. The potential for digital transformation to stimulate economic growth, inspire creativity, and improve the quality of life in these countries is considerable. However, there are several challenges on the road to digital transformation, such as inadequate infrastructure, digital illiteracy, and regulatory roadblocks.

The ability to bounce back quickly from technological setbacks is essential. This necessitates not only the resilience to endure and recover from setbacks, but also the flexibility to adjust to new circumstances and grow through time. Developing such toughness calls for a comprehensive strategy. In order to lay the groundwork for digital technologies, investment in digital infrastructure is essential. Increasing people's and groups' digital literacy is critical for them to be able to fully engage in the online economy.

Policies that foster growth are also crucial. The digital transformation process can be aided by governments that remove legislative barriers and provide enabling frameworks for digital technologies. In addition, these regulations can ensure that the advantages of digital transformation are shared by as many people as possible.

Some effective methods of dealing with digital disruptions are highlighted by case studies from Asia's developing economies. These best practices provide useful insights for other markets on their digital transformation journeys, including how to drive innovation through super-apps, promote financial inclusion, leverage partnerships and collaborations, and create a supportive policy environment.

Resilience is becoming increasingly important in this age of fast digital transformation. In order to survive in the digital era, Asia's rising economies must develop the resilience to take advantage of the opportunities presented by the Fourth Industrial Revolution (4IR) while also meeting the obstacles it presents head-on. The background of digital disruptions is discussed in this chapter, along with the significance of adopting appropriate tactics to successfully navigate them. Others, both in Asia and around the world, can benefit from the lessons learned by Asia's emerging markets as they undergo digital transformation.

Summary

The consequences of the Fourth Industrial Revolution (4IR) were examined in the context of digital disruptions in Asia's rising economies in this chapter. Opportunities and threats posed by 4IR technologies including automation, AI, IoT, and blockchain were examined. Infrastructure, digital literacy, and policy challenges were all discussed in this chapter as they pertain to digital transformation. It highlighted the need for infrastructure, digital literacy, and enabling policies as means of building resilience in the face of digital disruptions. Case studies of Asian markets that have been particularly fruitful were given, and lessons learned from these markets were discussed. The chapter ended by emphasizing once again the significance of resilience in successfully completing the digital transformation process.

References

Adiningsih, S. (2019). *Indonesia's Digital-Based Economic Transformation: The Emergence of New Technological, Business, Economic, and Policy Trends in Indonesia*. Gramedia pustaka utama.

Brunetti, F., Matt, D. T., Bonfanti, A., De Longhi, A., Pedrini, G., & Orzes, G. (2020). Digital transformation challenges: Strategies emerging from a multi-stakeholder approach. *The TQM Journal, 32*(4), 697–724.

Cascio, W. F., & Montealegre, R. (2016). How technology is changing work and organizations. *Annual Review of Organizational Psychology and Organizational Behavior, 3*, 349–375.

Da Xu, L., He, W., & Li, S. (2014). Internet of things in industries: A survey. *IEEE Transactions on Industrial Informatics, 10*(4), 2233–2243.

Dash, S. P. (2020). The impact of IoT in healthcare: Global technological change And the roadmap to a networked architecture in India. *Journal of the Indian Institute of Science, 100*(4), 773–785.

Falloon, G. (2020). From digital literacy to digital competence: The teacher digital competency (TDC) framework. *Educational Technology Research and Development, 68*, 2449–2472.

Foster, C., & Azmeh, S. (2020). Latecomer economies and national digital policy: An industrial policy perspective. *The Journal of Development Studies, 56*(7), 1247–1262.

Giustiniano, L., Clegg, S. R., e Cunha, M. P., & Rego, A. (Eds.). (2018). *Elgar introduction to theories of organizational resilience*. Edward Elgar Publishing.

Gochhwal, R. (2017). Unified payment interface—An advancement in payment systems. *American Journal of Industrial and Business Management, 7*(10), 1174–1191.

Grau, J. M. (2020). *The effect of synchronous online versus traditional instruction in teaching jazz music* (Doctoral dissertation, University of Georgia).

Jengwa, E., & Pellissier, R. (2022). An operational excellence strategy implementation model for growth in a volatile, uncertain, complex, and ambiguous environment. *Acta Commercii, 22*(1), 1–11.

Jie, Y. U., Subramanian, N., Ning, K., & Edwards, D. (2015). Product delivery service provider selection and customer satisfaction in the era of internet of things: A Chinese e-retailers' perspective. *International Journal of Production Economics, 159*, 104–116.

Khanna, T., & Palepu, K. G. (2010). *Winning in emerging markets: A road map for strategy and execution*. Harvard Business Press.

Khanna, T., Palepu, K. G., & Sinha, J. (2015). Strategies that fit emerging markets. In *International business strategy* (pp. 615–631). Routledge.

Kitsara, I. (2022). Artificial intelligence and the digital divide: From an innovation perspective. *Platforms and Artificial Intelligence: The Next Generation of Competences* (pp. 245–265). Springer International Publishing.

Kumar, A. (2020). Digitalization impact on entrepreneurial competencies of business in India. *International Journal of Economic Perspectives, 14*(7), 61–66.

Kwon, S., & Kim, E. (2022). Sustainable health financing for COVID-19 preparedness and response in Asia and the Pacific. *Asian Economic Policy Review, 17*(1), 140–156.

La Torre, M., Dumay, J., & Rea, M. A. (2018). Breaching intellectual capital: Critical reflections on Big Data security. *Meditari Accountancy Research, 26*(3), 463–482.

Lee, S. M., & Lee, D. (2021). Opportunities and challenges for contactless healthcare services in the post-COVID-19 Era. *Technological Forecasting and Social Change, 167*, 120712.

Ma, C., Mao, J. Y., & An, X. P. (2022). The driving forces behind the phenomenal rise of the digital economy in China. *Management and Organization Review, 18*(4), 803–815.

Manners-Bell, J., & Lyon, K. (2019). *The logistics and supply chain innovation handbook: Disruptive technologies and new business models*. Kogan Page Publishers.

Mehla, A., & Deora, S. S. (2022). Use of machine learning and IoT in agriculture. *IoT based smart applications* (pp. 277–293). Springer International Publishing.

Nair, V. P. (2016). Eschewing cash: The challenges of cashless transactions in the Philippines. *Journal of Southeast Asian Economies (JSEAE), 33*(3), 387–397.

Neumann, M. M., Finger, G., & Neumann, D. L. (2017). A conceptual framework for emergent digital literacy. *Early Childhood Education Journal, 45*, 471–479.

O'Donovan, N. (2020). From knowledge economy to automation anxiety: A growth regime in crisis? *New Political Economy, 25*(2), 248–266.

Onyeaka, H., Anumudu, C. K., Al-Sharify, Z. T., Egele-Godswill, E., & Mbaegbu, P. (2021). COVID-19 pandemic: A review of the global lockdown and its far-reaching effects. *Science Progress, 104*(2), 00368504211019854.

Pallathadka, H., Ramirez-Asis, E. H., Loli-Poma, T. P., Kaliyaperumal, K., Ventayen, R. J. M., & Naved, M. (2023). Applications of artificial intelligence in business management, e-commerce and finance. *Materials Today: Proceedings, 80*, 2610–2613.

Patrikios, A. (2008). The role of transnational online arbitration in regulating cross-border e-business–Part I. *Computer Law and Security Review, 24*(1), 66–76.

Petrenko, S. (2022). *Cyber security innovation for the digital economy: A case study of the Russian federation.* CRC Press.

Reisdorf, B., & Rhinesmith, C. (2020). Digital inclusion as a core component of social inclusion. *Social Inclusion, 8*(2), 132–137.

Rikap, C. (2021). *Capitalism, power and innovation: Intellectual monopoly capitalism uncovered.* Routledge.

Sahay, M. R., von Allmen, M. U. E., Lahreche, M. A., Khera, P., Ogawa, M. S., Bazarbash, M., & Beaton, M. K. (2020). *The promise of fintech: Financial inclusion in the post COVID-19 era.* International Monetary Fund.

Spöttl, G., & Windelband, L. (2021). The 4th industrial revolution–Its impact on vocational skills. *Journal of Education and Work, 34*(1), 29–52.

Su, L., Peng, Y., Kong, R., & Chen, Q. (2021). Impact of e-commerce adoption on farmers' participation in the digital financial market: Evidence from rural China. *Journal of Theoretical and Applied Electronic Commerce Research, 16*(5), 1434–1457.

Van Dijk, J. A. (2006). Digital divide research, achievements and shortcomings. *Poetics, 34*(4–5), 221–235.

Vera, D., Samba, C., Kong, D. T., & Maldonado, T. (2020). Resilience as thriving: The role of positive leadership practices. *Organizational Dynamics.*

Wang, D., Zhou, T., & Wang, M. (2021). Information and communication technology (ICT), digital divide and urbanization: Evidence from Chinese cities. *Technology in Society, 64*, 101516.

Wang, Y., Han, J. H., & Beynon-Davies, P. (2019). Understanding blockchain technology for future supply chains: A systematic literature review and research agenda. *Supply Chain Management: An International Journal, 24*(1), 62–84.

World Bank Group. (2016). *World development report 2016: Digital dividends.* World Bank Publications.

Wu, X., Ramesh, M., Howlett, M., & Fritzen, S. A. (2017). *The public policy primer: Managing the policy process.* Routledge.

Yeganeh, H. (2019). An analysis of emerging patterns of consumption in the age of globalization and digitalization. *FIIB Business Review, 8*(4), 259–270.

Zhao, Z., Chen, M., & Zhang, W. (2019). Social community, personal involvement and psychological processes: A study of impulse buying in the online shopping carnival. *Journal of Electronic Commerce Research, 20*(4), 255–272.

Zreik, M. (2023). Analytical study on foreign direct investment divestment inflows and outflows in developing economies: Evidence of China. *The Chinese Economy, 56*(6), 415–430. https://doi.org/10.1080/10971475.2023.2193118

Dr. Mohamad Zreik a Postdoctoral Fellow at Sun Yat-sen University, is a recognized scholar in International Relations. His recent work in soft power diplomacy compares China's methods in the Middle East and East Asia. His extensive knowledge spans Middle Eastern Studies, China–Arab relations, East Asian and Asian Affairs, Eurasian geopolitics, and Political Economy, providing him a unique viewpoint in his field. Dr. Zreik is a proud recipient of a PhD from Central China Normal University (Wuhan). He's written numerous acclaimed papers, many focusing on China's Belt and Road Initiative. His groundbreaking research has established him as a leading expert in his field. Presently, he furthers his research on China's soft power diplomacy tactics at Sun Yat-sen University.

Disruption and the Gig Economy: What's Next?

Tobias Endress

Abstract The gig economy, a multibillion-dollar business, disrupts traditional industries like hotels and taxis by offering flexible income and efficient access to services. It has grown significantly with the rise of digital platforms like AirBnB, Freelancer.com, and Grab. The gig economy promotes financial and social inclusion, but challenges like labor rights, job security, and regulatory control persist. Independent gig workers enjoy a high work–life balance, flexibility, autonomy, and creative freedom, while contingent workers become a new precariat. Digital platforms like AirBnB; Fiverr; and Grab disrupt economic activity by resetting entry barriers, changing value creation, and playing regulatory arbitrage. They empower trust in service quality, democratize grassroots entrepreneurship, and create employment opportunities. Still, the gig economy faces frictions and there is significant consolidation in the industry. The business models might need to be refined when funding gets tighter and regulations prevent unfair competition and exploitation of workers. Additional governance structures, fair labor, regulation, and assistance for marginalized populations are needed to address these issues. Policymakers must create regulations and governance frameworks to ensure fair compensation, worker protection, and social inclusion.

Keywords Gig economy · Platform economy · Digital transformation · Disruption · Digital inclusion · HappyFresh · Asia

Introduction

The Gig Economy and its famous start-up companies like AirBnB, Freelancer.com, and Grab represent a multibillion-dollar business. This type of company is often described as disruptive to existing business models. This chapter discusses the current state of the so-called 'Gig Economy' in Asia and potential future developments. The Gig Economy is often described as disruptive for traditional industries (hotels, taxis,

---

T. Endress (✉)
Asian Institute of Technology (AIT), Bangkok, Thailand
e-mail: tobiasendress@ait.asia

© The Author(s), under exclusive license to Springer Nature Singapore Pte Ltd. 2024
T. Endress and Y. F. Badir (eds.), *Business and Management in Asia: Disruption and Change*, https://doi.org/10.1007/978-981-99-9371-0_7

etc.) and has become a multibillion-dollar business and is expected to keep growing fast. However, it seems that many of the disruptive business models struggle in many cases to achieve sustainable and profitable operations. Overall, the gig economy shapes current work organization and conduct. They allow individuals to earn flexible income and businesses and clients to rapidly and efficiently access a wide range of services. The gig economy also presents critical problems concerning labor rights, job security, and regulatory control, which vary by nation and are currently being debated and reformed. This chapter contributes to this discussion, reflects on the current situation, and presents best practices.

Gig Economy and the Disruptive Forces

The term was originally used in the music industry and jazz musicians used it to describe their engagements for an evening. Some authors see this as the origin of the term (e.g., Brandie, 2019; Pal, 2021; Wallace, 2019). The term evolved over time and was used increasingly to describe various jobs, especially temporary or freelance jobs (Cambridge Dictionary, 2023; Starr-Glass, 2017). These 'gigs' are often performed on an informal or on-demand basis. The Gig Economy consists of many different types of work arrangements but is characterized by a significant volume of labor provided by independent contractors or informal workers rather than by organizational employees. Those gig workers are generally hired on a short-term basis to complete specific tasks. The gig economy landscape continues to be extremely varied in the kinds of work being done. Several types of services are available, ranging from food delivery to merchandise sales. With the rise of the internet and the creation of digital platforms, the gig economy reached new heights. In 2005, Amazon opened Mechanical Turk, a crowdsourcing marketplace for simple, repetitive tasks that AI can't do well. Also, in 2005, Airbnb was founded to rent out (private) rooms, and despite some initial struggles, it became a multi-billion-dollar company (Wallace, 2019). Still, the gig economy is not limited to the digital space. Gig workers can also work for more traditional companies, which might have changed their staffing approach. Delivery drivers, for example, might also be employed on a piece-by-piece delivery basis, even though their employer might not have tech start-up origins or be a digital platform often associated with this type of work (Kobie, 2018). Other terms often used in similar contexts are 'platform economy' or 'sharing economy,' which in particular refers to the digital platform respective a business model often described as disruptive for existing industries. There are also some terms like 'the Precariat,' or 'the 1099 Economy' that refer more to the type of employment of gig-workers and how they are compensated (Kenney & Zysmann, 2016; Starr-Glass, 2017). These terms already indicate somehow the controversy about this form of business. While the gig economy is booming (Charro et al., 2022) and many workers appreciate the advantages of this form of work, especially the flexibility, it is not an easy work environment for many gig workers.

According to a recent survey conducted in South Korea, nearly 80 percent of respondents stated that the leading reason why they would like to work as gig workers is due to the offered flexibility (see Table 1). Still, authors (e.g., Wu et al., 2019) question the stated flexibility, asserting that workers actually have significantly less flexibility than commonly believed. This is attributed to the labor control techniques employed by the platform. The authors analyze three approaches of "soft" management, specifically economic control, emotional labor, and consent making, to illustrate that the notion of "being one's own boss" is not always straightforward. The authors highlight the necessity for platforms to proactively manage drivers' online availability to meet the increased demand for rides during peak hours. They emphasize that bonuses serve as a highly efficient economic mechanism for exerting control (Wu et al., 2019).

More than 40% appreciate not being involved in intrapersonal relationships with the company and almost 35 percent stated to become gig workers because they would then be able to continue working after retirement (Saramin, 2022). Some authors conclude that the gig economy combines both demographic factors and technological advancements to facilitate the advancement of financial and social inclusion. The emergence of the future of work has materialized, establishing platform employment as a permanent part of the labor landscape (Ramachandran & Raman, 2021).

Still, gig work is not only about job flexibility. The consideration of financial aspects is an obvious and integral component. According to a BCG survey on the gig economy in India in 2022, the primary reason to take up a job among both gig and non-gig workers was to meet their monthly household expenses. Notable differences are that finance and monthly household expenses are for 43% of non-gig workers the main reason but only for 32% of primary gig-workers. Whereas about 27 percent took gig work to fund their other expenses (as compared to 15% of non-gig workers). To gain more financial independence was also a major motivation to take up gig work (Augustinraj & Bajaj, 2020). However, there is also the downside of the gig economy. There are several severe issues that are of concern for many gig workers, including inconsistency of work assignments, fair pay, healthcare, and lack of protection (see also Charro et al., 2022; Kobie, 2018; Sperow, 2023).

McFeely and Pendell (2018) argue that there are two different types of gig workers: independent and contingent gig workers. Independent gig workers, such as online platform workers and freelancers, experience high levels of work–life balance, flexibility, autonomy, meaningful feedback, and creative freedom. In fact, Gallup data suggests they score even higher on these factors compared with traditional workers

Table 1 Leading reasons for becoming a gig worker in South Korea in 2022 (Saramin, 2022)

Flexibility of work	79.2%
Not being influenced by interpersonal relationships in the company	40.7%
Possibility of working after retirement	34.8%
Because it is becoming a trend	24.7%
Possibility to use my skills	20.3%

and other types of gig workers (McFeely & Pendell, 2018). In contrast, contingent workers, such as temporary workers and on-call workers, say they receive less feedback and few actually report their performance metrics are within their control. In many aspects of their work, including belongingness, passion, autonomy, creativity, feedback, performance metrics, and hours, these contingent gig workers are more similar to traditional workers than they are to independent gig workers (McFeely & Pendell, 2018). McFeely and Pendell conclude that only independent gig workers can truly be their own boss and enjoy the often-praised benefits of gig work more regularly, in particular flexibility and freedom. Meanwhile, contingent gig workers experience their workplace almost like regular employees do, just without the perks of a traditional job: benefits, pay, and security (McFeely & Pendell, 2018). There is a risk that this divide with increase further. NITI Aayog (2022), a think tank of the Government of India, reports for the year 2021, only around 22% of gig work in India to be in high-skilled jobs, while the highest rate of 46% is actually in medium-skilled and 31 percent in low-skilled gig work. The trends reflect a gradual increase in high- and low-skilled jobs till 2030 (see Fig. 1).

It is clear that not all gig workers are the same and that the differences are great. Some authors try to group roles to analyze the different positions and requirements. While differentiation in independent and contingent gig workers is an important criterion (fair) payment is another important factor. While freelance work in general can be very profitable. Burke and Cowling argue that "comparing the new dynamic economy to earlier more static form, we observe the evolution of freelancing from lower paid substitutes for employees to higher paid complements of employees." (2020, p. 396). However, they acknowledge that some freelancers will still serve the typically low-paid, vulnerable informal workers (Burke & Cowling, 2020). In some cases, gig workers might already achieve higher income compared to traditional workers. Digital platforms can be inclusive and might even offer a higher

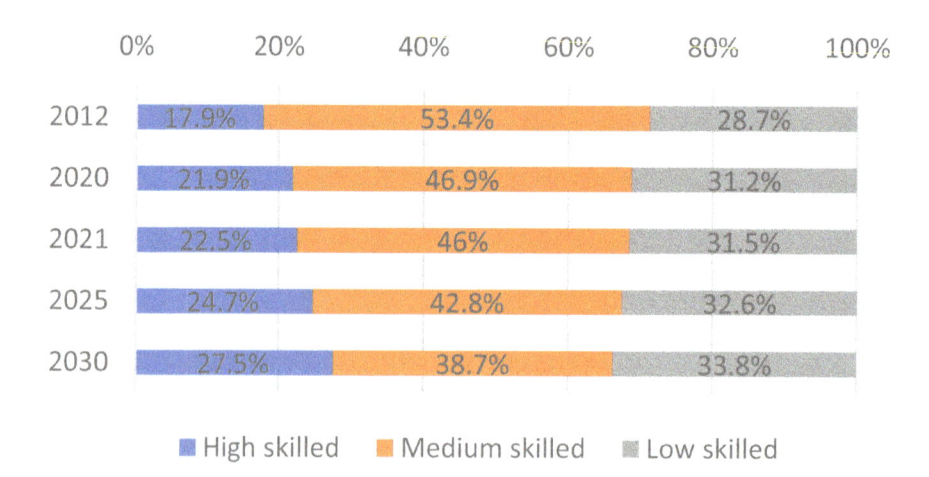

Fig. 1 Share of gig work employment by skill category (NITI Aayog, 2022)

earning potential (Ramachandran & Raman, 2021). Still, it can be observed that freelancers, especially gig-workers, are overrepresented in low-income groups (see Statista, 2023a, 2023b, 2023c, 2023d). The severity of the problem is worsened when gig workers fail to complete their assigned duties within the specified timeframe, resulting in a payment delay. According to a survey conducted in South Korea in 2021, there are three main difficulties experienced by gig-workers: 1. "Not being paid for the work," 2. "Paying for unjustified costs and losses," and 3. "Pay reduction without notice" (Statista, 2022). All these issues are related to the financial aspects. Furthermore, without projects or tasks, gig workers are unable to generate any kind of income (Gusai et al., 2022). During the peak of the COVID-19 epidemic, in March 2020, slightly under 52% of gig economy employees globally had no income due to the coronavirus situation and its restrictions. Only 2% of the respondents said their income had increased due to the pandemic (appjobs.com, 2020). An initial proposed solution, mostly pushed by labor unions, entails classifying gig workers as regular employees, taking into account the level of control exerted by platforms over these workers. The current legislation and regulatory framework would remain in effect, so maintaining the applicability of existing laws to gig workers (see also: Aloisi, 2015; De Stefano, 2015; Koutsimpogiorgos et al., 2020). Consequently, gig employees would continue to receive the benefits associated with that job status, thereby also social protection. The inevitable consequence of such a trajectory would be that the majority of platforms would be unable to sustain their existing business models (Koutsimpogiorgos et al., 2020). It seems to be vital to create regulatory frameworks that preserve flexibility while promoting improved social inclusion and working standards.

The Benefits of the Gig Economy

While there is already a growing body of academic literature, the overall benefit of the gig economy is hard to estimate. "What we do know is that these platforms are in many cases, disrupting the existing organization of economic activity by resetting entry barriers, changing the logic of value creation and value capture, playing regulatory arbitrage, repackaging work, or repositioning power in the economic system" (Kenney & Zysmann, 2016).

The Role of Platforms

Platforms play a special role in the gig economy ecosystem. Platforms are not only drive innovation and develop new business models, they are also facilitators and intermediaries (Table 2). The gig economy relies on platforms to link people and businesses with freelancers and independent workers who can deliver specific services. In the gig economy, platforms play several roles:

1. Matching Supply and Demand: Gig economy platforms connect service seekers and providers. These platforms leverage algorithms and data to match worker talents, availability, and location with consumer or corporate needs. This applies not only to goods but also to a broad talent pool. Platforms offer a diverse and global freelance labor pool. Gig economy platforms give workers and clients

flexibility. Workers can work when and how much they choose, while clients can get help with occasional tasks without long-term contracts. Businesses and individuals can access products, specialized skills, and experience that may not be available locally.
2. Transparency, Trust, and Reputation Building: Many gig economy platforms provide gig worker evaluations, ratings, and profiles to help clients make decisions. These platforms help workers gain credibility. Positive ratings and reviews can increase gig worker job possibilities and pay. Platforms may require background checks and safety safeguards for gig workers and clients, depending on the gig. This can empower trust in service quality but is also described as an opportunity to "democratize grassroots entrepreneurship and create employment opportunities that uplift disadvantaged communities" (Saijai, 2023).
3. Escrow and Payment Processing: Platforms secure and efficiently process client-gig worker payments. From a business perspective, it can make sense to become part of the payment process, but there are different ways in which platforms fulfil this function. Sometimes, platform deducts the money from the order and credits it only after delivery to the provider. It could be considered as a form of escrow but embedded in the gig economy transaction. The platform a neutral third-party providing service for both sides of the transaction: seekers and providers. This can help improve both the convenience and confidence in a smooth transaction. They may even offer invoicing and payment tracking. Platforms often feature dispute resolution methods for clients and gig workers (Sperow, 2023).
4. Job Management: Platforms with project management, communication, and collaboration tools help clients and workers organize tasks and deliverables.
5. Regulatory Compliance, Income Tracking, and Reporting: Many gig economy platforms ensure workers follow local tax and regulation requirements. This includes appropriately categorizing workers as employees or independent contractors and withholding and paying taxes. Platforms may help gig workers track their income and expenses, simplifying tax reporting and financial management. However, it could be observed that various of these platforms also try to exploit regulatory loopholes or do arbitrage (Kenney & Zysmann, 2016).
6. Innovation and Technology: Gig economy platforms invest in technology and innovation to improve their services, making it easier for participants to identify and source products and services.

Table 2 Types of digital platforms

Types of digital platforms	Examples
Service-providing platforms	Amazon web services, Microsoft's azure, and google cloud platform
Platforms mediating work	Amazon mechanical Turk, Fiverr, LinkedIn, UpWork, Urban Company
Retail platforms	AliExpress, Etsy, Lazada, Meituan, Shopee
Service-providing platforms	AirBnB, Grab, Foodpanda, HappyFresh, Lineman, Saijai, Tujia

Overall, gig economy platforms play a pivotal role in shaping the way work is organized and conducted in the modern economy. They provide opportunities for individuals to earn income on a flexible basis while enabling businesses and clients to access a wide range of services quickly and efficiently. However, the gig economy also raises important questions about labor rights, job security, and the need for regulatory oversight, which vary from country to country and are the subject of ongoing debate and reform efforts. Many freelancers see platform management capabilities as limiting and disrupting control over work availability, client relationships, and reputation, resulting in new types of precarity. As a result, Alvarez De La Vega et al. (Alvarez De La Vega et al., 2021) suggest that freelancing platforms, as they are now constituted, should not be presumed to be the same as traditional forms of freelance labor because their features and restrictions ultimately determine the degree of control freelancers have over their work.

Social Disparity and Inclusion

The question about social disparity and inclusion needs to be taken seriously. The ability to access technology and the internet is necessary for digital transformation. It is possible that people who do not have access to these resources, which are often individuals with lower incomes, may be excluded from the opportunities given by the gig economy, further increasing the digital divide. While some advocates for the gig economy claim that it enables the workforce and opens new opportunities (Ramachandran & Raman, 2021). Still, the employment income in the gig-economy is often of a problematic nature. Some authors make a distinction between "voluntary" and "involuntary" entrepreneurship (Karaivanov & Yindok, 2022). Banerjee and Dunflu famously outline in Poor Economics that some poor people are driven to start entrepreneurs because of the lack of other opportunities (Banerjee & Duflo, 2012). For many, this is not an ideal start to entrepreneurship and they are overwhelmed with many things and are not very successful. Maybe this is a reason for other authors to discuss the need for "Digital Unions" (Galipeau, 2023; Wood et al., 2018) and argue that union leaders are responsible for building a strong digital presence. "Informal workers are becoming more technologically savvy and are discovering new networking models that coordinate collective action on a global scale. As the negative impacts of IR4.0 technologies outweigh the positive effects even slightly, workers' resistance will grow as they try to rebalance the power dynamic" (Galipeau, 2023, p. 96). It can be stated that the gig economy may lack inclusivity for all. Various marginalized groups may suffer limited prospects as a result of discrimination and bias, while various forms of gig work may demand specialized physical qualities or equipment that certain individuals may not have.

It is evident that the digital revolution and the gig economy present prospects for economic engagement and empowerment. However, it is important to acknowledge that these developments also pose potential dangers of amplifying social inequalities and marginalization, particularly if not adequately monitored and regulated. To tackle these difficulties, a holistic approach encompassing technology advancements, just labor practices, regulatory measures, and assistance for marginalized populations is necessary. This approach aims to promote a more equitable distribution of the advantages offered by the digital economy.

Financial Constraints Drive Consolidation in the Industry

Various companies in the gig economy industry have already begun to consolidate operations. HappyFresh, for example, was founded in 2014 and claimed to be the first and fastest-growing online grocery platform in Southeast Asia (HappyFresh, 2015). This growth story could probably be considered a success. The venture capital company Samena Capital, for example, sold its stake in 2021 as part of a series d deal with an ROI of 2.37x (Saraf & Hassan, 2021). The company grew fast and expanded in new markets, even targeting second-tier regions in Thailand (Leesa-Nguansuk, 2022). In 2022, HappyFresh was ranked number six among the leading e-commerce platforms for grocery shopping in Malaysia (Vase.ai, 2022). HappyFresh grew fast to an estimated annual revenue of $103.5 M per year (Growjo, 2023).

However, the growth of the company faced severe restrictions. Already in 2016, only about 2 years after the start of the company, financial investors seemingly urged the company to focus on their strategy. The company managed to secure series B funding and simultaneously announced to withdraw from Taiwan and the Philippines (Khaw, 2022). The COVID-19 situation boosted the food delivery services, and HappyFresh has experienced significant growth over that period in the three remaining active markets (Indonesia, Malaysia, and Thailand). The company even seemed to observe a shift in customers' behavior toward online groceries (Ahmad, 2021). Still, it didn't persist and the growth story got more cracks. The growth rate after the pandemic slowed down and the grocery delivery service industry is very competitive. This led to further consolidation in the industry. Grab, which also has a stake in HappyFresh, closed its dark store operations in Singapore, Vietnam, and the Philippines in 2022 as part of its efforts to streamline its delivery ecosystem (Tan, 2022). The year 2022 was also a difficult year for HappyFresh. The company managed again to secure funding. From its founding in 2014 till 2022, the company raised a total of $97 million over 8 rounds in both equity and debt funding but apparently, the investors had some influence on the company's strategic development. The investors urged the company, again, to focus on core markets. Having only three markets left implied concentrate on operations in its biggest market, Indonesia. The operations in Thailand and Malaysia are discontinued (Maheshwari & Diela, 2022).

In general, it seems to get harder for low-margin business models (or companies in the growth stage with negative margins) to secure funding—especially for growth ventures and market development activities. The HappyFresh case illustrates very vividly how investors, potentially driven by increased interest rates, have a direct impact on the company's strategy. Investors might question the viability and sustainability of business models more intensely in the current environment. However, it is by far not the only example and indication for consolidation in the industry. Gojek, an Indonesian ride-hailing and on-demand delivery service has merged with Tokopedia to form GoTo Group (Daga & Potkin, 2021). Other companies in the industry also announced strategic consolidation. Delivery Hero, as another prominent example, announced its plan to sell its Foodpanda business in selected markets in Southeast

Asia including Singapore, Cambodia, Laos, Malaysia, Myanmar, the Philippines, and Thailand (Bast & Hesse, 2023; More, 2023). Economic environment, inflation, and interest rates might play an important role in the consolidation of the industry.

What's Next? The Future of the Gig Economy

It seems that the Gig Economy is at a turning point. Technology and markets become more and more mature and the question regarding the sustainability of business models is becoming eminent. Gig economy disruptions might have some similarities with the First Industrial Revolution (IR). 1. It changed the way how people work and get compensated. 2. It enabled innovation and economic growth. 3. New social rules and standards needed to be established. Especially, the third point is a process where eventually the "new normal emerges." However, this process might not be without friction. Some might see here, again, a similarity to the first IR or even be reminded on Schumpeter's "Creative Destruction" (Schumpeter, 1942). He pointed out that "every piece of business strategy acquires its true significance only against the background of that process and within the situation created by it. It must be seen in its role in the perennial gale of creative destruction; it cannot be understood irrespective of it" (Schumpeter, 1942, pp. 82–83).

It is hard to say how the Gig Economy as a whole might develop. However, we have a few indications and trends that might give us some idea about the future status of the industry. In 2022, the value of the global Ride Sharing market amounted to US$96.9 billion and is expected to amount to around US$226 billion by 2028 (Statista Company Insights, 2023) and this segment represents only a part of the overall gig economy.

It is extremely challenging to determine the amount to which the platforms contribute to the provision of income to those who might otherwise have no income at all (i.e., the inclusive impacts of the platforms), while also considering the extent to which they might even foster exploitative practices. Several factors are currently evolving and might even be getting additional momentum in the near future (see Fig. 2).

However, it becomes clear that the digital footprint on a large digital platform gives at least some visibility. As digital platforms need a certain size (to achieve sufficient reach and economies of scale), it is more difficult for them to operate permanently "under the radar" of regulation. This allows policymakers to develop (labor) rules for those platforms. It might also be possible to implement and enforce additional governance structures with a direct impact on the gig economy, including the informal work sector. These instruments facilitate the establishment of a favorable business environment in dynamic economies, enabling the recruitment of highly productive and high-earning freelancers. They also provide support to vulnerable freelancers who fall within the lower end of the earnings and precarious spectrum, protecting them from exploitation. Additionally, these instruments aim to identify and minimize instances of false self-employment, while simultaneously recognizing and promoting

Fig. 2 Important participants shaping the gig economy

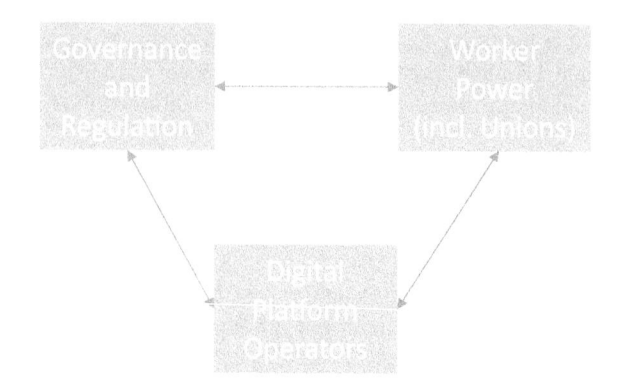

the milestones towards the digital work future and on the way to a stable regulatory framework (promoting labor rights and innovation). Some of the newer gig economy platforms, e.g., SAIJAI and Yindii, take on the challenge to include sustainability in the business models and it might ignite further innovation and inspire other platforms to enhance their business models accordingly. Still, some argue that digital gig economy platforms are a form of natural monopoly. New economic models and technological change appear to increase concentration compared to older, traditional/physical markets. Data collection and analysis, prediction technologies, and algorithmic matching services create economies of scale that were not available before. These changes make the natural monopoly paradigm an interesting starting point to evaluate market power concerns in current digital gig economy platforms, and about competition, entry, and market fragmentation. It can also help our understanding of efficient concentration and winner-takes-all policy approaches. There is no doubt that some elements that typically compromise natural monopoly, especially the economies of scale, apply to gig economy platforms (Ducci, 2020). Still, the digital platform does not provide an entrance barrier as we know it from telecom or utility companies. This makes them more vulnerable to new market entrances than other natural monopolies that require large infrastructure investments (like water supply or utilities). Still, it might be reasonable to expect that the consolidation in the gig economy continues.

Summary and Conclusion

The chapter reviews the gig economy in Asia and examines future trends. The gig economy, which involves on-demand or temporary work, is worth billions and anticipated to rise. Digital platforms like Airbnb, Fiverr, and Grab have grown the gig economy. The gig economy in Asia is rising rapidly and has both opportunities and concerns. The gig economy gives job flexibility and revenue to cover monthly costs or achieve financial independence. It offers workplace flexibility and income, but fair compensation, worker protection, and social inclusion are problems. Additional drawbacks, include unpredictable work assignments, lack of healthcare, and limited gig worker protection. Different gig workers and compensation levels exist in the gig economy. Some gig workers may make more than regular labor, but others may be vulnerable and underpaid.

The gig economy may challenge business models and empower workers. However, it poses social inequality and inclusion concerns. Without technology and internet connection, gig economy opportunities may be unavailable, expanding the digital divide. Due to a lack of prospects, some people may be driven into gig employment, which makes entrepreneurship difficult. Technology, regulation, and marginalized population assistance are needed to solve these problems. Education programs and initiatives to reduce the digital device are needed. This method seeks to distribute the gig economy and digital economy benefits more evenly.

A turning point is coming for the gig economy. Gig economy business models are under threat as technology and markets mature. The pressure from the financial market increases and we can observe a tendency towards consolidation. The gig economy, like the earlier industrial revolution, is transforming work and societal norms. However, this technique may be difficult. Policymakers need to create gig economy regulations and governance frameworks to encourage business, labor rights, and innovation. Platforms require robust regulatory frameworks to shape their business models. Once platforms reach a certain size and importance it might be possible to impose rules to increase worker protection. A holistic approach is needed to address these concerns and guarantee gig economy advantages are distributed more evenly. How policymakers and stakeholders handle gig economy issues and possibilities will determine its destiny.

References

Ahmad, S. (2021, October 13). *The roller-coaster years of Indonesian e-grocer HappyFresh*. Tech in Asia. https://www.techinasia.com/rollercoaster-years-indonesian-egrocer-happyfresh

Aloisi, A. (2015). Commoditized Workers The Rising of On-Demand Work, A Case Study Research on a Set of Online Platforms and Apps. *SSRN Electronic Journal*. https://doi.org/10.2139/ssrn.2637485

Alvarez De La Vega, J. C., Cecchinato, M. E., & Rooksby, J. (2021). "Why lose control?" A study of freelancers' experiences with gig economy platforms. *Proceedings of the 2021 CHI conference on human factors in computing systems* (pp. 1–14). https://doi.org/10.1145/3411764.3445305

appjobs.com. (2020, March). *Current financial situation of gig workers worldwide due to the COVID-19 pandemic as of March 2020 [Graph]*. Statista. https://www.statista.com/statistics/1128318/gig-workers-worldwide-current-financial-situation-covid-19/

Augustinraj, R., & Bajaj, S. (2020). *Unlocking the Potential of the Gig Economy in India*. https://media-publications.bcg.com/India-Gig-Economy-Report.pdf

Banerjee, A. V., & Duflo, E. (2012). *Poor economics: A radical rethinking of the way to fight global poverty* (Paperback ed). PublicAffairs.

Bast, C., & Hesse, L. (2023, September 20). *Delivery Hero SE confirms negotiations regarding a potential sale of its foodpanda business in selected markets in Southeast Asia – Delivery Hero*. https://ir.deliveryhero.com/news/delivery-hero-se-confirms-negotiations-regarding-a-potential-sale-of-its-foodpanda-business-in-selected/180a664d-7f27-4f1e-8a0a-590dd6278023/

Brandie, P. (2019, October 23). *The history of the modern gig economy. WriterAccess.* https://www.writeraccess.com/blog/the-history-of-the-modern-gig-economy/

Burke, A., & Cowling, M. (2020). On the critical role of freelancers in agile economies. *Small Business Economics, 55*(2), 393–398. https://doi.org/10.1007/s11187-019-00240-y

Cambridge Dictionary. (2023, September 27). *Gig.* https://dictionary.cambridge.org/dictionary/english/gig

Charro, G., Dua, A., Ellingrud, K., Luby, R., & Pemberton, S. (2022). *Freelance work, side hustles, and the gig economy | McKinsey.* https://www.mckinsey.com/featured-insights/sustainable-inclusive-growth/future-of-america/freelance-side-hustles-and-gigs-many-more-americans-have-become-independent-workers

Daga, A., & Potkin, F. (2021, May 17). *Indonesia's Gojek, Tokopedia to create biggest local tech group | Reuters.* https://www.reuters.com/technology/indonesias-gojek-tokopedia-merge-countrys-biggest-deal-2021-05-17/

De Stefano, V. (2015). The rise of the "just-in-time workforce": on-demand work, crowd work and labour protection in the "gig-economy." *SSRN Electronic Journal.* https://doi.org/10.2139/ssrn.2682602

Ducci, F. (2020). *Natural monopolies in digital platform markets* (1st ed.). Cambridge University Press. https://doi.org/10.1017/9781108867528

Galipeau, D. (2023). How Industry 4.0 influences our work environment. In T. Endress (Eds.), *Digital project practice for new work and Industry 4.0* (1st ed., pp. 75–98). Auerbach Publications. https://doi.org/10.1201/9781003371397-6

Growjo. (2023). *HappyFresh: Revenue, competitors, alternatives.* https://growjo.com/company/HappyFresh

Gusai, O. P., Rani, A., & Yadav, P. (2022). Digital Industrial Revolution 4.0 and sustaining gig economy: Challenges and opportunities ahead. In A. Gupta, T. Tewary, & B. N. Gopalakrishnan (Eds.), *Sustainability in the gig economy* (pp. 187–198). Springer Nature Singapore. https://doi.org/10.1007/978-981-16-8406-7_14

HappyFresh. (2015). *Home.* HappyFresh. https://www.happyfresh.com/

Karaivanov, A., & Yindok, T. (2022). Involuntary entrepreneurship—Evidence from Thai urban data. *World Development, 149*, 105706. https://doi.org/10.1016/j.worlddev.2021.105706

Kenney, M., & Zysmann, J. (2016, April 1). The rise of the platform economy. *Issues in science and technology.* https://issues.org/rise-platform-economy-big-data-work/

Khaw, C. (2022, September 23). A timeline of HappyFresh's tumultuous 7-year journey in M'sia, from launch to closure. *Vulcan Post.* https://vulcanpost.com/804408/happyfresh-malaysia-shutdown-history-funding-expansion/

Kobie, N. (2018, September 14). What is the gig economy and why is it so controversial? *Wired UK.* https://www.wired.co.uk/article/what-is-the-gig-economy-meaning-definition-why-is-it-called-gig-economy

Koutsimpogiorgos, N., Van Slageren, J., Herrmann, A. M., & Frenken, K. (2020). Conceptualizing the gig economy and its regulatory problems. *Policy and Internet, 12*(4), 525–545. https://doi.org/10.1002/poi3.237

Leesa-Nguansuk, S. (2022, July 22). HappyFresh keen on expansion into provinces. *Bangkok Post.* https://www.bangkokpost.com/business/general/2351361/happyfresh-keen-on-expansion-into-provinces

Maheshwari, A., & Diela, T. (2022, September 22). *HappyFresh resumes Indonesia grocery deliveries after new funding.* Nikkei Asia. https://asia.nikkei.com/Spotlight/DealStreetAsia/HappyFresh-resumes-Indonesia-grocery-deliveries-after-new-funding

McFeely, S., & Pendell, R. (2018, August 16). *What workplace leaders can learn from the real gig economy.* Gallup.Com. https://www.gallup.com/workplace/240929/workplace-leaders-learn-real-gig-economy.aspx

More, R. (2023, September 20). Delivery Hero confirms talks on partial sale of Asian business. *Reuters.* https://www.reuters.com/markets/deals/delivery-hero-planning-partial-sale-asia-business-media-report-2023-09-20/

NITI Aayog. (2022, June 25). *India: Share of gig work employment by skill category 2030*. Statista. https://www.statista.com/statistics/1318281/india-share-of-gig-work-employment-by-skill-category/

Pal, B. (2021). Rising popularity in gig economy: A case study from India. *International Journal of Religious and Cultural Studies, 3*(2). https://doi.org/10.34199/ijracs.2021.09.08

Ramachandran, S., & Raman, A. (2021). *Unlocking jobs in the platform economy*. Ola Mobility Institute. https://static.investindia.gov.in/s3fs-public/2021-06/OMI_Platform%20Economy%20Report.pdf

Saijai. (2023). *Find maid, child care, elderly care, driver, pet care, tutor, beauty care, Handyman | SaiJai*. https://saijai.io/en

Saraf, S., & Hassan, R. (2021, August 1). *HappyFresh exit announcement*. https://www.samenacapital.com/investor-relations/latest-news/2021/10/12/happyfresh-exit-announcement

Saramin. (2022, June 22). *Leading reasons for becoming a gig worker in South Korea in 2022 [Graph]*. Statista. https://www.statista.com/statistics/1334884/south-korea-reasons-for-becoming-gig-workers/

Schumpeter, J. A. (1942). *Capitalism, socialism and democracy*. Harper.

Sperow, J. L. (2023). Arbitrating gig economy mass claims. *Dispute Resolution Journal, 76*(4). https://kluwerlawonline.com/api/Product/CitationPDFURLfileJournals\DRJ\DRJ2023010.pdf

Starr-Glass, D. (2017). Psychological Contracts and Strategic Leadership. In V. X. Wang (Ed.), *Encyclopedia of strategic leadership and management*. IGI Global. https://doi.org/10.4018/978-1-5225-1049-9

Statista. (2022, October). *Gig economy in South Korea*. Statista. https://www.statista.com/study/117955/gig-economy-in-south-korea/

Statista. (2023a, August). *Target audience: Self-employed people and freelancers in Indonesia*. Statista. https://www.statista.com/study/126966/self-employed-people-and-freelancers-in-indonesia/

Statista. (2023b, August). *Target audience: Self-employed people and freelancers in Japan*. Statista. https://www.statista.com/study/126969/target-audience-self-employed-people-and-freelancers-in-japan/

Statista. (2023c, August). *Target audience: Self-employed people and freelancers in Malaysia*. Statista. https://www.statista.com/study/126972/self-employed-people-and-freelancers-in-malaysia/

Statista. (2023d, August). *Target audience: Self-employed people and freelancers in Singapore*. Statista. https://www.statista.com/study/126984/self-employed-people-and-freelancers-in-singapore/

Statista Company Insights. (2023, July 12). *Top 100 companies: Sharing Economy*. Statista. https://www.statista.com/study/140121/top-100-companies-sharing-economy/

Tan, J. (2022, September 8). *HappyFresh next to reportedly make job cuts*. Marketing-Interactive. https://www.marketing-interactive.com/happyfresh-job-cuts-review-financials

Vase.ai. (2022, September 12). *Malaysia: Leading e-commerce platforms for grocery shopping 2022 [Graph]*. Statista. https://www.statista.com/statistics/1335958/malaysia-leading-e-commerce-platforms-for-grocery-shopping/

Wallace, B. (2019, December 9). *The history and future of the gig economy*. LinkedIn. https://www.linkedin.com/pulse/history-future-gig-economy-brian-wallace/

Wood, A. J., Lehdonvirta, V., & Graham, M. (2018). Workers of the Internet unite? Online freelancer organization among remote gig economy workers in six Asian and African countries. *New Technology, Work and Employment, 33*(2), 95–112. https://doi.org/10.1111/ntwe.12112

Wu, Q., Zhang, H., Li, Z., & Liu, K. (2019). Labor control in the gig economy: Evidence from Uber in China. *Journal of Industrial Relations, 61*(4), 574–596. https://doi.org/10.1177/0022185619854472

Dr. Tobias Endress is an Assistant Professor and Program Director for Business Analytics & Digital Transformation at the Asian Institute of Technology (AIT) | School of Management. He has more than 20 years of professional experience in digital project business and innovation management. His former (non-academic) roles include project manager, product owner, and business analyst for leading financial companies in Europe and the United States. He has completed professional training for banking, graduated in Computer Science and Business Administration at VWA Frankfurt/Main, and in Business Economics at Avans+ in Breda (NL). He got a Master's Degree in Leadership in Digital Communication at Berlin University of the Arts (UdK Berlin), as well as a Doctorate in Business Administration at the University of Gloucestershire in Cheltenham (UK).

Adopting Tele-migration in Developing Asian Market: Exploring Drivers in the Face of Change

Tayyaba Irum Shakil, Adeel Tariq, Mumtaz Ali Memon, and Marko Torkkeli

Abstract The Industrial Revolution and globalization have brought about major changes in all industries, which have a direct impact on corporate success. Tele-migration is an emerging strategy that allows individuals to work remotely from foreign countries to gain several advantages while also favorably impacting the corporate environment. This study offers a unique exploration of the tele-migration phenomenon by utilizing diffusion of innovation theory as a theoretical framework. This research looks at the internal and external factors that drive individuals in the developing Asian market to use tele-migration. The internal factors that encourage the adoption of tele-migration include mainly freedom and flexibility, cultural immersion, financial incentives, and skills development, while the external factors comprise limited job prospects, government favorable policies, technological advancements, and skill-based compensation. Moreover, tele-migration is changing the performance of individuals in terms of their routine, work performance, and quality, resulting in increased productivity and improved skills. This study has practical implications such as adopting tailored tactics like tele-migration to address the industrial revolution and globalization opportunities and changes, moreover, individuals and start-ups can overcome geographical constraints and tap into the potential of expanding Asian markets by exploiting the benefits of tele-migration.

Keywords Tele-migration · Internal drivers · External drivers · Developing country · Expanding Asian markets

---

T. I. Shakil · A. Tariq (✉)
NUST Business School, National University of Sciences and Technology, Islamabad, Pakistan
e-mail: adeel.tariq@lut.fi

A. Tariq · M. Torkkeli
Industrial Engineering and Management Department, Lappeenranta-Lahti University of Technology (LUT), Kouvola Unit, Kouvola, Finland
e-mail: marko.torkkeli@lut.fi

© The Author(s), under exclusive license to Springer Nature Singapore Pte Ltd. 2024
T. Endress and Y. F. Badir (eds.), *Business and Management in Asia: Disruption and Change*, https://doi.org/10.1007/978-981-99-9371-0_8

Introduction

The Fourth Industrial Revolution and globalization are driving forces behind the fast-paced development of emerging market companies in the Asian area. Due to these factors and the advent of digital technologies, many industries have experienced substantial changes and disruptions (Tsapenko & Grishin, 2022). The rise of telecommunication services and the ability to work remotely from any location, including one's home, has increased the significance of distant employees in showing their professional skills and talents (Tsapenko & Grishin, 2022). This creative working structure enables Asian markets to export their services directly, as opposed to the conventional strategy of creating goods with local labor and then exporting them (Baldwin, 2019). This lucrative opportunity for the Asian market has resulted in the overall expansion of the service trade which is likely to be an export gain for them (Baldwin & Forslid, 2020). This trade in services gives rise to "tele-migration," in which an employee with recognizable skills while sitting in a foreign country, works in offices in another country and interacts with foreign employers using online platforms and digital gadgets (Serrat, 2021; Tsapenko & Grishin, 2022).

Tele-migration is an innovative approach to personnel management that helps employers, small businesses, and companies save expenses related to setting up foreign branches in the regions where experts and specialists reside (Tsapenko & Grishin, 2022). This also saves them from the costs related to the relocation of in-demand foreign workers to their country of employment. All the interactions between the employer and employees happen via online platforms that only require internet connectivity and technological gadgets (Nash et al., 2018). Tsapenko and Grishin (2022) documented that employers, including small businesses, can have access to a pool of talented workers and performers across the globe and enable them to quickly hire the most suitable candidate who is an expert in his field.

Tele-migration also facilitates the formation of international teams of workers willing to solve the personnel problems of the companies and improve work efficiency. Distributing the tasks among such mixed work teams allows businesses to concentrate their resources on the primary areas of business activity, enhancing maneuverability and flexibility (Kuek et al., 2015). Hiring foreign employees from different geographical backgrounds fosters cultural diversity in the workforce which as previous studies show, stimulates creativity, increases efficiency, and makes the organization more appealing to potential foreign employees (Kovács-Ondrejkovic et al., 2021). Moreover, organizations with virtual and online communication channels and procedures that promote routine cooperation, idea sharing, and cross-cultural understanding among personnel, even when they are dispersed across multiple locations, are more like to reap higher benefits from cultural diversity. Ultimately, these factors enhance the competitiveness and effectiveness of business operations (Tsapenko & Grishin, 2022). Furthermore, this practice effectively spares employees from the financial burdens associated with relocating to the employment country (Martin, 2017). Tele-migration allows talented workers from abroad to telecommute into the workplaces of another country and compete for the service sector and professional jobs there. Working productively while saving cost has led to an increase in tele-migration (Gousev & Yurevich, 2021).

Baldwin (2019) has attributed tele-migration as an opportunity for many economies, such as Asian economies employees to secure worldwide employment opportunities. Tele-migrants get to offer and deliver their services at high-wage rates, making no compromise on the quality of the service. Baldwin and Forslid (2020) suggested that it is a win–win situation for both the employer and employee as companies in high-income countries can hire a tele-migrant at a low-wage rate as compared to the employee they can hire from their own country at a standard wage rate (higher than they pay to a tele-migrant). The global transactions are between the workers (sellers of services) from countries with low cost and the employers (buyers of services) from high-cost countries who are willing to pay high wages (Graham & Anwar, 2019). A tele-migrant is also able to earn more due to the dollar exchange rate of his own home country (Brinatti et al., 2021). The significant price differential enables both workers and employers to benefit in the global market for information services and other related services without the need for physical migration (Graham & Anwar, 2019).

This research has its own merits in explaining how digital disruption is creating opportunities for individuals and start-ups in the Asian region, for this reason, this research delves into a specific aspect that holds immense significance: the study of internal and external factors that motivate the adoption of tele-migration. This research intends to provide a thorough understanding to practitioners of the factors that influence the success of tele-migrants, considering the growing significance of tele-migrants in Asian economies and their impact on the global workforce. This research provides practitioners with invaluable insights and practical knowledge to manage tele-migrant teams effectively, maximize their performance, and navigate the complexities of this evolving paradigm by looking at both the internal motivation factors and the external factors influencing the tele-migration landscape. Moreover, it is also significant for policymakers to understand the factors for strategically designing the policies to enhance the export of services that lead to overall economic growth and in the meantime, dealing with economic factors such as unemployment. It can also help to design flexible policies and procedures that support employees' desire to adopt tele-migration. Moreover, the findings of the research can also help startups and organizations to know about the factors that encourage their domestic talent to work for foreign companies instead of working for them. Lastly, the study may assist prospective tele-migrants in understanding the effects of tele-migration, particularly how it will change their performance and routines before entering the world of tele-migration.

Adoption of Innovation Model

In this era of innovation, corporations, and startups are interested and enthusiastic about new and innovative concepts that can be beneficial for their businesses (Modgil et al., 2022). To date, the benefits and drawbacks of globalization and automation have been primarily experienced by the manufacturing sector in both developing and developed countries (Baldwin & Forslid, 2020). But in the future, professional and service-sector jobs are also likely to experience the advantages of this concept.

We operationalized innovation adoption theory to understand the factors that influence the adoption of tele-migration among individuals in Pakistan, this theory has been extensively used to analyze technological innovation adoption in management and business research (Clohessy & Acton, 2019; van de Weerd et al., 2016). Moreover, the adoption of the innovation model best suits the context of this research as it elaborates on the decision-making process and individual factors that influence the adoption of tele-migration. In this study, the term "innovation" refers to tele-migration, an innovative approach to work that enables individuals to perform their job responsibilities remotely from foreign countries. Tele-migration is a departure from conventional working conditions and offers potential advantages such as cost savings, talent access, and flexibility. Adoption in this context refers to the decision-making process that leads people in growing Asian market, Pakistan, to choose tele-migration as a work strategy. Adoption includes learning about tele-migration, developing an opinion of it, deciding to use it, carrying it out, and reaffirming its use. Thus, adopting the innovation model provides a vital foundation for understanding the factors that influence the adoption of tele-migration by individuals in Pakistan, a developing Asian nation.

Tele-migration supports the innovative working arrangements from developed countries into developing countries where the labor in the developed countries is overpriced as compared to the developing countries, so it mostly represents an export opportunity for developing countries and an import opportunity for developed countries (Baldwin & Forslid, 2020). The consequences of this innovation in developing nations can be counted as desirable which opens multiple opportunities for the skillful workers of developing countries to work in foreign offices and avail monetary and non-monetary benefits.

According to a BCG survey conducted by Kovács-Ondrejkovic et al. (2021), the most attractive and appealing countries for cross-border remote work are high-wage nations like the United States, Australia, Canada, Germany, and Great Britain. The main things for this attraction are the compensation package, the nature of the job, and the dependability of the employer (Kovács-Ondrejkovic et al., 2021). The BCG survey further highlighted that the United States is the most sought-after location among all these advanced economies. According to the statistics employers who are importing services from tele-migrants are concentrated with 75% located in just 4 countries, namely, US (53.4%), Australia (8.3%), UK (7.4%), and Canada (6.4%). Moreover, majority of the workers (over 60%) exporting their services abroad are concentrated in just 3 Asian countries, namely India, Philippines, and Pakistan

(Bayudan-Dacuycuy et al., 2020). According to Hanson et al. (2018), a significant percentage of online workers are from the People's Republic of China, India, Russia, Ukraine, Vietnam, and Pakistan and they export their services in the field of software development/technology.

The analysis done by Brinatti et al. (2021) regarding remote wages shows that employee's location is a significant factor that accounts for almost one-third of the variability in remote wages. Their research indicates that the observed wage difference is strongly linked with the GPD per capita of the employee's location and is not influenced by the employer's location. Moreover, the wages expressed in the local currency are subject to fluctuations due to purchasing power parity and tele-migrants are likely to earn higher amounts in local currency reflecting the exchange rate dynamics (Brinatti et al., 2021).

Tele-migration—A Different Type of Remote Work

The difference between tele-migrants from other types of remote work is explained in Table 1.

Table 1 Examples of different types of remote work

Terms	Examples
Tele-migration	A tele-migrant can occupy a highly skilled occupation or strategic position in foreign companies that require higher education. These are accountants, engineers, architects, software developers, programmers, creative writers, designers, etc. For instance, a copywriter of advertisements from Pakistan virtually teleports into the office in New York using digital technology in the evening and teleports back at midnight. This would surely help the New York firm to get the job done at a lower wage rate and would allow the Pakistani copywriter to earn a higher salary (Baldwin, 2019)
Outsourcing	An organization transfers the responsibility of its functions on a contractual basis such as HR, finance, legal, IT services, advertising, and software development. These independent vendors are responsible for executing and sourcing their services to these businesses with fee-for-service outsourcing (McIvor, 2010)
Freelancing	Freelance work is independent and self-directed and formed by a freelancer identified as an independent contractor. A freelancer works for different clients and gets compensation on a project basis often associated with providing expert services such as in writing and creative occupations (Kuhn & Galloway, 2019; Stephany et al., 2021)
Gig work	Gig work is assessed through digital platforms and traditional ways like advertising or networking. Gig work engages a gig worker mainly in task-based work that requires lower skills such as ridesharing or microwork and sometimes in knowledge-intensive or creative work for a longer time such as IT consulting, graphic designing, and coaching (Caza et al., 2022)

The Location of the Worker Differentiates Tele-migration

In alignment with these definitions and the concept of tele-migration, it can be inferred that the location of the worker or employee differentiates tele-migration from all other types of remote work, i.e., a tele-migrant remains in his city/country and works for an overseas company. Such companies adopt the technology and make the work arrangements easy for the tele-migrants to work for them. According to Baldwin, (2019), a tele-migrant virtually teleports to the office in another country in the morning using digital platforms and gadgets and then teleports back to his home in the evening. However, in telework and telecommuting an employee performs his duties and responsibilities from his home, or any other location and that location does not necessarily have to be in another country like in the case of tele-migration (Ollo-López et al., 2021). Furthermore, unlike tele-migration gig work and outsourced activities that can be performed by any local or global vendor, it does not necessarily have to be performed by workers overseas (McIvor, 2010).

The Role of a Tele-migrant Differentiates Tele-migration

The participation of the tele-migrant as an employee or as a team member of his international office differentiates tele-migration from other modes of remote work. Baldwin and Forslid, (2020) state that tele-migration is when a person is virtually going to the office in another country and is participating as a team member using his different gadgets, online tools, and platforms. However, in other types of remote work, it is not necessary for a person who is working online to be an employee or team member of the firm he is working for, i.e., a freelancer is self-employed and is an independent worker who works for any organization without being its permanent employee (Akhmetshin et al., 2018) and is compensated on the project basis (Kuhn & Galloway, 2019; Stephany et al., 2021). Furthermore, a gig worker engages in task-based work (Caza et al., 2022) and is not bound to any organization, he gets the assigned gig or task and moves to the next one (Barlage et al., 2019). In terms of outsourcing, tele-migration is different from a company outsourcing its operations or projects to external suppliers on a contract base that is not for a long term. Such companies need temporary expertise for any specific task or project. An organization pursues selective outsourcing involving the transfer of limited responsibilities and activities related to the business process, transitional outsourcing involving outsourcing a process temporarily, or pursue total outsourcing involving the outsourcing of an entire process to the local or global vendor (McIvor, 2010).

Methodology

The study is qualitative and was conducted following the phenomenological approach to interpret the meanings of the participants' experiences in relation to the tele-migration phenomenon. The study focuses on understanding the meaning of tele-migrants' experiences by searching the themes and interpretatively engaging with the data following the interpretative phenomenology (Gohar et al., 2022; Neubauer et al., 2019). The researcher for this study collected data from a homogenous population taking semi-structured interviews and probing questions were also asked to evoke in-depth information. The interview questions addressed the encouraging factors of the participants for tele-migration adoption and how it is altering the performance of these tele-migrants. Sixteen interviews were conducted, including interviews from experienced and knowledgeable tele-migrants in different foreign offices. Interviews were coded using ATLAS software and categories were created based on it.

Internal Factors that Encourage Tele-migration Adoption

Financial Incentives and Enhanced Compensation

Tele-migrants from developing Asian countries experience difficulties in earning competitive wages in local enterprises, prompting them to seek better financial opportunities through tele-migration. Converting their salary into the currency of their native nation yields two to three times the amount they could earn locally. Tele-migration is an appealing alternative for freshers seeking improved living standards in a shorter time due to limited income rates and a lack of experience. Most of the participants adopted tele-migration to become financially independent while studying and the late working hours due to the different time zones helped them to manage their jobs while studying in the daytime.

Foreign employers particularly respect the pay for working longer hours, which is uncommon in the local job market. When compared to traditional work in local companies, tele-migration provides better payment in terms of salary, hourly rates, bonuses, commissions, and overtime pay. Moreover, the majority of the respondents adopted tele-migration after experiencing exploitation by the local companies as they did not get the deserved appreciation or compensation and were often asked to work extra hours without any compensation (Memon et al., 2020). Another major issue for them was limited communication with their employer where limited mutual respect and information was shared between the employee and the employer.

Furthermore, tele-migration provides huge cost savings to enterprises in a variety of ways. Physical office space is no longer required, allowing them to function digitally (Baldwin et al., 2021). Businesses can obtain qualified and skilled personnel from anywhere in the country through tele-migration. Additionally, expenses such as energy, office supplies, equipment, and the upkeep of power backup systems are decreased. Tele-migrants control their resources; therefore, companies no longer need to give physical assets to employees (Tsapenko & Grishin, 2022). This allows tele-migrants to create cash that may be used for personal needs rather than transportation, office meals, clothing, and grooming.

International Job Experience and Cultural Immersion

Tele-migrants are driven by the ability to explore and get exposure to worldwide markets, including overseas companies' work culture, ethics, and practices. Tele-migration facilitates participants' strong desire to learn about and broaden their awareness of foreign workplace culture, ethics, the legal environment, and interacting with international clients and consumers. Their interest extends to comprehending multinational clientele's ideas and beliefs and this versatile exposure is regarded as beneficial to their self-esteem and confidence.

Moreover, a healthy employee–employer relationship at work helped in the development of mutual trust and respect between tele-migrants and their employers, paving the way for high employee morale, effective communication between them, and improved tele-migrant performance. According to the participants, the clear and precise guidelines of the foreign employers improve their work quality. It helps them to understand their tasks and what the employer is expecting from them. So, putting effort into the right tasks allows them to meet and exceed the expectations of their company.

Additionally, tele-migration allows people to gain much-needed exposure to working with diverse cultures without physically relocating to another country. Foreign employers' and teams' timeliness and dedication to work inspired tele-migrants to develop punctuality, time management skills, self-control, and encourage them to improve their work ethics and performance. The majority of participants agree that observing their colleagues' professionalism, skillfulness, and work quality from around the world assists them in developing their own work quality, skills, and professional qualities.

Freedom of Mobility

Freedom is one of the most prominent internal factors that encouraged the participants to tele-migration adoption. The freedom of mobility that comes with tele-migration helped the participants to do their jobs from anywhere and not be location-bound for their jobs. As mentioned by the participants, they can even do their jobs while traveling, when they are on vacation, and even when they are managing other activities side by side. Moreover, participants adopted tele-migration to avoid the massive struggles that come with relocation, where they had to take a clean slate of their lives in another country or continent. So, instead of relocating, they can get the experience of working across the border while sitting in the comfort of their homes, saving their expenses, travel hassles, and time.

Flexible Working Hours and a Secure Work Environment

Flexibility in working hours, which allows tele-migrants to do their tasks whenever they wish, is another motivating element that encouraged tele-migration adoption. This flexibility allows people who are balancing their academics with this profession to work whenever it is convenient for them. All tele-migrants say that their productivity and job efficiency have increased and improved because of working from their comfort zones when their brains are relaxed, and they can take breaks between work (Choudhury, 2020; Mehmood et al., 2021). Their efficiency increases as well because when they do not need the entire working hour to complete a task, they efficiently complete their tasks before the deadline and enjoy the rest of the time, as opposed to traditional jobs where they must be physically present and sit idle to complete the working hours. Furthermore, few participants are satisfied with their work schedules because they believe tele-migration helps them to keep a healthy lifestyle, offers them more time for physical activities, hobbies, and interests, and enhances their connections.

This flexibility of hours also allows female tele-migrants who are mothers or stay-at-home spouses to manage their family life while working. Moreover, security is one of the key reasons for the female participants, as they and their families were concerned about their workplace security and other connected issues such as workplace harassment. Because relocation was not an option for them, they were drawn to tele-migration to earn a living while sitting in a safe and secure location of their choice.

Fostering Productive Boundaries

For most of the participants, another internal factor in this adoption was that they did not want to be watched by someone while working and being answerable to them on the spot as then they felt anxious. Also, they wanted to avoid physical interaction with their employer and other colleagues because of their introverted personalities so tele-migration provided them with the freedom of working in isolation without socializing with colleagues. This trend is likely to increase in the future where people would like to maintain a specific distance from their colleagues in hostile work environments (Lodovici et al., 2021).

Transparency in Process

Transparency in the processes and communication proved to be another reason for enhancing the work performance of the tele-migrants as the digital platforms assist in smooth, transparent, and effective communication between the tele-migrants and their employers. When there is no communication gap and tele-migrants are provided with all the necessary information at the appropriate times it increases their work efficiency. Furthermore, the transparency in the work processes does not allow organizational politics or personal conflicts to obstruct tele-migrants' productivity and efficiency.

Skill Development in Tele-migration

Tele-migrants are provided with different necessary tools, equipment, and on-the-job training that in their opinion help in using their skills to complete their tasks with the highest standards. Most of the participants agreed that tele-migration has helped them in learning and enhancing their skills including communication skills, technological skills, problem-solving, and time management skills. According to the participants, it has enhanced their adaptivity, helping them grow in the industry, and they are learning multiple skills at the same time.

Many people are motivated to become technologically savvy as they recognize the growing importance of tele-migration and its expected growth in the coming years. Adopting this career allows individuals to obtain insights into this phenomenon, comprehend its mechanics, and investigate how to capitalize on technological advancements to gain considerable experience and exposure to firms and communities abroad while remaining in their home nation.

External Factors that Encourage Tele-migration Adoption

Limited Job Prospects in the Local Market

One of the most significant external factors influencing individuals' decision to earn a living through tele-migration is the lack of opportunities. The majority of tele-migrants had difficulty finding stable and well-compensated jobs in their home nation based on their education, aptitude, and skills. They believe that there are currently very few possibilities accessible, particularly for students, recent graduates, and persons with no work experience. These individuals subsequently researched worldwide marketplaces and took advantage of the opportunities available, leading to the introduction of tele-migration. Another external aspect highlighted by participants was in-demand skills that are determined by factors like technological development, economic growth, demographic change, and globalization (Hoftijzer & Gortazar, 2018). Various skills were in demand in the European market, where employers recognized their skills and offered them a better job than they were doing in local organizations.

Skill-Based Compensation by Overseas Employers

According to the participants' home countries, no matter how skilled they are, they can only make a certain amount of money. Many of them are now compensated on a skill-based basis by overseas corporations. Furthermore, it was simple for participants to export their services depending on their talents, which were valued and generously compensated by overseas companies. Another external element that influenced the participants' adoption of tele-migration was Pakistan's emerging economy. This was a motivating element for them because the foreign currency conversion rates in Pakistan are fairly high, allowing them to earn a sizable wage when translated into Pakistani money. Furthermore, a few participants stated that by utilizing tele-migration, their foreign exchange gains are viewed as critical to their country's economic prosperity.

Government Policies and Regulator Flexibility for Empowering Tele-migration

Pakistan's government laws and regulators regulating and encouraging tele-migration and other associated types of labor are flexible, which benefits tele-migrants. These policies, as noted by the participants, encouraged them to migrate more and acted as an external element in this adoption. These policies, as stated by the participants, enable them to obtain bank loans, credit cards, and the simplicity of sending and receiving payments abroad in exchange for their services, software purchases, online platform usage, and other similar charges.

Technological Advancements

Tele-migration is being driven by technological advancements and altering work paradigms (Baldwin & Forslid, 2020), which make it simpler for individuals to interact, find work on online markets, and receive money through cross-border platforms. Tele-migration not only opens more lucrative prospects but also allows participants to keep up with changing work trends and technology breakthroughs. Businesses and labor migrating to internet platforms (Baruah et al., 2021) caused a spike in tele-migration during the COVID-19 pandemic. Because tele-migrants were unable to find physical occupations in their native countries or relocate elsewhere for work, several participants chose tele-migration.

Challenges and Impact of Tele-migration on Tele-migrant

Work Demands and Impact on Routines and Holidays

Tele-migrants typically receive national, public, regional, official, and unofficial holidays observed in the country in which they work, hence they are mostly working on holidays observed in their home country. To accomplish their jobs before such holidays, individuals must work extra hours every week, which disrupts their routines during this time.

Isolation, Loneliness, and Mental Health Challenges

Few individuals stated that their performance is hampered in some way by isolation, loneliness, and night shifts. They grow bored and sluggish, and it becomes difficult for them to find time for themselves and other activities, which affects their mental and physical health. They become agitated and less motivated to complete their jobs when they are unable to be physically present in an office setting. So, in tele-migration, they lack the drive that they can get from being part of a large team and having an in-person connection with them. Tele-migrants have a lack of personal development chances due to a lack of socialization and in-person engagement.

Summary

This research has explored the acceptance of tele-migration in the developing Asian market—Pakistan. The acceptance of tele-migration is driven by financial incentives and higher compensation, which raises wages and improves the standard of living for people from developing Asian nations. International work experience and cultural immersion also contribute by raising employee morale, facilitating effective communication, and enhancing performance. Moreover, the freedom of movement that comes with tele-migration to accomplish their jobs from anywhere and not be location-bound for their occupations, encourages its adoption, in addition to flexible working hours and secure working hours. Other internal factors that play a significant role include skills development, transparency in the process, and fostering productive boundaries. External factors that support tele-migration adoption include limited employment opportunities, skill-based compensation, flexible government regulations, and technological advancements. These factors attract tele-migrants with high-demand abilities, facilitate cross-border transactions, and provide opportunities for accessing financial services. Policymakers and practitioners can further encourage the adoption of tele-migration successfully by addressing the difficulties faced by tele-migrants, finding the best practices, and implementing them. The main obstacles that must be considered and minimized include disruptions to routines, isolation, and mental health issues.

To maximize the benefits of tele-migration, businesses should make substantial infrastructure investments, maintain secure work environments, and develop efficient communication and collaboration solutions. They should also put tele-migrants' well-being first by providing support networks, encouraging work–life balance, and encouraging a feeling of community. Professionals who tele-migrate should actively manage their work–life balance, keep up their social networks, and ask for help when they need it. By creating flexible legislation, encouraging digital literacy, and supporting programs that ease cross-border transactions and access to financial services, policymakers may play a significant role.

References

Akhmetshin, E. M., Kovalenko, K. E., Mueller, J. E., Khakimov, A., Yumashev, A., & Khairullina, A. (2018). Freelancing as a type of entrepreneurship: Advantages, disadvantages and development prospects. *Journal of Entrepreneurship Education, 21*(2), 1528–2651.

Baldwin, R. (2019). Globalisation 4.0 and the future of work. *Economistas, 165*, 63–75.

Baldwin, R., & Forslid, R. (2020). *Globotics and development: When manufacturing is jobless and services are tradable.* National Bureau of Economic Research.

Barlage, M., van den Born, A., & van Witteloostuijn, A. (2019). The needs of freelancers and the characteristics of 'gigs': Creating beneficial relations between freelancers and their hiring organizations. *Emerald Open Research, 1*, 8.

Baruah, N., Chaloff, J., & Dumont, J. (2021). *Labor migration in Asia: Impacts of the COVID-19 crisis and the post-pandemic future.* Tokyo: Asian Development Bank Institute, Organization for Economic Co-Operation and Development, and International Labour Organization. [Google Scholar].

Bayudan-Dacuycuy, C., Orbeta, A. C., Serafica, R. B., & Baje, L. K. C. (2020). *Online work in the Philippines: Some lessons in the Asian context.* PIDS discussion paper series.

Brinatti, A., Cavallo, A., Cravino, J., & Drenik, A. (2021). *The international price of remote work.* National Bureau of Economic Research.

Caza, B. B., Reid, E. M., Ashford, S. J., & Granger, S. (2022). Working on my own: Measuring the challenges of gig work. *Human Relations, 75*(11), 2122–2159.

Choudhury, P. (2020). Our work-from-anywhere future. *Harvard Business Review, 98*(6), 58.

Clohessy, T., & Acton, T. (2019). *Investigating the Influence of Organizational Factors on Blockchain Adoption: An Innovation Theory Perspective., 119*(7), 1457–1491. https://doi.org/10.1108/IMDS-08-2018-0365

Gohar, M., Abrar, A., & Tariq, A. (2022). The role of family factors in shaping the entrepreneurial intentions of women: A case study of women entrepreneurs from Peshawar, Pakistan. *The Role of Ecosystems in Developing Startups: Frontiers in European Entrepreneurship Research, 40.*

Gousev, A., & Yurevich, M. (2021). Globalization of employment amid COVID-19 pandemic. *MGIMO Review of International Relations, 14*(1), 148–173.

Graham, M., & Anwar, M. (2019). The global gig economy: Towards a planetary labour market? *First Monday, 24*(4).

Hanson, G. H., Kerr, W. R., & Turner, S. (2018). *High-skilled migration to the United States and its economic consequences.* University of Chicago Press.

Hoftijzer, M., & Gortazar, L. (2018). *Skills and Europe's Labor Market.*

Kovács-Ondrejkovic, O., Strack, R., Baier, J., Antebi, P., Kavanagh, K., & Gobernado, A. L. (2021). *Decoding global talent, onsite and virtual.* Boston Consulting Group.

Kuek, S. C., Paradi-Guilford, C., Fayomi, T., Imaizumi, S., Ipeirotis, P., Pina, P., & Singh, M. (2015). *The global opportunity in online outsourcing.*

Kuhn, K. M., & Galloway, T. L. (2019). Expanding perspectives on gig work and gig workers. *Journal of Managerial Psychology, 34*(4), 186–191.

Lodovici, M. S., Ferrari, E., Paladino, E., Pesce, F., Frecassetti, P., & Aram, E. (2021). *The impact of teleworking and digital work on workers and society.* Study Requested by the EMPL Committee.

Martin, P. L. (2017). *Merchants of labor: Recruiters and international labor migration.* Oxford University Press.

McIvor, R. (2010). *Global services outsourcing.* Cambridge University Press.

Mehmood, M. S., Jian, Z., Akram, U., & Tariq, A. (2021). Entrepreneurial leadership: The key to develop creativity in organizations. *Leadership and Organization Development Journal.*

Memon, M. A., Salleh, R., Mirza, M. Z., Cheah, J.-H., Ting, H., Ahmad, M. S., & Tariq, A. (2020). Satisfaction matters: The relationships between HRM practices, work engagement and turnover intention. *International Journal of Manpower, 42*(1), 21–50.

Modgil, S., Dwivedi, Y. K., Rana, N. P., Gupta, S., & Kamble, S. (2022). Has Covid-19 accelerated opportunities for digital entrepreneurship? An Indian perspective. *Technological Forecasting and Social Change, 175*, 121415.

Nash, C., Jarrahi, M. H., Sutherland, W., & Phillips, G. (2018). *Digital nomads beyond the buzzword: Defining digital nomadic work and use of digital technologies* (pp. 207–217).

Neubauer, B. E., Witkop, C. T., & Varpio, L. (2019). How phenomenology can help us learn from the experiences of others. *Perspectives on Medical Education, 8*, 90–97.

Ollo-López, A., Goñi-Legaz, S., & Erro-Garcés, A. (2021). Home-based telework: Usefulness and facilitators. *International Journal of Manpower, 42*(4), 644–660.

Serrat, O. (2021). Techtonic: The role of technology in organizations. *Unpublished Manuscript, The Chicago School of Professional Psychology.*

Stephany, F., Kässi, O., Rani, U., & Lehdonvirta, V. (2021). Online labour index 2020: New ways to measure the world's remote freelancing market. *Big Data and Society, 8*(2), 20539517211043240.

Tsapenko, I., & Grishin, I. (2022). Virtualization of cross-border labor migration. *Herald of the Russian Academy of Sciences, 92*(5), 580–589.

van de Weerd, I., Mangula, I. S., & Brinkkemper, S. (2016). Adoption of software as a service in Indonesia: Examining the influence of organizational factors. *Information and Management, 53*(7), 915–928.

Tayyaba Irum Shakil is an MS Innovation and Entrepreneurship student at NUST Business School in Islamabad, Pakistan. With a strong academic background and a passion for learning, Tayyaba has actively engaged in various research projects in collaboration with reputable institutions. Her research interests include entrepreneurial learning, new venture creation, design thinking, innovative work arrangements that drive organizational success, and advanced qualitative research methods.

Dr. Mumtaz Ali Memon is an associate professor and research coordinator at the business school of Sohar University in Oman. He is the managing editor of applied structural equation modeling journal JASEM. Dr. Mumtaz has published in several international refereed journals and earned "Best Paper" honors. He has spoken at several international conferences. Additionally, he proudly has the "2018 Emerald Literati Award for Outstanding Paper." His research interests include advanced quantitative methods, performance management systems, green HRM, and high-performance work systems.

Prof. Marko Torkkeli is a Professor of Technology and Business Innovations at the Lappeenranta-Lahti University of Technology (LUT), Kouvola Unit in Finland. His research interests focus on technology and innovation management, strategic entrepreneurship, growth venturing, and decision support systems. He has published over 300 articles in academic journals and conferences. He serves as the Director of Publications of the International Society for Professional Innovation Management (ISPIM) and is one of the founding editors of the open-access, multidisciplinary Journal of Innovation Management. He was leading the EU flagship project on the European Academic Network for Open Innovation, designed to promote cooperation on open innovation topics in European Higher Education Curricula and Institutes within the knowledge triangle for the benefit of EU competitiveness (52 partners from 35 countries).

Back to Work or Remote Work: Trends and Challenges

Anita Maharani

Abstract Businesses around Asia are pushing workers to return to conventional workplaces and offices. Several workers have indicated a desire to continue working from home or in a hybrid setting. Employers and governments are responding by providing incentives to encourage people to return to work. As workplaces continue to transform, new possibilities and hazards for all stakeholders are emerging. The purpose of this research is to examine the trend experienced in a number of Asian countries related to working mode policies, during which more companies practiced remote work during the pandemic, now that a number of Asian countries have opened access to mobility for their citizens and foreigners, a number of companies have also returned the policy from remote work to back to work. However, this does not imply that all companies are solely implementing back-to-work; there are several companies that are still surviving with the same working model as before the pandemic; thus, the purpose of this article is to highlight the characteristics of companies that implement remote work and back to work.

Keywords Workplace · Mode of work · Asia · Business

Introduction: The Stand Point

The issue of pandemics still seems interesting to be raised as a research theme, even though the focus is indeed increasingly diverse from time to time, in line with changes in society. Several years ago, a number of studies dealing with themes related to COVID-19 flourished and are still considered interesting to be raised as research themes even when entering 2023 with a focus on recovery. The research that emerged in the early days of the pandemic focused mainly on the adaptation of companies and individuals related to mobility restrictions imposed by many countries, then, from a focus on adaptation to issues regarding the management of human resources related to mental health, however, studies that raise the conditions in the organizational

---

A. Maharani (✉)
Master Management, BINUS Business School, Jakarta, Indonesia
e-mail: anita.maharani@binus.edu

© The Author(s), under exclusive license to Springer Nature Singapore Pte Ltd. 2024
T. Endress and Y. F. Badir (eds.), *Business and Management in Asia: Disruption and Change*, https://doi.org/10.1007/978-981-99-9371-0_9

or corporate environment related to post-pandemic decisions have not been widely explored.

On the other hand, a number of studies have seen that the positive side resulting from the pandemic is that a number of employee management policy initiatives have emerged in almost all companies. Among them is the working mode policy, and if prior to the pandemic the term flexible working arrangement was better known, then during the pandemic complementary terms were used, including work from office, work from anywhere, or work from home, which are actually similar to flexible working arrangements. In the context of location. However, studies that address the application of this policy post-pandemic have yet to be widely explored as several practices in the field still apply policies similar to the pandemic, and several practices in the field have "returned" the working mode policy to full onsite in the company.

However, habits that arose because of the COVID-19 pandemic did not change immediately. Long before the COVID-19 pandemic, the industry was actually familiar with the term work arrangements, where basically the term telecommuting was known for a long time, to be precise in the 1970s when Jack Nilles who worked at NASA mentioned the term "telecommuting" because working from home (Newport, 2020), and continued without how long later with IBM conducting experiments by allowing a number of its employees to work from home (Allen, 2020).

How about the current developments? When a number of countries decided to revoke the obligation to use masks in public spaces? From the results of a survey conducted was stated that 74% of the total respondents who participated in the study stated that they planned to change their employee work patterns from having to come to the office to "remote" (Lavelle, 2020). Similar conditions are also experienced by workers who carry out their work in project mode, which may not be possible for the rest of their lives to apply the working mode from the office due to the varying scope of work and locations, and those who saw the potential for the enforcement mode flexible working is still relevant in jobs that do allow the practice (de Laat, 2023).

A research found that the impact of a pandemic on a person's work performance is enormous, one that is highlighted in the research is feelings of fatigue and problems in managing work completion because working people must also share time with family and personal issues related to COVID-19 (Chong & Huang, 2020). So, in a number of studies, it is suggested that companies also provide solutions as a form of company attention to employees, which can be utilized by employees, especially related to work completion problems.

Remote Work: As not so Brand New Concept

Before the Industrial Revolution, remote work existed, but when the idea of telecommuting was first presented, it became its current shape. Jack Nilles first used the word "telecommuting" in 1972 to refer to working remotely on a NASA project, as mentioned earlier in this chapter. While remote work and telecommuting are distinct concepts, they complement one another. Moreover, remote working is a flexible work arrangement in which people operate in areas far from their central offices or production facilities, the worker has no human contact with co-workers there, but can interact with them using technology (Di Martino & Wirth, 1990).

Interestingly, remote work was always connected with a balance between family and work life, or, to put it another way, a family–work life before the epidemic. One research that highlights the connection between the two (Sullivan, 2012). As a result, even if remote work is common during a pandemic, the work–family balance problem is nothing new. However, it will always be fascinating to investigate the connection between the two from time to time, particularly when work–family life is connected to remote work during a pandemic and reviewed and compared to when it was still normal, and even when it is still the new normal.

General Findings in Current Studies

As long as the COVID-19 pandemic is considered a phenomenon, almost all industries implement different work arrangements than before. One that is popular during the pandemic is remote work. Remote work is considered something that is commonly done during a pandemic because, after all, business must continue, while on the other hand, there are also concerns about health problems. Therefore, in several years during the pandemic, several studies emerged that explored remote work practices in companies, then went inland regarding the effects of remote work on various aspects of a worker, such as work-family conflict, productivity, job performance, and work–life balance.

Study found that remote working is carried out by an employee due to a policy regulating working mode and is expected to be carried out from home; instead of reducing work–family conflict, it has intensified (Wang et al., 2021). The study found that remote work adoption has more positive relations than negative ones among professionals, with cost-reduction and work–life balance being the most positive outputs, while communication and technical problems, as well as management issues, are the main concerns (Ferreira et al., 2021). Condition is caused because workers consider remote work to interfere with family life. After all, everything that should be done in an office environment is carried out simultaneously with domestic life. It differs from one study found someone who try to see the relationship between remote work policies, which raise the problem of social isolation (Toscano & Zappalà, 2020). Social isolation in the research findings means that workers who were previously used to meeting and collaborating with other workers are limited and disconnected due to remote work. However, communication can be done online, including via short messages, electronic mail, or teleconferences. However, the loss of physical presence could better impact workers' job satisfaction. Thus, the impact of remote work can generate stress, reducing workers' perceptions of work productivity.

Remote work and stress levels are related and are experienced by both men and women. A study conducted before the pandemic found that workers who work in remote work mode must try hard to manage time between work and family time

(Eddleston & Mulki, 2017). In reality, managing time between work and family is not easy. This study also found that workers' efforts to integrate work–family will increase family-to-work conflict and work-to-family conflict. On the other hand, a worker is unable to detach from work, which can increase work-to-family conflict. Nonetheless, different findings mentioned someone who found that remote work can have a positive impact, including flexibility in working time and autonomy at work (Adekoya et al., 2022). Thus, apart from the potential problems caused by remote work, it can be assumed that if workers can manage their time properly, remote work will provide benefits related to flexibility and autonomy.

Sometime after the world was declared to be experiencing a pandemic, several studies about remote work began to link it to other factors besides productivity and job satisfaction. For example, a study seeks to explore the needs and challenges of remote work and compare it to a hybrid mode of work, which is seen from the perspectives of individuals, groups, and leadership in companies (Chafi et al., 2022). This study is interesting because it finds that remote work can provide benefits such as increased flexibility, autonomy, work–life balance, and individual performance. Nonetheless, the results of this study note that there are social aspects such as loss of friendship and feelings of alienation or social isolation due to remote work, so the hybrid work mode is considered an alternative. Hybrid working mode represents working from any location and at any time (Gratton, 2021). Although only a few companies have attempted to establish a hybrid work mode, this research shows that companies can overcome problems that arise among workers, especially due to remote work, by changing policies from remote work to hybrid.

In the pre-pandemic period, there was no longer any worry about the emergence of studies that attempted to confirm the results of research during the pandemic and even compared them with pre-pandemic conditions, and the impact of remote work on work productivity and also related to work-life balance (Rañeses et al., 2022). What is interesting is that previously remote work was considered to harm work–family life. When this research was conducted, it was found that remote work did not significantly impact employees' work–life balance; in other words, remote work cannot be expected to help employees balance their work life. Furthermore, a study explored the work productivity of workers in remote work mode, in general types of work (Morikawa, 2023). The results of this study break the notion that remote work will only positively impact workers who are engaged in creative types of work. However, on the contrary, it will harm workers engaged in monotonous work.

It is important for companies to pay attention to employee expectations regarding remote work (Carraher-Wolverton, 2022). In his study, it was found that workers' feelings toward remote work, which lead to dissatisfaction, can lead to decreased performance and involvement in cyberslacking. Thus the results of this study recommend that companies can manage working modes to provide satisfaction and maintain worker productivity when working remotely.

A study highlights the difficulties that telework employees encountered during the pandemic, as well as the relevance of organizational support in minimizing the negative consequences of task failures. The findings may assist organizations in better understanding how to support their employees and improve their telework experiences (Chong & Huang, 2020). Pandemic has setbacks, and it was positively connected to end-of-day emotional tiredness in the study. Employees who faced task setbacks were exhausted at the end of the day. Furthermore, employees with a higher level of task interdependence with coworkers showed a larger positive association between task failures and weariness; this implies that employees who rely on their teammates for coordinated job efforts are more vulnerable to task failures.

Findings on Hybrid and Remote Work

In order to support several discussions that raise the research that has been done, the researcher considers it important to present some data that can strengthen the discussion in this paper.

There is a change in trend in the way of working remotely that occurred due to COVID-19 in the United States, where after COVID-19, there was an increase in working mode to remote for five days compared to before the pandemic (Statista, 2023a). In other words, the company is trying to adapt and make it part of the company policy in setting its working mode.

Several countries even show a trend of companies implementing remote work policies. The country with the most companies practicing remote working is North America, Asia, and Europe. However, other parts of the world also show information about countries with companies that practice remote working modes, such as the Middle East, South America, the Pacific, and Africa. It is clear that some businesses had already adopted remote work as a mode of operation before COVID-19. However, as a result of the outbreak, fewer businesses continued to do so. Conversely, during the pandemic, the number of days designated for remote work increased significantly. The information above demonstrates that the pandemic has altered corporate practices, despite the existence of complementing evidence on businesses that continue to believe that remote labor is not required during a pandemic.

There are nations where businesses use remote labor to operate (Buildd, 2021). North America has the most, followed by Asia and Europe in population. While, there is also a survey found about comparisons between employers and employees regarding the success of remote work practices in the United States in 2020. The results show that both employers and workers think remote work is successful (Statista, 2023).

Next, some data came from Gartner in 2020, showing how big the company's interest is in practicing remote work after the pandemic. As organizations struggle with the continued business interruptions caused by COVID-19, permanent remote employment might supplement cost-cutting initiatives that CFOs have already implemented or plan to implement. According to Gartner's poll, 20% of respondents have delayed on-premise technology spending, with another 12% planning to do so. An additional 13% of respondents stated that they have already reduced their real estate expenditures, with another 9% planning to do so in the future. However, several areas for improvement are needed for the data above to require validation, wherein the explanation of the methodology, Gartner only states that this survey was conducted involving 371 Chief Financial Officers and leaders in the financial industry in 2020 (Lavelle, 2020).

Next is data from the Pew Research Center, which released the results of its survey on remote work using the term teleworking. The survey conducted by the Pew Research Center involved 5,889 Americans working part-time or full-time and only working in one type of profession and more than two professions but considering choosing one. This survey was conducted in January 2022 for six days; the results obtained from the survey were more than 50% of respondents thought it was easier to balance work and personal life and less connected to co-workers since working from home is practiced (Parker et al., 2020).

What About Remote Work in Asia?

There needs to be more data to show for the Asia Pacific specifically. However, this article will describe a few updates related to countries in the Asia Pacific. One of the quotations from CNBC is rather fascinating (Tong, 2023). Singaporean workers have a phenomenon where they still prefer remote work, but employers are beginning to consider limiting this option and inviting workers to return to work in traditional settings. This phenomenon was covered in a news report by CNBC in 2023.

Additionally, Thailand has fascinating things to offer in terms of remote employment. Thailand implemented work-from-home legislation, allowing businesses to authorize workers to do official business from home using devices like computers and smartphones (Koty, 2023). On the other hand, Jobstreet claimed that most businesses in Indonesia treated policies as before the pandemic, namely that all workers completely returned to the workplace, and diverse experiences were discovered in Indonesia (Sadya, 2023).

The circumstances in Japan are especially intriguing since businesses are attempting to exercise caution when choosing whether or not to switch from remote work to conventional workplaces. One of the indicators is that Japanese workers choose remote work modes of operation (Hiratsuka, 2023).

From the explanations mentioned above, it is clear that the main issue with remote work is not the company's regulations but rather the workers' adaption process, which has led to a reaction from the workforce when the firm tries to correct the situation.

Considerations for Mode of Work: Health Impacts

Findings indicated that factors such as the workers' place of residence, marital status, managerial positions, and employee status had an impact on the work mode choice. Employees who work in remote work mode changed their behaviors more than office workers did during the crises. 67.0% of the people in the remote work mode group exercised less, according to their exercise habits (Niu et al., 2021). So, this can have a serious impact on the health of workers who are undergoing remote work mode. While remote work has helped firms adapt and survive the COVID-19 epidemic, it has also increased the risk of physical and mental health issues for employees.

Long before the pandemic, researcher shared their thoughts on the benefits of remote work, cited from several sources (Mann & Holdsworth, 2003). They found as follows: 1) employees with remote work mode of work will have a better balance between home and work life, 2) employees with remote work mode of work will have the possibility of having more flexibility, 3) employees with remote work mode of work will be able to reduce cost from commuting that will relate a lot with time and mental health, 4) employers that implement remote work as a mode of work will be able to reduce overheads, 5) employers that implement remote work as a mode of work will be able to increase skill base, and 6) employers and employees will engage more and able to increase total productivity. However, this argument was challenged as much more research was released concerning health issues related to remote work.

Several studies contradict each other regarding the health impacts that will arise from remote work practices. First, some studies say that the potential for telework or remote work to inversely correlate with a change to better lifestyles and lengthen idle time is also present. Before the COVID-19 epidemic, there was little intervention research on teleworking, and mental stress indicators depended on societal and individual circumstances (Godderis et al., 2019) Then secondly, some researchers recommend continuing teleworking post-COVID-19 due to its benefits on their working and social life. Telework would enable employers to adapt and satisfy the teleworkers' expectations to maintain their work and productivity (Zalat et al., 2021).

More reliable data on the connection between remote work and employee health still needed to be discovered (Lunde et al., 2022). The lack of studies on several pertinent and significant health consequences, according to the research, suggests a significant information gap that must be filled in order to decide how to integrate remote work in the future working life.

So, when it is explored further, the World Health Organization and the International Labor Organizations are already aware of and trying to advocate for the community through related parties regarding the importance of Occupational Health and Safety for workers who work in remote work mode, regardless of the type of industry.

Both organizations released the Technical Brief regarding Healthy and Safety in Telework document in Geneva in 2021. The document is divided into five important parts, namely, the introductory part, which contains the definition of telework, and the prevalence of telework then. The second part is about the health impacts resulting from telework; the third part is about protecting and promoting health, safety, and well-being when carrying out telework; the fourth part regarding the roles and responsibilities of employers, workers, and the government, and finally before the conclusion is the fifth part which describes the roles and responsibilities of occupational health services.

In the document (Technical Brief regarding Health and Safety in Telework) mentioned before, remote work is implemented, employees should get education on the possible threats to their physical and mental health and well-being from occupational health personnel, national health, safety authorities, or other suitable individuals. Referring to an ergonomic evaluation should be done, and steps should be taken to optimize the workplace for the worker and the duties. In-person or online ergonomic risk assessments and access to occupational and physical therapy treatments to address work-related musculoskeletal injuries and eye strain should all be included in occupational health services.

Important details about the company's decisions on remote employment need to be addressed. At the same time, the remote work policy was implemented as a response to the pandemic issue that had already happened. Businesses must consider the best course of action in the event of a pandemic to ensure their operations' continuity. Therefore, it is not unexpected that despite having remote work rules in place, businesses still feel unprepared, especially in light of potential problems like decreased productivity, poor employee mental health, etc.

Recent research has revealed that remote work mandated by employers can have negative implications for workplace social support and disrupt both work and personal activities, thus jeopardizing employee well-being (Kaltiainen & Hakanen, 2023). An assessment carried out by the Indian industry found that companies were not fully equipped to incorporate remote work into their operations (Kurland & Egan, n.d.; Shah & Manna, 2020). The study exposed a lack of essential policies, culture, training, and resources required to facilitate remote work, which was merely adopted as a crisis management measure with little change to business practices.

Other Considerations: Organizational Justice for Employees Work in Remote Work Versus Back to Work

As remote work becomes more common, businesses must get it right to ensure the enjoyment and well-being of their remote workforce. Remote work can improve how fair workers perceive organizational interactions and processes (Kurlan et al., 1999). In remote work, unresolved concerns of organizational justice might have negative effects, such as greater turnover rates and lower employee motivation. A research concerning the likelihood that full-time remote workers will leave their jobs, a quantitative relationship analysis of organizational justice and its subcomponents distributive, procedural, informational, and interactional justice, and this was urgent to conducted (Truitt, 2023). Whereas, before Truitt, a research found a relationship between informational justice and distributive, interpersonal, and informational justice interactions with remote working (Lane & Aplin-Houtz, 2021).

Employers who welcomed the remote work revolution recognized its potential to strengthen company resilience, develop their best personnel, and save some money on office space. Unfortunately, oversights in how companies handle remote workers might undermine much of that goodwill, harming their reputation and putting them at risk for heavy financial fines (Chávarro, 2023).

According to the preceding explanation, businesses need to ensure that workers who work remotely and those who have returned to their official sites experience the same level of justice. The business can act by establishing performance standards tailored to the circumstances of its workers' jobs. Organizational control is a crucial management issue in remote work settings (Errichiello & Pianese, 2016). Then, social isolation is mentioned in much research on the phenomena of distant work. According to a study, the detrimental impacts of social isolation on the happiness of remote work are growing among employees who are particularly concerned about COVID-19. In contrast, employees less concerned about the virus are likelier to report favorable opinions of productivity and contentment with remote work (Toscano & Zappalà, 2020).

Then, organizational justice is not just about what employees feel but also about their rights as employees, in addition to providing incentives and benefits and the opportunity for growth that was often acquired before the pandemic. Employees may still take advantage of these possibilities even during a pandemic. The phenomena investigated by connected to employee development utilizing technology, in this case, a learning management system, is intriguing for businesses to follow up on concerning employee development prospects (Mikołajczyk, 2022).

However, whether it will be back to work or remain remote work, one interesting article found discussing the preparation that must be made by companies, 1) considering the companies position in the market, 2) planning for bouncing back in order to achieve objectives in the future, 3) the readiness of culture to deal with any crisis, 4) the challenge of new business initiatives, and 5) preparation of executing plans and projects (Pedersen & Ritter, 2020).

If Still Remote Work then What Companies Must Do?

Based on the explanation above, the authors see that several aspects must be considered before a company adopts a remote work policy, regardless of the pandemic conditions, which may be controllable in several countries. Companies that decide to continue implementing remote work must be able to build clear communication channels to coordinate employees working in offices and remote work. Then, to ensure equality and fairness, companies must be able to set clear goals and expectations for employees.

Establish a remote-friendly company culture to avoid the social isolation that may occur in employees working in remote workplaces. However, companies that have implemented a mode of working back to formal locations also need to see the importance of the transition for employees, as when employees are trying to transition from normal times to a pandemic.

Then, in terms of employee quality of life, companies should consider cultivating a collaborative environment, which can lead to increased innovation, sharing of ideas, and problem-solving among employees working in remote workplaces. Then, create a team building to build trust and connection between employees, managers in companies then must be able to understand mental health among employees by giving them ways to separate work life.

If Back to Work, then What Companies Must Do?

Something that is always in our mindset going back to work is whether we will get the benefits of working on-site as we would compared to working remotely. Then, the problem may be related to work-life balance. During remote work, employees will experience dysfunction in becoming ideal workers (Thomason & Williams, 2020). However, one interesting finding states that companies must support employees who will "join" back to work by designing spaces that support communication and concentration (Appel-Meulenbroek et al., 2022). Thus, even though they are practiced temporarily, remote work practices can leave behind an experience and even give rise to the view that employees can receive many benefits from this practice. It is known that many companies see remote work as no longer relevant when countries open restrictions caused by the pandemic, especially in companies that still recognize that employee presence in the workspace is important. However, even though companies are returning to the beginning, it is also a good idea to consider facilitating habits that have emerged among employees. Namely, remote work encourages people to feel the need to have a workspace that suits their needs. Therefore, consideration of contemporary workspaces is important for consideration by the company. More importantly, companies must be able to help employees adopt the habit of going back to work in a new mode after the pandemic.

References

Adekoya, O. D., Adisa, T. A., & Aiyenitaju, O. (2022). Going forward: Remote working in the post-COVID-19 era. *Employee Relations, 44*(6), 1410–1427.
Allen, N. (2020). The pioneers of modern remote work. *Wrkfrce*.
Appel-Meulenbroek, R., Kemperman, A., van de Water, A., Weijs-Perrée, M., & Verhaegh, J. (2022). How to attract employees back to the office? A stated choice study on hybrid working preferences. *Journal of Environmental Psychology, 81*.https://doi.org/10.1016/j.jenvp.2022.101784
Buildd. (2021). *State of Remote Work 2021: Remote is the new normal*.
Carraher-Wolverton, C. (2022). The co-evolution of remote work and expectations in a COVID-19 world utilizing an expectation disconfirmation theory lens. *Journal of Systems and Information Technology, 24*(1), 55–69.
Chafi, M. B., Hultberg, A., & Yams, N. B. (2022). Post-pandemic office work: Perceived challenges and opportunities for a sustainable work environment. *Sustainability (Switzerland), 14*(1). https://doi.org/10.3390/su14010294
Chávarro, J. M. (2023). *Work-From-Home Regulations Are Coming. Companies Aren't Ready*.
Chong, S., & Huang, Y. (2020). Supporting interdependent telework employees: A moderated-mediation model linking daily COVID-19 task setbacks to next-day work withdrawal. *Journal of Applied Psychology*.https://doi.org/10.1037/apl0000843.supp

de Laat, K. (2023). Remote Work and post-bureaucracy: unintended consequences of work design for gender inequality. *ILR Review, 76*(1), 135–159. https://doi.org/10.1177/00197939221076134

Di Martino, V., & Wirth, L. (1990). Telework: A new way of working and living. *International Labour Review, 129*(5), 529–554.

Eddleston, K. A., & Mulki, J. (2017). Toward Understanding remote workers' management of work-family boundaries: the Complexity of workplace embeddedness. *Group and Organization Management, 42*(3), 346–387. https://doi.org/10.1177/1059601115619548

Errichiello, L., & Pianese, T. (2016). Organizational control in the context of remote work arrangements: A conceptual framework. *Performance Measurement and ....* https://doi.org/10.1108/S1479-351220160000031009

Ferreira, R., Pereira, R., Bianchi, I. S., & da Silva, M. M. (2021). Decision factors for remote work adoption: Advantages, disadvantages, driving forces and challenges. *Journal of Open Innovation: Technology, Market, and Complexity, 7*(1), 70. https://doi.org/10.3390/joitmc7010070

Godderis, L., Leuven, K., Okubo, T., Yoshimura, R., Furuya, Y., Nakazawa, S., Fukai, K., & Tatemichi, M. (2019). *Health impacts with telework on workers: A scoping review before the COVID-pandemic.* https://www.crd.york.ac.uk/prospero/

Gratton, L. (2021). How to do hybrid right. *Harvard Business Review*, 1–19.

Hiratsuka, Y. (2023). *Japan poll finds half of workers against returning to office after COVID.* The Mainichi.

Kaltiainen, J., & Hakanen, J. J. (2023). Why increase in telework may have affected employee well-being during the COVID-19 pandemic? The role of work and non-work life domains. *Current Psychology.* https://doi.org/10.1007/s12144-023-04250-8

Koty, A. C. (2023). *Thailand Adopts work from home bill: Implications for employers.* ASEAN Briefing.

Kurland, N. B., & Egan, T. D. (n.d.). Telecommuting: Justice and control in the virtual. In *Source: Organization Science* (Vol. 10, Issue 4).

Lane, E. K., & Aplin-Houtz, M. (2021). "FAIR OR NOT?": The impact of remote working on. *Proceedings of the Eleventh International Conference on Engaged Management Scholarship-EMS 2021*, 1–27. https://ssrn.com/abstract=3944901

Lavelle, J. (2020). *Gartner CFO Survey Reveals 74% Intend to Shift Some Employees to Remote Work Permanently.* https://twitter.com/share?text=Learn+more+about+recent+Gartner+press.&url=https%3A%2F%2Fwww.gartner.com%2Fen%2Fnewsroom%2Fpress.

Lunde, L. K., Fløvik, L., Christensen, J. O., Johannessen, H. A., Finne, L. B., Jørgensen, I. L., Mohr, B., & Vleeshouwers, J. (2022). The relationship between telework from home and employee health: A systematic review. *BMC Public Health, 22*(1). https://doi.org/10.1186/s12889-021-12481-2

Mann, S., & Holdsworth, L. (2003). The psychological impact of teleworking: Stress, emotions and health. *New Technology, Work and Employment, 18*(3), 196–211. https://doi.org/10.1111/1468-005X.00121

Mikołajczyk, K. (2022). Changes in the approach to employee development in organisations as a result of the COVID-19 pandemic. *European Journal of Training and Development, 46*(5–6), 544–562. https://doi.org/10.1108/EJTD-12-2020-0171

Morikawa, M. (2023). Productivity dynamics of remote work during the COVID-19 Pandemic. *Industrial Relations, 62*(3), 317–331.

Newport, C. (2020). Why Remote Work Is So Hard—and How It Can Be Fixed _ The New Yorker. *The New Yorker.* https://www.newyorker.com/culture/annals-of-inquiry/can-remote-work-be-fixed

Niu, Q., Nagata, T., Fukutani, N., Tezuka, M., Shimoura, K., Nagai-Tanima, & Aoyama, T. (2021). Health effects of immediate telework introduction during the COVID-19 era in Japan: A cross-sectional study. *PloS One, 16*(10).

Parker, K., Horowitz, J. M., & Minkin, R. (2020). *How the Coronavirus Outbreak Has—and Hasn't—Changed the Way Americans Work.*

Pedersen, C. L., & Ritter, T. (2020). *Preparing Your Business for a Post-Pandemic World*.

Rañeses, M. S., Nisa, N. un, Bacason, E. S., & Martir, S. (2022). Investigating the impact of remote working on employee productivity and work-life balance: A study on the business consultancy industry in Dubai, UAE. *International Journal of Business and Administrative Studies, 8*(2). https://doi.org/10.20469/ijbas.8.10002-2

Sadya, S. (2023). *Mayoritas Perusahaan di Indonesia Kembali WFO pada 2022/2023*. DataIndonesia.Id.

Shah, J. A., & Manna, I. (2020). An empirical assessment of telework readiness on Indian industries. *Journal of Organisation and Human Behavior, 9*(1), 50–61.

Statista. (2023). *Employers' and employees' views on the success of remote work in the United States in 2020*.

Sullivan, C. (2012). Remote working and work-life balance. In *Work and Quality of Life: Ethical Practices in Organizations* (pp. 275–290). Springer Netherlands. https://doi.org/10.1007/978-94-007-4059-4_15

Thomason, B., & Williams, H. (2020). *What Will Work-Life Balance Look Like After the Pandemic?*

Tong, G. C. (2023). *Singapore's workers want to stay remote, but employers are backtracking on flexibility*. CNBC.

Toscano, F., & Zappalà, S. (2020). Social isolation and stress as predictors of productivity perception and remote work satisfaction during the COVID-19 pandemic: The role of concern about the virus in a moderated double mediation. *Sustainability (Switzerland), 12*(23), 1–14. https://doi.org/10.3390/su12239804

Truitt, T. (2023). *Navigating the "New Normal": Investigating the Relationship Between Full-Time Remote Work, Organizational Justice, and Turnover Intentions*.

Wang, B., Liu, Y., Qian, J., & Parker, S. K. (2021). Achieving effective remote working during the COVID-19 Pandemic: A work design perspective. *Applied Psychology, 70*(1), 16–59. https://doi.org/10.1111/apps.12290

Zalat, M. M., Hamed, M. S., & Bolbol, S. A. (2021). The experiences, challenges, and acceptance of e-learning as a tool for teaching during the COVID-19 pandemic among university medical staff. *PLoS ONE, 16*. https://doi.org/10.1371/journal.pone.0248758

Dr. Anita Maharani is one of the Faculty Members of the Binus Business School Master Program (AACSB Accredited). Anita has been studying Management, specializing in Human Resource Management since 2015. Research she has conducted has been published in various journals and continues. Her interest in human resource management also encouraged her to participate as one of the authors of this book chapter. This article hopes to light the phenomena that occurs in organizations, especially regarding remote work, which was previously practiced in many organizations when the pandemic occurred.

Managing the 3 Ps in Workplace Disruption: People, Place, and Process in the Case of Co-working Space

Aqilah Yaacob, Goh See Kwong, Gu Manli, and Karen Tsen Mung Khie

Abstract The push for digitalization and the impact of the pandemic have transformed how organizations design their workspaces. In the past, Asian organizations heavily invested in physical workspaces and required employees to be present at the workplace. Flexible work arrangements were merely discussed superficially before the pandemic. However, the pandemic forced companies to adopt remote working and integrate digital tools into their continuity plans. Having experienced remote or flexible working, employees now find it challenging to revert to conventional in-person work setups. Consequently, organizations are reevaluating the need for extensive workspace, leading many to consider redesigning their offices as co-working spaces (also referred to as activity-based offices). This book chapter offers recommendations for contemporary organizations in designing co-working offices that fulfill users' needs. Drawing upon empirical research and case studies from corporate and higher education sectors, we integrate three key factors—people, place, and process—underlying the transition and implementation of co-working spaces. By identifying challenges and opportunities arising from this disruption, we provide guidance for organizations and employees to navigate this rapidly changing landscape. Ultimately, this chapter seeks to enhance understanding of workplace disruption caused by co-working spaces and provide practical assistance for organizations and employees striving to thrive in this evolving environment.

Keywords 3Ps · Workplace disruption · People · Place · Process · Co-working space

---

A. Yaacob (✉) · G. Manli · K. T. M. Khie
Faculty of Business and Law, Taylor's University, 47500 Subang Jaya, Selangor, Malaysia
e-mail: aqilah.yaacob@taylors.edu.my

G. S. Kwong
Monash School of Business, Monash University, 47500 Subang Jaya, Selangor, Malaysia

© The Author(s), under exclusive license to Springer Nature Singapore Pte Ltd. 2024
T. Endress and Y. F. Badir (eds.), *Business and Management in Asia: Disruption and Change*, https://doi.org/10.1007/978-981-99-9371-0_10

Introduction

Before the pandemic, co-working spaces gained popularity in many major cities worldwide and these spaces are known to be modern and innovative. It offers a dynamic and flexible atmosphere for professionals from various industries and backgrounds to work in a common place (Fuzi, 2015; Spinuzzi, 2012). Co-working spaces are known as a common space in a building where multi-tenants from numerous organizations use the space by sharing common facilities and/or services (Weijs-Perrée et al., 2019). This trend has been fueled by several factors, including the growth of the knowledge-sharing economy and new work models (Bouncken & Reuschl, 2018; Weijs-Perrée et al., 2019).

One of the most significant benefits of co-working spaces is that they provide a low-cost alternative to traditional office setups (Weijs-Perrée et al., 2019). Besides, co-working spaces foster a sense of community by bringing together professionals from different fields who can share their knowledge and experiences. This can promote collaboration between fields (Fuzi, 2015; Weijs-Perrée et al., 2019). This has led to a growing demand for flexible work arrangements.

The key characteristics of co-working spaces gained significant momentum during the COVID-19 pandemic. Furthermore, with the accelerated rise of technology partially induced by the pandemic, there has been a growing trend toward more flexible and collaborative workspaces in many Asian countries. In a relatively short period of two to three years, many employees have shifted their working preferences toward flexibility, often associating it with achieving a better work-life balance.

In response, organizations have begun to recognize the benefits of co-working spaces and move toward designing an activity-based office (ABO) within their facilities, rather than relying on external public spaces, and have started revising their work policies to support work-from-home arrangements. ABO refers to a workspace design strategy that specifically adapts the physical work environment to align with the demands and needs of activities carried out within an organization (Gerdenitsch et al., 2018). They further suggest that the characteristic of ABO derives from office location, layout, and use. To compare, ABO refers to spaces created from within the organization to enable daily work operations, meanwhile, co-working space is frequently used to refer to facilities outside the organization that are shared by the public. However, as more people get accustomed to the idea, co-working is becoming a more commonly used phrase in the business world including spaces within the organization. The research in this article focuses on workspace design, which includes both co-working spaces and ABO, two terms that are used interchangeably.

With the introduction of new technologies and the rise of the knowledge-sharing economy, workers and employers are increasingly seeking more flexible and dynamic work environments. A "2022 Global Talent Trend" study conducted by Mercer shows that 7 in 10 employers across Asia have supported a shift to a hybrid work model, where employees have some freedom to determine their work schedule. Companies in the Asia–Pacific region are also undergoing a shift away from fixed office seating toward activity-based office, according to CBRE's "Spring 2022 Asia–Pacific Occupier Survey—Crafting the Post-Pandemic Office." Employers increasingly recognize the benefits of empowering employees to work where and when they are most productive.

Co-working spaces and ABO suit the current trend significantly of promoting hybrid working in improving employees' productivity, well-being, and work–life balance. However, implementing activity-based offices is not merely about redesigning the space but also about how employees fit within the space. It also requires a fundamental rethinking of how work is organized and conducted within an organization. The present study investigates the challenges associated with implementing activity-based offices, and how such implementations can impact the 3Ps—People, Place, and Process—within organizations. In addition, this book chapter provides practical recommendations for organizations seeking to design an effective activity-based office.

Workplace Disruption Due to Pandemic

The COVID-19 pandemic has profoundly impacted how work is conducted and organized around the world. Prior to the pandemic, many organizations had already begun to embrace flexible work arrangements, such as telecommuting and remote work (Hornung et al., 2008; Breaugh & Farabee, 2012), as a means of increasing productivity (Spinuzzi, 2012; Bentley et al., 2016) and reducing costs (Richardson & McKenna, 2014). However, the pandemic accelerated this trend, as millions of workers were forced to work from home in order to comply with social distancing measures. Now, in the wake of the COVID-19 pandemic, employees and employers are reevaluating traditional work arrangements. It has become clear that a return to pre-pandemic work norms is unlikely. Meanwhile, employees can't be working remotely or virtually on a permanent basis. It is clear that new approaches to work must be adopted. With this change, organizations are moving toward hybrid work arrangements. Such work arrangement provides the maximum benefit to both employees and the organization, it allows the flexibility of employees to work remotely or work-from-home (WFH) on certain days while returning to the office when it is needed.

Although this hybrid plan is welcomed, the shift toward remote work or WFH has had significant implications for both employees and employers (Soga et al., 2022). On the one hand, workers have had to adapt to new technologies and work environments, often facing increased workloads and blurring of the boundaries between work and personal life. On the other hand, employers have had to invest in new technologies and infrastructure to support remote work, while also grappling with challenges such as employee monitoring, communication, and collaboration (Soga et al., 2022). Central to this shift are changes to working styles, working locations, and the implications of these changes for well-being, productivity, and costs.

i. Working styles: WFH and flexible schedules have become increasingly popular among employees, with many citing the benefits of reduced commuting time and increased autonomy (Charalampous et al., 2022). For example, remote workers may be able to set their own schedules, take breaks when needed, and work in environments that suit their preferences.

ii. Employee Well-being—Employees have more control over their work schedules, which can help to reduce stress and improve work–life balance. They also have the opportunity to work from home, which can be particularly beneficial for employees. Such as for those who must commute far to work or those who need to take care of family members (Wang et al., 2021). In contrast, some may experience a negative impact on their well-being due to social isolation and a lack of connection with colleagues (Charalampous et al., 2022). This can lead to feelings of isolation and disengagement. Working remotely can also induce a fear of potential job loss, particularly among frequent homeworkers (Tsen et al., 2023). In addition, remote employees may struggle to separate their work and personal lives. The perception of needing to be "always on" can harm their mental health (Wang et al., 2021).

iii. Productivity—As mentioned above, saving commute time, and having flexible planning in time helps productivity and employees have greater autonomy to plan when and where can be completed (Soga et al., 2022). Having such flexibility would also help employees to reduce distractions that may be present in a traditional office setting, such as interruptions from coworkers or noise from the office environment. However, employees may experience difficulty in collaborating and communicating effectively with their coworkers. This can lead to miscommunication and delays in completing projects (Charalampous et al., 2022). Also, managers may also have challenges in monitoring work progress and output that may ultimately influence the productivity of the team (Wang et al., 2021).

iv. Hybrid work locations—employees may split their time between working remotely and working in the office, which have also become more common in the post-pandemic world (De Klerk et al., 2021). This approach allows employees to enjoy the benefits of remote work, such as flexibility and autonomy, while also providing opportunities for in-person collaboration and socialization. However, to accommodate hybrid working, the office space needs to be reconfigured for collaborative work, rather than individual work, as employees may be spending more of their individual work time at home. This may involve creating more open and flexible spaces that can be easily reconfigured to support different types of collaboration and work (Vyas, 2022).

v. Cost—With a growing number of employees working from home or adopting flexible work arrangements, some employers have recognized that large office spaces, personalized workstations, and expensive commercial leases may no longer be necessary or cost-effective (Vyas, 2022; Soga et al., 2022). In a competitive market, maintaining underutilized resources can be seen as counterproductive by senior leadership teams. Additionally, the rising cost of raw materials and living expenses has prompted many organizations to take strategic measures to ensure their financial viability.

Based on the above shift and changes in the workplace, it is likely that many organizations will continue to embrace flexible work arrangements, albeit in a more hybrid form that combines both remote and in-person work. As such organizations need to consider adapting, a flexible work policy with effective activity-based offices (or co-working spaces) where they can ensure effective collaboration, communication, and engagement among remote and in-person workers.

Activity-Based Offices

Due to the workplace challenges and disruption, activity-based offices have emerged as a transformative approach for the modern-era workplace. Recognizing that work is no longer confined to individual desks and rigid structures, activity-based offices emphasize the integration of three vital elements: People, Place, and Process. By prioritizing these Ps, organizations should aim to create dynamic environments that foster collaboration, flexibility, and productivity. People become the center of attention, with their diverse needs and preferences taken into account. Place focuses on creating versatile spaces that accommodate various work styles, encouraging movement and interaction. The process entails the seamless transition of change management that supports efficient work practices. Together, these interconnected Ps form the foundation of activity-based offices, revolutionizing the way employees work while enhancing overall organizational performance. Figure 1 summarizes the 3 Ps (people, place, and process), which will be discussed in the subsequent paragraphs.

People

One of the primary challenges in managing workplace disruptions is to ensure that employee satisfaction and productivity remain unaffected. A key strategy to optimize employee well-being is to design a workplace that caters to the needs of its users. According to the Person–environment fit theory, people are more likely to thrive in environments that are compatible with their individual attributes such as needs, preferences, values, and goals (Van Vianen, 2018). This theory suggests the importance of designing an employee-centric activity-based office, one that recognizes that the employee characteristics such as personality, job demands, psychological needs, and workstyles play a crucial role in shaping their experience and performance in the workplace.

A study published in the Journal of Research and Personality (Baranski et al., 2023), for example, found that people who are more extroverted are often happier and more focused in offices with open seating arrangements, while introverts feel

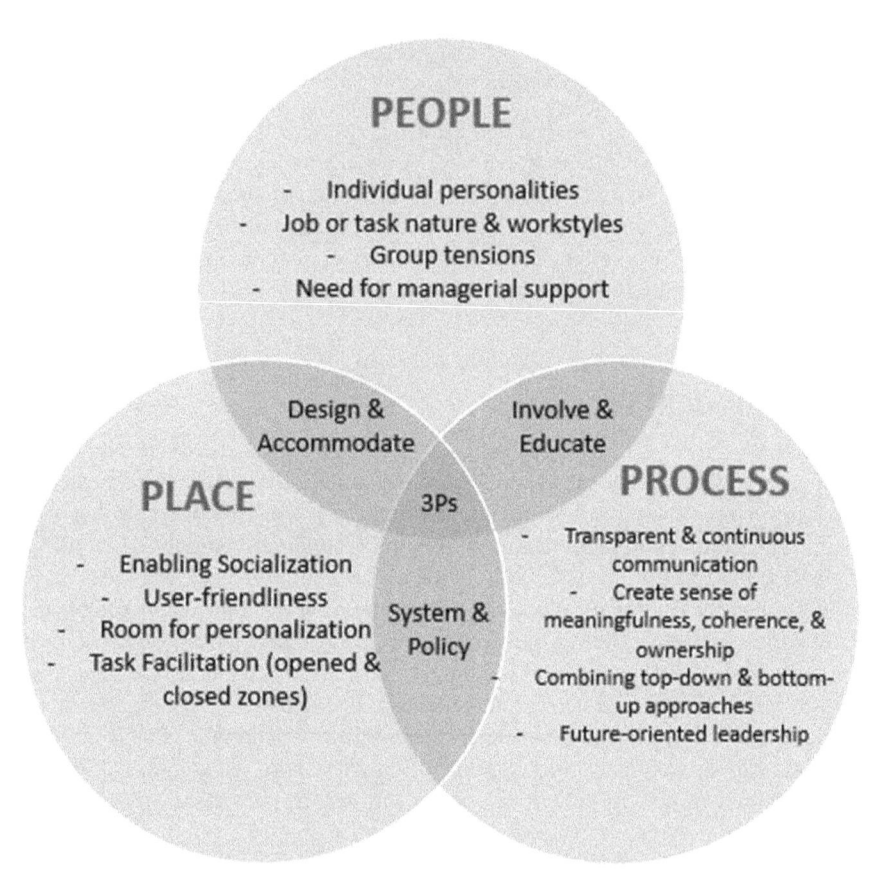

Fig. 1 Diagram of the 3 Ps (People, Place, and Process)

more at ease and perform better in enclosed environments such as cubicles and private offices. In designing activity-based offices, inclusivity therefore is a crucial consideration for employers. It is essential to create an environment where all employees feel that their needs are being acknowledged and supported. While extroverted employees may appreciate the benefits of open seating arrangements that facilitate casual interaction and collaborative work, introverts require isolated space to be able to concentrate better on work. Inclusivity means providing options that cater to the needs of different groups of employees. To achieve this, employers need to ensure that sufficient workspaces are allocated for quiet, uninterrupted work with minimum distractions, such as small, enclosed rooms that are soundproof. In her famous book, "Quiet, The Power of Introverts in a World That Can't Stop Talking," author Susan Cain explains that introverted individuals are more easily overwhelmed by external stimuli in their surroundings than extroverts. However, one of their strengths is their ability to engage in deep, reflective thinking, which can often lead to creative solutions (Cain, 2013).

In addition to individual personalities, employers would also need to consider the nature of the job tasks people do in the company. For certain roles that involve extensive research, such as information search, data analysis, and report writing, a "transparent" office design can be overstimulating. Financial analysts, editors, and legal investigators, for instance, work best when some degree of privacy is preserved. In comparison, jobs in marketing, information technology, and sales often require face-to-face discussions with team members to generate ideas and strategies. Employees in this category are more likely to benefit from an open and social work environment that facilitates quick exchanges and conversations.

Employers, however, must recognize that providing open spaces for collaboration doesn't always lead to increased interaction and communication among employees. Harvard University research has found that open office designs can reduce face-to-face interaction by up to 70%, resulting in more email communication and decreased productivity (Bernstein & Turban, 2018). While the exact factors contributing to this outcome are not fully understood, privacy appears to be a key factor, given that it is a fundamental human need. This suggests that although an open-plan layout is a main feature of activity-based offices, it should not overshadow the importance of providing other workspaces that cater to employees' privacy needs. The lack of privacy is often reported to be a stressor among those working in such an office environment. People feel uncomfortable, for example, having confidential conversations in the open space, as they are concerned about their own privacy and the potential disruption to others (De Been et al., 2015). This discomfort may be a reason why some individuals resort to written communication instead.

Moreover, activity-based offices operate under the assumption that people choose the type of workspace that best fits their activities. In practice, however, not everyone feels the need to switch between work zones and settings. Research shows that employees have a tendency to occupy the same spot or have their own "preferred" stations. It is also the case that some workplace types are more popular than others, resulting in overcrowding in certain areas while other spaces remain underutilized (De Been et al., 2015). This creates an imbalance in the distribution of available workspace and can lead to dissatisfaction and discomfort among employees. While offering a diverse range of workstations is important, a well-designed activity-based office should also take into account the specific types of workspaces that best suit employees' needs. Conducting a comprehensive assessment test, interview, or survey to evaluate workers' work habits and preferences is strongly recommended before designing and constructing the office space. This ensures an appropriate distribution of workspace types. (Engelen et al., 2019). Startups and consulting firms for example, due to their dynamic workstyles, may need a higher proportion of meeting rooms or open collaboration spaces compared to research institutions that might prioritize individual private workstations.

Additionally, if not managed properly, activity-based offices can create ingroup-outgroup tensions. For instance, some employees may prefer to work from home for convenience and the reduced stress of commuting, while others may lack a well-functioning home office or rely on office time for networking, training, and mentorship, particularly if they are new or junior staff members (Gratton, 2021).

Furthermore, the flexibility afforded by activity-based work settings regarding when and where to work can make it difficult for some employees to regularly engage with their colleagues face-to-face, potentially hindering social bonding. To foster a strong social cohesion in the activity-based work environment, managers should actively work toward creating opportunities for employee interaction and connection outside of formal work settings. Activities such as social events, off-site retreats, or team-building workshops can help to create a more inclusive social atmosphere.

There is also research evidence that shared office spaces are associated with a decrease in the perception of supervisor support (Morrison & Macky, 2017). In some organizations, managers may retain their own dedicated desk or office, while in other cases, managers operate within the same activity-based environment as everyone else, which may make them less easily accessible compared to the traditional cellular office setting. To address the perceived reduced supervisory support, managers should establish open and effective communication channels. It is essential for managers to proactively engage with their team members, provide opportunities for regular meetings where employees can share their experiences, ideas, and feedback related to the use of the activity-based office. By actively listening to employees, managers can gain a better understanding of their motivations and preferences, enabling them to provide the necessary support and resources required for individuals to thrive in the activity-based work environment.

Place

Designing an effective ABO necessitates careful attention to accommodate the diverse needs of employees and ensure user-friendliness. In this section, we will discuss the two main zones of ABO (task completion and socializing) and how they should be designed to enhance social connectivity and minimize work distractions. Additionally, we will explore key considerations regarding technology integration, ergonomic furniture, space allocation, and indoor-outdoor connections to create a productive and engaging work environment.

To begin with, an ABO should incorporate different zones that cater to the types of activities employees engage in daily. Generally, these activities can be categorized into task completion and socializing. For *task completion*, we could further analyze the conditions that enable work productivity. ABO is unique because it covers both *"open"* and *"closed"* circulations (Richardson, 2017). A free-seating space can be seen as a ground for knowledge exchange and opportunities for collaborations, representing the *"open"* circulation. However, it is important to note that the benefits of geographical proximity are most likely to occur with the support of social proximity, as mentioned by Parrino (2015).

To boost social proximity within an ABO, employers can take certain steps. Firstly, they can introduce activities that stimulate collaboration among employees. This can include brainstorming sessions, team-building exercises, or project-based group work. Secondly, establishing a communication channel between employees, such as a dedicated messaging platform or shared project management tools, can facilitate interaction and information sharing. Lastly, having a welcome board with descriptions and photos of all employees can help foster a sense of community and familiarity within the workplace (Parrino, 2015).

Furthermore, within the free-seating space (Fig. 2), it may be beneficial to segment a portion into a quiet zone where employees can work without noise distractions (Bouncken et al., 2021). Employers can explore installing partial partitions between desks to minimize visual distractions and reduce direct visual interferences.

On top of that, certain work tasks that demand privacy and focused attention work best in "*closed*" circulations, particularly when dealing with sensitive and confidential information. To facilitate this, private rooms should be designed with doors featuring frosted glass, allowing individuals inside to be seen without disturbing their work. Additionally, installing soundproof rooms can minimize noise disruptions and provide privacy by reducing noise transmission. In situations where private rooms are not a must, employers can provide a designated "phone booth" where employees can make brief calls without disturbing their colleagues.

Alongside areas designed for focused work, there should also be communal spaces for *socializing* purposes, such as a pantry or break room (Fig. 3). Similarly, designated meeting rooms should be available for hosting external parties like clients, suppliers,

Fig. 2 Example of open-seating space

Fig. 3 Example of communal space

or business partners. It is advisable to position these rooms near the office entrance to minimize disruptions to other employees.

The COVID-19 pandemic has brought significant changes to the workplace, with teleconferencing emerging as a vital component of modern hybrid work, and this trend seems to continue in a post-pandemic era (Green et al., 2020). In light of this, technology has become an essential aspect of an ABO. To facilitate effective communication in a modern workplace, it is essential for employers to ensure they have the necessary hardware. Although many ABOs spaces offer conference rooms with screens, their audio systems may not be optimized for teleconferencing (Fig. 4). A more advanced conference room typically has a ceiling mic installed in a suspended or recessed manner on the ceiling, allowing them to pick up sound from all directions. They are designed to have a wide coverage pattern, which ensures that everyone in the room can be heard clearly without the need to pass around a handheld microphone.

Additionally, considering the limited availability of individual and discussion rooms, implementing an online booking system for these spaces is necessary to maximize their utility. The system should typically consist of a web-based application accessible to all employees with relevant log-in credentials. It will display the available spaces, their location, and the available time slots. Besides, cloud storage should be made available to enable employees to access their files from anywhere in the office or at home.

Fig. 4 Example of conference room

In an ABO, where employees do not have assigned workstations, it is essential to avoid relying on one-size-fits-all furniture options and consider the diverse needs of all individuals, including those with disabilities. Prioritizing ergonomic furniture that caters to individual differences is vital not only to prevent back pain and other physical discomforts but also to ensure accessibility and inclusivity within the workplace. Height-adjustable tables, ergonomic chairs, and angle-adjustable monitor arms are effective solutions that promote good posture and comfortable work setups for employees. Furthermore, accessibility features should be integrated to accommodate employees with disabilities. Installing sliding doors and carefully considering the presence of stairs ensures easy navigation for disabled individuals. Wheelchair-accessible desks, adjustable keyboard trays, and Braille signage are additional measures that enhance accessibility and inclusivity. Furthermore, it is crucial to create designated spaces within the office to cater to specific needs. By establishing a dedicated mother's room, nursing mothers can attend to their infants in a comfortable and private setting. Similarly, setting up a designated Muslim prayer room allows employees to observe their religious practices in a respectful and appropriate environment. These spaces contribute to a workplace that values and accommodates the diverse needs of its employees.

The next step is to ensure sufficient space. It is important to consider the appropriate number of seats to provide, especially for companies with flexible working arrangements. Given that not all employees will be present at the office at the same time, we recommend companies study the occupancy rate of the office before designing an ABO. A general rule of thumb is to allocate 60% to 70% of seats based on the total number of employees for both the open spaces and individual rooms. However, this figure should exclude discussion rooms and other common areas as they are not designed for long hours of work. In addition to seating arrangements, physical storage is another crucial factor to consider. Employees may feel a lack of sense of ownership when they do not have a designated space to display their personality. Therefore, ample physical storage such as lockers and drawers not only help in storing personal items but also provides opportunities for personalization. Employers could also encourage employees to add personal touches to shared spaces, such as bulletin boards or common areas, so that a sense of pride could be instilled. Mobile storage solutions, such as trolleys or drawers with wheels, are also recommended to help employees move items between spaces more easily.

Lastly, establishing indoor–outdoor connections within the physical space of an ABO can greatly enhance employees' general well-being by reducing stress and increasing positive moods (Sander et al., 2019). By incorporating natural light and introducing plants, the office environment can come alive, transforming it from a cold, sterile space into an energetic and vibrant living environment (Gray & Birrell, 2014). This infusion of nature creates a positive atmosphere that promotes friendly conversations and increases energy levels that could eventually enhance productivity.

Process to Implement Change

Besides managing the people and place in the case of co-working space, the organization should also address concerns related to the transition and change process due to the workplace disruption. This is because the future of smooth transition among employees in adapting to the workplace disruption caused by the introduction of the new co-working space may be determined by how well the managers handle the challenges related to resistance, expectation, and transition process. There are several opportunities that arise from this disruption; hence the managers need to learn to navigate this disruptive landscape by managing workers' expectations during the change process and guiding people in adapting to the new work styles to optimize the benefits of co-working space while mitigating its potential challenges. Although some studies have highlighted the impact of process factors such as information on employees' satisfaction with their new office arrangements (e.g., Brunia et al., 2016; Rolfö et al., 2018; Babapour Chafi and Rolfö, 2019), the significance of the implementation process for a successful workplace relocation is often overlooked in research studies (Nielsen & Randall, 2013).

Change is inevitable; however, workplace disruption can be challenging if not carefully crafted and managed accordingly. Brunia et al. (2016) found out that employee satisfaction on the activity-based office concept is not only influenced by the physical characteristics of the work environment, but also by the implementation process. To stay relevant, organizations need to assist employees to embrace change through an effective change management process of guiding employees from the earliest stages of conception and preparation, through implementation and, finally, to resolution. This management strategy can ensure organizations successfully transition and adapt to the changes that are occurring. This is because introducing a new co-working space can certainly disrupt the workplace arrangements, therefore it is important to manage the transition process among employees carefully.

Firstly, transparent, and frequent communication about the changes and what employees can expect is vital. For example, the top management should explain the reasons for the change and how it will benefit the growth of the company and employees' productivity. If the purpose of introducing this new co-working space is to encourage collaboration and networking opportunities, this message needs to be loud and clear in employees' minds. This can also include sharing details about the new space, outlining how it will affect their workday, and providing updates throughout the transition process. A study conducted by Wijk et al. (2020) conquered that communication before relocation to activity-based workplaces was crucial. Employees often experience a "Sense of coherence" (SOC) when they understand why a change is being made in their organization (Vogt et al., 2016). When employees are informed about the reasons behind a change, they are better able to make sense of it and understand how it fits into the overall vision and strategy of the organization. This understanding can help employees feel more engaged, committed, and motivated to support the change. When employees do not have a clear understanding of why a change is being made, they may feel confused, uncertain, and resistant to the change. They may also feel that the change lacks meaning and that their work is no longer aligned with the goals and values of the organization. This may lead to negative attitudes, reduced productivity, and increased turnover. Wijk et al. (2020) findings suggested that to prevent decreases in satisfaction with the physical and psychosocial work environment, organizations that adopt activity-based workplaces should focus on enhancing employees' perceived sense of meaningfulness throughout the process.

Secondly, the management should consider creating a committee made up of employees to help plan the transition in which it will provide a sense of ownership over the process and ensure that their needs are considered. Involving employees in the planning process means that they are more likely to be invested in the success of this new workplace arrangement and they will feel more responsible for its outcomes. Brunia et al. (2016) suggested a balance between a top-down and a bottom-up approach and clear instructions on how to use activity-based workplaces. In conjunction with prior research, thorough preparation before implementing significant changes in the workplace and involving employees in the change process are deemed to be significant (Morrison & Macky, 2017; Berthelsen et al., 2018). The management should also be open in addressing concerns from the employees and take their feedback into consideration by making the necessary changes. It is one thing to redesign the office space from the management's point of view, but also to understand employees fit within the new office landscape. Employees' unique insights and perspectives can also help to shape the planning process and encourage collaboration that can build stronger relationships and foster a more positive workplace culture.

Thirdly, guidance, instructions, and continuous support should be given to help employees transition quicker and smoother (i.e., assisting employees through the four stages of the change process including denial, resistance, exploration, and commitment). For instance, employees may need guidance on how to use the new co-working space and its features in the form of short briefing, demo videos, initial tour of the new space as well as follow-up emails. To ensure a smooth transition, managers should also pay attention to the ease of using the technological facilities. Introducing this equipment in a user-friendly manner can effectively minimize the technostress experienced by employees during the initial phases of hybrid work (Molino et al., 2020). This continuous guidance and support can also help employees to better understand how to make the most of the new working space. Throughout the implementation process, Bergsten et al. (2021) also suggested a change-oriented leadership behavior to avoid productivity loss among employees when implementing the new activity-based workplaces. This change-oriented leadership (i.e., future-oriented managers) is needed in the transition process to act as the promoter of change that can guide employees' well-being and performance in the new activity-based workplaces (Bergsten et al., 2021; Yukl, 2019; Nielsen & Abildgaard, 2013).

Finally, once the transition is complete, the management should celebrate the new co-working space and its benefits in which it can help to create a positive atmosphere and encourage employees to embrace the change. Celebrating and guiding employees in adapting to the new office concept is crucial in embracing this distinctive phenomenon of sharing economy toward building collaborative environments post-pandemic society (Berbegal-Mirabent, 2021). Celebrating the new workplace culture should also be done in a way that fosters the appropriate etiquette of using the space. For example, the management should reinforce certain rules and guidelines for using the space to avoid any mishap incidents (e.g., instructions on how to use the space in the form of infographics such as no seat hogging and no telephone calls in quiet zones as well as details of the person-in-charge should be posted on the wall). The management team should also go the extra mile in actively listening to employees even after the implementation has successfully taken place by welcoming suggestions every now and then. Table 1 summarizes the changes before and after the co-working space took place from the 3 Ps perspectives.

Conclusion

Overall, to enhance resource efficiency and work productivity, organizations seeking to implement activity-based offices should accord priority to three fundamental aspects, namely, people, place, and processes. In the workspace transformation strategy, it is critical to avoid concentrating entirely on cost-cutting initiatives that can jeopardize the well-being and productivity of the staff. A well-planned workspace has the potential to be useful and advantageous for a long time. A well-rounded strategy must strike a balance between economic factors and the three pillars of people, place, and processes. A change of this magnitude may also require significant staff support

Table 1 The effects of co-working space: the perspective of 3 Ps

Dimension	Before Co-working space	After Co-working space
People		
Employee Relationship	Limited interaction across departments and relationships is likely dictated by formal hierarchy	Enhanced inter-departmental collaboration and informal networking if social proximity is present. However, the flexibility afforded might hinder social bonding and regular face-to-face interaction
Supervisory Support	Managers are more easily accessible to employees	Potential decrease in the perception of supervisor support when managers may no longer have dedicated offices or desks
Workspace Allocation and Styles	Fixed allocation of workspace based on job titles or seniority	Flexibility in choosing and customizing workspace based on individual preferences, needs, and working styles, which may promote employees' autonomy
Inclusivity	One-size-fits-all office design	Emphasis on inclusivity through diverse workspace options catering to various personality types, individual needs, and roles
Distraction	Minimal workplace distractions from co-workers	Potential noise and visual distractions from shared spaces, particularly because of unwelcome conversations or activities
Place		
Office Design	Traditional office layouts (i.e., fixed desks, cubicles, and furniture) with compartmentalized floor and minimal flexibility	Dynamic and versatile office designs, supporting various work styles, which enable socializing and task completion (e.g., board rooms, consultation room, open seating areas)
Privacy	Personal workspaces provide higher privacy levels	Emphasis on providing a balance between private workspaces (e.g., meeting rooms) and open collaboration areas
Technology	Less reliance on digital tools for remote work	Increased reliance on technology for remote work, collaboration, and productivity
Personalization	More rooms for personalization and customization (e.g., the entire workspace)	Limited room for personalization and customization (e.g., only lockers)
Cost	Typically higher, as organizations often lease dedicated office spaces regardless of occupancy rate	Potential cost savings due to the shared and flexible nature of co-working spaces with occupancy rate taken into consideration
Process		

(continued)

Table 1 (continued)

Dimension	Before Co-working space	After Co-working space
Communication	Reliance on in-person meetings and formal communication	Adaptation to digital communication tools and more informal interactions. Combining top-down and bottom-up perspectives
Leadership	Mainly conventional leadership approach	Future-oriented leadership incorporating technology and twenty-first century workspace settings
Ownership	Clear ownership of workspace and resources	Shared responsibility for workspace and resources
Policy	No strong reinforcement and policy in space utilization as it is an individual setting	More emphasis on etiquette to avoid mishap accidents as it involves many stakeholders

Source Information obtained from the interview with respondents from private organizations in Malaysia

and buy-in because it will probably affect how effectively and efficiently, they operate within the organization. Thus, it is imperative to adopt a well-rounded strategy that guarantees effective execution while prioritizing the overall triumph and contentment of both the organization and its workforce.

Acknowledgements This research was supported by Taylor's University through the Taylor's Internal Research Grant Scheme—Impact Lab Grant (TIRGS-ILG/1/2023/SMK/002).

Special thanks to Taylor's University for the co-working space facilities.

References

Babapour Chafi, M., & Rolfö, L. (2019). Policies in activity-based flexible offices-'I am sloppy with clean-desking. We don't really know the rules'. *Ergonomics, 62*(1), pp.1–20.

Baranski, E., Lindberg, C., Gilligan, B., Fisher, J. M., Canada, K., Heerwagen, J., ... & Mehl, M. R. (2023). Personality, workstation type, task focus, and happiness in the workplace. *Journal of Research in Personality, 103*, 104337.

Bentley, T. A., Teo, S. T. T., McLeod, L., Tan, F., Bosua, R., & Gloet, M. (2016). The role of organisational support in teleworker wellbeing: A socio-technical systems approach. *Applied Ergonomics, 52*, 207–215.

Bernstein, E. S., & Turban, S. (2018). The impact of the 'open' workspace on human collaboration. *Philosophical Transactions of the Royal Society b: Biological Sciences, 373*(1753), 20170239.

Berbegal-Mirabent, J. (2021). What do we know about co-working spaces? *Trends and Challenges Ahead. Sustainability, 13*(3), 1416.

Berthelsen, H., Muhonen, T., & Toivanen, S. (2018). What happens to the physical and psychosocial work environment when activity-based offices are introduced into academia? *Journal of Corporate Real Estate, 20*(4), 230–243.

Bergsten, E. L., Haapakangas, A., Larsson, J., Jahncke, H., & Hallman, D. M. (2021). Effects of relocation to activity-based workplaces on perceived productivity: Importance of change-oriented leadership. *Applied Ergonomics, 93*, 103348.

Bouncken, R. B., Aslam, M. M., & Qiu, Y. (2021). Coworking spaces: Understanding, using, and managing sociomateriality. *Business Horizons, 64*(1), 119–130.

Bouncken, R. B., & Reuschl, A. J. (2018). Coworking-spaces: How a phenomenon of the sharing economy builds a novel trend for the workplace and for entrepreneurship. *Review of managerial science, 12,* 317–334.

Brunia, S., De Been, I., & van der Voordt, T. J. (2016). Accommodating new ways of working: Lessons from best practices and worst cases. *Journal of Corporate Real Estate, 18*(1), 30–47.

Cain, S. (2013). *Quiet: The power of introverts in a world that can't stop talking.* Crown.

Charalampous, M., Grant, C. A., & Tramontano, C. (2022). It needs to be the right blend: A qualitative exploration of remote e-workers' experience and well-being at work. *Employee Relations: The International Journal, 44*(2), 335–355.

De Been, I., Beijer, M., & Den Hollander, D. (2015). How to cope with dilemmas in activity based work environments-results from user-centred research. In *Conference paper 14th EuroFM Research Symposium. EuroFM research papers* (pp. 1–10).

De Klerk, J. J., Joubert, M., & Mosca, H. F. (2021). Is working from home the new workplace panacea? Lessons from the COVID-19 pandemic for the future world of work. *SA Journal of Industrial Psychology, 47*(1), 1–14.

Engelen, L., Chau, J., Young, S., Mackey, M., Jeyapalan, D., & Bauman, A. (2019). Is activity-based working impacting health, work performance and perceptions? A systematic review. *Building Research and Information, 47*(4), 468–479.

Fuzi, A. (2015). Coworking spaces for promoting entrepreneurship in sparse regions: The case of South Wales. *Regional Studies, Regional Science, 2*(1), 462–469.

Gray, T., & Birrell, C. (2014). Are biophilic-designed site office buildings linked to health benefits and high performing occupants? *International Journal of Environmental Research and Public Health, 11*(12), 12204–12222.

Gratton, L. (2021). How to do hybrid right. *Harvard Business Review, 99*(3), 65–74.

Green, N., Tappin, D., & Bentley, T. (2020). Working from home before, during and after the Covid-19 pandemic: Implications for workers and organisations. *New Zealand Journal of Employment Relations, 45*(2), 5–16.

Gerdenitsch, C., Korunka, C., & Hertel, G. (2018). Need–supply fit in an activity-based flexible office: A longitudinal study during relocation. *Environment and Behavior, 50*(3), 273–297.

Morrison, R. L., & Macky, K. A. (2017). The demands and resources arising from shared office spaces. *Applied Ergonomics, 60*, 103–115.

Molino, M., Ingusci, E., Signore, F., Manuti, A., Giancaspro, M. L., Russo, V., Zito, M., & Cortese, C. G. (2020). Wellbeing costs of technology use during Covid-19 remote working: An investigation using the Italian translation of the technostress creators scale. *Sustainability, 12*(15), 5911.

Nielsen, K., & Randall, R. (2013). Opening the black box: Presenting a model for evaluating organizational-level interventions. *European Journal of Work and Organizational Psychology, 22*(5), 601–617.

Nielsen, K., & Abildgaard, J. S. (2013). Organizational interventions: A research based framework for the evaluation of both process and effects. *Work and Stress, 27*(3), 278–297.

Parrino, L. (2015). Coworking: Assessing the role of proximity in knowledge exchange. *Knowledge Management Research & Practice, 13*, 261–271.

Rolfö, L., Eklund, J., & Jahncke, H. (2018). Perceptions of performance and satisfaction after relocation to an activity-based office. *Ergonomics, 61*(5), 644–657.

Richardson, L. (2017). Sharing as a postwork style: Digital work and the co-working office. *Cambridge Journal of Regions, Economy and Society, 10*(2), 297–310.

Richardson, J., & McKenna, S. (2014). Reordering spatial and social relations: A case study of professional and managerial flexworkers. *British Journal of Management, 25*(4), 724–736.

Sander, E. J., Caza, A., & Jordan, P. J. (2019). The physical work environment and its relationship to stress. *In Organizational behaviour and the physical environmen*t (pp. 268–284). Routledge.

Soga, L. R., Bolade-Ogunfodun, Y., Mariani, M., Nasr, R., & Laker, B. (2022). Unmasking the other face of flexible working practices: A systematic literature review. *Journal of Business Research, 142,* 648–662.

Spinuzzi, C. (2012). Working alone together: Coworking as emergent collaborative activity. *Journal of Business and Technical Communication, 26*(4), 399–441.

Tsen, M. K., Gu, M., Tan, C. M., & Goh, S. K. (2023). Homeworking and employee job stress and work engagement: A multilevel analysis from 34 European Countries. *Social Indicators Research,* 1–28.

Van Vianen, A. E. (2018). Person–environment fit: A review of its basic tenets. *Annual Review of Organizational Psychology and Organizational Behavior, 5,* 75–101.

Vogt, K., Hakanen, J. J., Jenny, G. J., & Bauer, G. F. (2016). Sense of coherence and the motivational process of the job-demands–resources model. *Journal of Occupational Health Psychology, 21*(2), 194.

Vyas, L. (2022). New normal at work in a post-COVID world: Work–life balance and labor markets. *Policy and Society, 41*(1), 155–167.

Wang, B., Liu, Y., Qian, J., & Parker, S. K. (2021). Achieving effective remote working during the COVID-19 pandemic: A work design perspective. *Applied psychology, 70*(1), 16–59.

Weijs-Perrée, M., van de Koevering, J., Appel-Meulenbroek, R., & Arentze, T. (2019). Analysing user preferences for co-working space characteristics. *Building Research and Information, 47*(5), 534–548.

Yukl, G., Mahsud, R., Prussia, G., & Hassan, S. (2019). Effectiveness of broad and specific leadership behaviors. *Personnel Review.*

Dr. Aqilah Yaacob is a Senior Lecturer and program coordinator at the School of Management and Marketing, Faculty of Business and Law, Taylor's University, Malaysia. She obtained her Doctor of Philosophy (Business Studies), Master of Science in Social Science Research Methods, and Master of Science in Finance from Cardiff University, UK. Her research work has appeared in scholarly journals such as the Journal of Business Research, Journal of Content, Community and Communication, and SEARCH Journal of Media and Communication Research. She has presented her work at international conferences including the British Academy of Management Conference, Royal Bank International Research Conference, BLM2-ICAM4 An International Joint E-Conference, and International Conference on Responsible Tourism and Hospitality. She has won several Gold Awards and APJBA Awards of Excellence by Asia-Pacific Journal of Business Administration, Emerald. She has also received Research Grant Awards for the Provision of MCMC Digital Society Research, Seed Funding from Taylor's University, and FRGS from the Ministry of Higher Education, Malaysia. She has won several awards for innovation in teaching and learning. She has also been active in community projects such as competition judge and trainer for entrepreneurship programs for the underprivileged groups.

Professor Dr. Goh See Kwong is currently the Professor of Marketing and Deputy Head of School (Education) at the School of Business, Monash University Malaysia. He specializes in the area of marketing, strategy, and entrepreneurship. He obtained his Doctorate qualification from the University of Newcastle, Australia. His publications in international refereed journals include the Journal of Business & Industrial Marketing, the Journal of Vacation Marketing, Information Technology & People, the Journal of Retailing and Consumer Services, and the Journal of Cleaner Production.

Dr. Gu Manli received her Ph.D. from Monash University. She is currently a Senior Lecturer and postgraduate stream coordinator at the School of Management and Marketing in Taylor's University, Malaysia. Her research interest is in the area of cross-cultural management and organizational behavior. Her work has been published in international peer-reviewed journals such as the Journal of Cross-Cultural psychology, Asian Journal of Social Psychology, Employee Relations, Evidence-based HRM, International Journal of Sociology and Social Policy. She also serves as a reviewer for high-impact refereed journals such as International Business Review, The Sociological Quarterly, Personality and Individual Differences, cross-Cultural Research, and Asian Business and Management.

Dr. Karen Tsen is a Lecturer at the School of Management and Marketing, Faculty of Business and Law, Taylor's University, Malaysia. She obtained her Bachelor in Psychology (Hons) at HELP University, Malaysia, and completed her Master's in Management and Doctor of Philosophy (Business) at Taylor's University, Malaysia. Her research interest is organizational behavior and talent management, particularly in workplace flexibility which is also her thesis topic. She is leading a hub, Employees' Wellbeing and Productivity, under Impact Lab 8, Mental Health and Well-Being. The hub's aim is guided by Goal 3 and Goal 8 from the United Nations Sustainable Development Goals (SDGs) to empower different communities by focusing on various societal problems.

Organizational Resilience, Innovation Capabilities, and SME Performance in High-Risk Contexts

Nadia Zahoor, Ahmad Arslan, Donman Miri, and Zaheer Khan

Abstract This chapter aims to establish a link between innovative capabilities and organizational performance of SMEs under the condition of organizational resilience, in relatively high-risk contexts such as emerging economies of Asia. By establishing links between the two distinct innovation capabilities—explorative and exploitative and organizational performance, the current book chapter contributes to the innovation literature by establishing the vital role of these capabilities for SMEs operating in a high-risk context to survive and improve their performance. Finally, our book chapter conceptualizes organizational resilience as a contingency factor for the utilization of explorative and exploitative innovation capabilities to enhance SMEs' organizational performance, in relatively high-risk contexts.

Keywords Dynamic capabilities · Explorative innovation · Exploitative innovation · Organizational performance · Resilience · And SMEs

---

N. Zahoor (✉)
Queen Mary, UK & InnoLab, University of London, University of Vaasa, Vaasa, Finland
e-mail: n.zahoor@qmul.ac.uk

Adnan Kassar School of Business, Lebanese American University, Beirut, Lebanon

A. Arslan
Department of Marketing, Management & IB, University of Oulu, Finland & Innolab, University of Vaasa, Vaasa, Finland
e-mail: ahmad.arslan@oulu.fi

D. Miri
Teeside University, Middlesbrough, UK
e-mail: d.miri@tees.ac.uk

Z. Khan
UK & InnoLab, University of Aberdeen, University of Vaasa, Vaasa, Finland
e-mail: zaheer.khan@abdn.ac.uk

© The Author(s), under exclusive license to Springer Nature Singapore Pte Ltd. 2024
T. Endress and Y. F. Badir (eds.), *Business and Management in Asia: Disruption and Change*, https://doi.org/10.1007/978-981-99-9371-0_11

Introduction

Small and medium-sized enterprises (SMEs) represent most businesses worldwide and significantly contribute to economic development and job creation (The World Bank, 2021). They account for over 90% of all businesses and generate 50% of employment worldwide. Particularly, as Asian countries are gaining prominence globally—SMEs are playing a vital role in the economic growth of these countries (Lopes de Sousa Jabbour et al., 2020; Yang et al., 2020). This suggests that SMEs in this region are critical for job creation, as well as economic development. With the growing importance of SMEs—they are forced to seek new ways (e.g., developing distinctive expertise and technology) to achieve a competitive advantage to compete with other industry players, particularly large firms (Saleem et al., 2020; Shashi et al., 2019; Velamuri & Liu, 2017). In this concern, prior studies have argued that innovation plays a critical role to survive and thrive in an increasingly competitive environment, especially for SMEs (Oura et al., 2016; Rosenbusch et al., 2011). Innovation offers SMEs the possibility to enhance the performance of their newly developed products (Najafi-Tavani et al., 2018) and transform their resources into innovative offerings that are more attractive to customers (Mazzucchelli et al., 2021; Singh et al., 2022). Due to the importance of innovation for SMEs, a significant body of research has analyzed the relationship between innovation and organizational performance (e.g., Exposito & Sanchis-Llopis, 2018; Love & Roper, 2015; Rosenbusch et al., 2011; Saridakis et al., 2019).

Despite significant research on the impact of innovation on SMEs' performance in recent years, the existing studies have mainly considered innovation as the ability to gather information and create the knowledge needed to develop products and processes (Schoenherr & Swink, 2015; Zhang & Hartley, 2018), with relatively fewer efforts to distinguish between two distinct capabilities—explorative and exploitative innovation capabilities as suggested by March's (1991) seminal work. Explorative innovation capability refers to *"experimentation with new alternatives whose returns are uncertain, distant, and often negative"* whereas exploitative innovation capability relates to *"the refinement and extension of existing competencies, technologies, and paradigms"* (March, 1991, p. 85). Explorative innovation capability departs from existing skills and capabilities and is geared toward new customers and new markets, but exploitation innovation capability leverages existing knowledge to serve the needs of existing customers and markets (Ferreira et al., 2020). Given the unique nature of explorative and exploitative innovation capabilities—their potential to influence organizational performance is different. Also, it should be highlighted that firms operating in high-risk environments experience challenges such as weak institutional systems, difficulties associated with financial system and foreign reserves, policy uncertainty, and higher levels of corruption, among others (e.g., Hanifah et al., 2019; Khan et al., 2023; Mei et al., 2019; Zeng et al., 2010). In a context mired by high volatility and risk, the specific role of explorative and exploitative innovation capabilities for SMEs is critical to be understood, as some prior studies have referred to those innovative capabilities are an important way for such SMEs to overcome external (including institutional) challenges and resource scarcity (Amankwah-Amoah et al., 2019; Burhan et al., 2021). Here, it is vital to stress that for SMEs operating in high risk and volatile environments, organizational resilience is a major factor that helps them overcome those risks, survive, and grow (Gölgeci & Kuivalainen, 2020; Gölgeci et al., 2020).

In this book chapter, we aim to offer a conceptual discussion where explorative and exploitative capabilities are linked with organizational performance of SMEs under the condition of organizational resilences. According to the dynamic capability view (Teece et al., 1997), explorative and exploitative innovation are vital dynamic capabilities that allow SMEs in a high-risk context to survive and improve their performance. While explorative capabilities enable organizations to explore new markets, technologies, and business models, exploitative capabilities focus on optimizing current operations, improving efficiency, and leveraging existing assets to generate value. To support organizational performance, a dynamic capability view suggests that organizations should invest in both explorative and exploitative capabilities. Further, the dynamic capability view emphasizes the importance of organizational resilience in supporting both explorative and exploitative innovation. By fostering adaptability, organizations can proactively identify and capitalize on new opportunities for explorative innovation. They can also quickly respond and adapt to feedback and insights gained through exploitative innovation, making necessary adjustments to improve efficiency and effectiveness.

By conceptualizing a link between the two distinct innovation capabilities—explorative and exploitative and organizational performance, this book chapter strengthens the innovation's understanding in both academic and practical contexts. The presented argumentation establishes that both explorative and exploitative innovation are vital dynamic capabilities that allow SMEs in a high-risk context to survive and improve their performance. Further, our book chapter specifically highlights organizational resilience as a contingency factor for the utilization of explorative and exploitative innovation capabilities to enhance SMEs' organizational performance.

The next section offers a literature review on the premise of explorative and exploitative capabilities and how they support organizational performance of SMEs. Further, we argue the critical role of organizational resilience to support the impact of explorative and exploitative capabilities on organizational performance of SMEs in turbulent environments. This discussion is followed by theoretical propositions addressing the conceptualization, innovation capabilities, organizational resilience, and organizational performance in the context of SMEs. After that implications, limitations, and future research directions are presented. Finally, the chapter concludes with the presentation of the conclusions section.

Literature Review

Innovation as a Multi-dimensional Concept

Innovation is an important organizational capability as it improves the sales, profits, and competing powers of organizations (Figueiredo et al., 2020; Sulistyo & Siyamtinah, 2016; Zahoor et al., 2021). It is defined as *"a means of changing an organization, whether as a response to changes in its internal or external environment or as a preemptive action taken to influence an environment"* (Damanpour, 1991, p. 556). The seminal study of March (1991) suggests that innovation is a multidimensional and complex phenomenon, including explorative and exploitative innovation. This multidimensional conceptualization addresses whether innovation is designed for completely new customers or markets (i.e., explorative) or whether innovation addresses the needs of existing customers (i.e., exploitative) (Benner & Tushman, 2003). Specifically, explorative innovation relates to using new knowledge and developing new products, services, and processes for new markets or customers (Jansen et al., 2006). It is captured by *"terms such as search, variation, risk-taking, experimentation, play, flexibility, discovery, and innovation"* (March, 1991, p. 71). In contrast, exploitative innovation concerns the use of existing knowledge and extending products, services, and processes for existing customers (Jansen et al., 2006; Levinthal & March, 1993). It is captured by "terms such as refinement, choice, production, efficiency, selection, implementation, and execution" (March, 1991, p. 71). As explorative and exploitative innovation draws upon unique resources and processes, they might produce different outputs and impact organizational performance differently (O'Reilly & Tushman, 2013). In this concern, the scholars have called to uncover the differential implications of explorative and exploitative innovations as they do not carry the same levels of risks and require different investments (Khan et al., 2019; Limaj & Bernroider, 2019; Zahoor et al., 2021).

It is important to further stress that the influences of innovation can be different for SMEs as compared to their larger counterparts (e.g., Dominguez, 2018; Zahoor et al., 2021). For example, explorative innovation capability in SMEs can promote an entrepreneurial mindset among employees, empowering them to take calculated risks, think innovatively, and pursue new opportunities (Raymond et al., 2020). It can help to assemble teams with diverse skills and expertise to foster cross-pollination of ideas and perspectives. Furthermore, exploitative innovation capability allows SMEs to seek and incorporate customer feedback to refine products, services, and user experiences. Due to their closed culture, SMEs can use exploitative capability to capture and document knowledge gained through experience and learning (Donbesuur et al., 2023; Zahoor et al., 2023). It encourages SMEs' employees to share best practices and lessons learned to drive efficiency and effectiveness (Limaj & Bernroider, 2019).

Dynamic Capability View and Innovation Capabilities

The dynamic capability view provides a valuable perspective for analyzing how firms achieve competitive advantage in changing market conditions (Teece et al., 1997). The dynamic capability view asserts that a firm must possess the ability to integrate, build, and reconfigure competencies to adjust to environmental changes (Teece, 2007). While scholars debate on the nature and characteristics of dynamic capabilities, the consensus view is that dynamic capabilities comprehend change creation and are influenced by market dynamism (Eisenhardt & Martin, 2000), are firm-specific (Amit & Schoemaker, 1993), are path-dependent and rooted in firm processes (Wang & Ahmed, 2007). To this end, explorative and exploitative innovation are dynamic capabilities that can play a vital role in addressing rapidly changing environments (Teece, 2014). In relatively risky emerging economies, explorative and exploitative innovation capabilities are vital for achieving competitive advantage due to lack of institutional support, resource scarcity and dynamic market conditions (Liu et al., 2020).

Despite the organizational performance potential of explorative and exploitative innovation capabilities, SMEs in such countries are exposed to prolonged external shocks such as political upheavals, natural disasters (e.g., COVID-19), market dynamism (e.g., demand variability), political instability, and shortening product lifecycle (Cao & Shi, 2021; Liu et al., 2019). SMEs that do not resist the storm of such changes fail and in many cases cease to exit (Shin et al., 2015). In such dynamic environments, organizational resilience is a vital capability that allows SMEs to prepare for unexpected events, respond to disruptions, and recover from crises by maintaining continuity of operations and control over functions (Ortiz-de-Mandojana & Bansal, 2016; Zahoor et al., 2022). Organizational resilience can allow SMEs to bounce back quickly from external shocks and respond to dynamic environmental signals and develop flexible resources to apply to a wide range of interchangeable alternatives (Li et al., 2021; Purnomo et al., 2021). As such, SMEs possessing organizational resilience can better utilize their explorative and exploitative innovation capabilities to improve organizational performance. Therefore, it can be argued that organizational resilience can (potentially) positively moderate (strengthen) the influences of two distinct capabilities—explorative and exploitative innovation capabilities on SMEs' organizational performance, particularly the ones operating in risky markets.

Innovation Capabilities, Organizational Resilience, and Organizational Performance in SMEs

Explorative innovation capability is defined as the ability to use new knowledge for the development of new products, processes, or services for new customers or markets (March, 1991). It requires the morphing of old knowledge with significantly new science to seek novel technological opportunities that are disruptive in nature (Ryan et al., 2018). When SMEs engage in explorative innovation, they put more effort into planning new innovation activities that can increase the growth expectations of firms (Hughes et al., 2021). In this context, explorative innovation capability serves as a specialized asset for SMEs that is tacit in nature and can be a source of organizational performance (Wu & Peng, 2020). Explorative innovation capability allows SMEs to develop new products, processes, or services with improved technical specifications that can offer higher benefits to the customer over existing products in the markets (Kyriakopoulos et al., 2016; Zahoor et al., 2021). For example, Xero—a New Zealand-based company—offered cloud-based accounting software. This explorative innovation-based software provided SMEs with a user-friendly accounting platform that leverages cloud technology. This simplified financial management, automated tasks, and provided real-time insights to SMEs about their financial health. Thus, the focus of SMEs on explorative innovation capability can advance new ways to make use of their resources to seize new rents and improve organizational performance. Specifically, Asian SMEs often exhibit entrepreneurial attributes (e.g., risk-taking and proactiveness) that encourage these firms to engage in risky activities (Dubey et al., 2020; Yang et al., 2019). An example is Zoho, an Indian software company, that offers suite of cloud-based business applications for SMEs. This business software allows small businesses to explore integrated solutions for customer management, finance, HR, and more, improving efficiency and collaboration. Such SMEs are more likely to utilize explorative innovative capability to improve their competitive position by offering novel products/services and in turn providing novel benefits to customers. This can also allow SMEs to gain a first-mover advantage in their markets, which can consequently increase the market share and return on sales (Huang et al., 2014; Zahoor et al., 2022). Based on the above discussion, we propose that:

Proposition 1: Explorative Innovation Capability in SMEs Positively Influences Organizational Performance.

Exploitative innovation capability is based on the use of existing knowledge and resources to extend existing products and services for existing customers. This can allow SMEs to use their repetitive processes to reap the benefits of improvement in their products and continue making incremental improvements (Li et al., 2011), which can allow SMEs to achieve superior performance. Moreover, exploitative innovation capability emphasizes process reliability and quality orientation (Limaj & Bernroider, 2019). This can allow SMEs to take initiatives for process improvement, which in turn can increase greater efficiency in innovation development (Saridakis et al., 2019). An example is Patagonia, a small outdoor apparel company, that is focusing on exploitative innovation. By using recycled materials, reducing water consumption in manufacturing, and extending the lifespan of their clothing through recycling programs, they have improved their products which align with their mission and appeal to eco-conscious consumers. Although returns from exploitation innovation can be lower than those of explorative innovation—SMEs prefer exploitative innovation over less specific and distant outcomes of explorative innovation. As Cooper (1993) suggests, about 20–80% of R&D projects are unsuccessful due to higher risks. In this regard, exploitation reduces the risks and failures in the production process by enhancing the preferences of SMEs for existing competencies that can improve not only product quality but also customer acceptance (Colclough et al., 2019; Loon & Chik, 2019)—thereby increasing organizational performance. Particularly, Asian SMEs often suffer from liability of smallness, limited availability of resources, and lack of institutional support (Su et al., 2020; Xiao et al., 2020). This can restrict the R&D budget of such SMEs and encourage them to efficiently use their limited resources (Lopes de Sousa Jabbour et al., 2020). Further, in the high-risk environment of Pakistan, exploitative innovation capability enables SMEs to invest in low-risk activities and utilize existing knowledge for innovation improvement and subsequent performance gains (Xiao et al., 2020). In this sense, exploitative innovation capability can allow SMEs to utilize their existing knowledge for improving product offerings and achieving higher performance. Hence, we propose that:

Proposition 2: Exploitative Innovation Capability in SMEs Positively Influences Organizational Performance.

Organizational resilience is the ability of organizations to anticipate, avoid, bounce back, and adjust to external environmental shocks (Harries et al., 2018). It is a path-dependent capability that *"organizations develop by noticing and correcting for maladaptive tendencies that help them cope with unexpected circumstances"* (Ortiz-de-Mandojana & Bansal, 2016, p. 1617). Organizational resilience is a vital operational-level capability for SMEs as they are highly vulnerable to crisis times given their constrained financial and human resources (Eggers, 2020). An example is the outbreak of the COVID-19 pandemic that caused the risk of failure for SMEs due to decline of financing options, employee quitting jobs, reduction of customer demands, and decrease in economic growth (Amankwah-Amoah et al., 2021; Brown & Cowling, 2021; Duarte Alonso et al., 2020). The risk of failure is even greater amongst Asian SMEs operating in risky countries as lack of institutional support and resources to cope with dynamic changes (Asia Development Bank, 2020; Burhan et al., 2021). However, at the same time, the constant exposure to such challenges in their markets tend to make SMEs more resilient to cope with external shocks and respond to new product demands (Bianchini & Kwon, 2021). As such, this can be argued that organizational resilience is a vital operational capability to take advantage of innovation capabilities for organizational performance. Stating differently, organizational resilience might moderate the impacts of explorative and exploitative innovation capabilities on organizational performance given that SMEs might find it difficult to balance and simultaneously pursue both these activities.

Explorative innovation capability entails variation, risk-taking, experimentation, and innovations (Benner & Tushman, 2003). This can allow SMEs to develop novel products, processes, or services that can increase market performance. However, Asian economies are dynamic with growing fluctuations in customers' demands and changes in political systems. In such a case, organizational resilience can enable these SMEs to cope with the external environments by effectively utilizing explorative innovation capability for organizational performance. Organizational resilience entails features like identification, response, experimentation, adaptation, and flexibility (Iborra et al., 2020). It allows SMEs to withstand stress and recover from external shocks by acquiring and using new knowledge for product innovations, thereby leading to enhanced market shares. This is consistent with the dynamic capability view suggesting that firms need to exploit complementary dynamic capabilities to overcome inertia and timely respond to environmental changes (Eisenhardt & Martin, 2000; Teece et al., 1997). While organizational resilience is vital to manage tensions effectively and have stability to survive (Duarte Alonso et al., 2020; Fath et al., 2021), explorative innovation is crucial to experiment with new ideas and develop new product offerings for new customers or markets (Hughes et al., 2021). As a result, the importance of combining organizational resilience with explorative innovation capabilities becomes more evident. Once SMEs identify threats and disruption in external environment, they can strategically respond to these threats by introducing technologically superior products, which in turn promotes market performance. Thus, we propose that:

Proposition 3a: The effect of explorative innovation capability on SMEs' organizational is conditioned on organizational resilience such that the relationship will be strengthened at a high level of organizational resilience.

Exploitative innovation capability allows SMEs to leverage their existing knowledge and resources for improving products, processes, or services (Ferreira et al., 2020). Exploitation innovation capability entails low-risk activities that can ensure SMEs' immediate survival and organizational performance. However, the external shocks and environmental jolts in Asia can threaten SMEs' engagement in successful exploitation activities (Afshar Jahanshahi & Brem, 2020; Lu et al., 2022). Organizational resilience can enable SMEs to respond to external shocks (Gölgeci et al., 2020), and continue their operations by maintaining control over functions (Gölgeci & Kuivalainen, 2020). More importantly, Asian SMEs with organizational resilience can extend their existing product and service portfolios and outperform competitors when faced with unexpected events (Darvishmotevali et al., 2020). When SMEs possess greater organizational resilience, they exhibit a greater response to market disruptions, opportunities, and customer requirements by modifying their product and service offerings promptly (Marcucci et al., 2022). Therefore, we expect that higher levels of organizational resilience can allow these SMEs to benefit from higher levels of exploitative innovation capability for organizational performance. Based on this discussion, we propose that:

Proposition 3b. The effect of exploitative innovation capability on SMEs' organizational is conditioned on organizational resilience such that the relationship will be strengthened at a high level of organizational resilience.

The following Fig. 1 presents our chapter's summary framework based upon the discussion presented above.

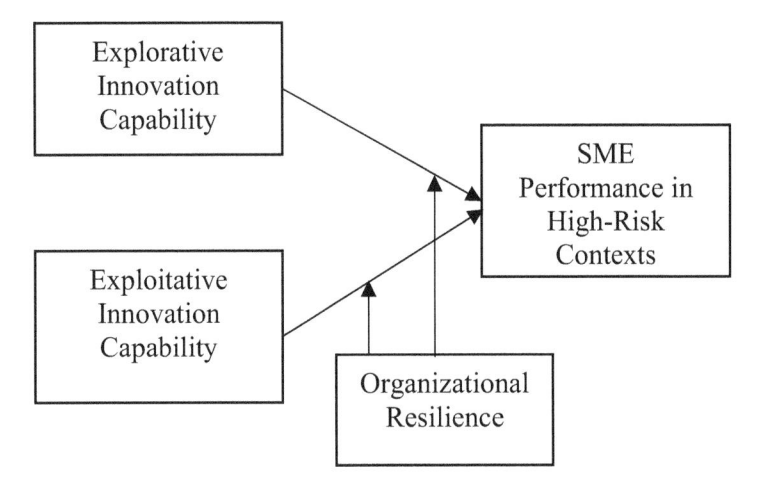

Fig. 1 Summary framework

Implications

The discussion presented in our chapter offers theoretical, practical, and policy implications. From a theoretical perspective, our chapter highlighted both explorative and exploitative innovation capabilities as two unique and distinct capabilities for SME performance. As the dynamic capability view suggests (Teece, 2007), SMEs need to build, integrate, and reconfigure capabilities to achieve a competitive advantage in a dynamic environment (e.g., Zahoor et al., 2022). Explorative innovation capability allows SMEs to benefit from new knowledge and resources for the development of new products/services that can offer performance gains in the long run, whereas exploitative innovation capability enables SMEs to take advantage of existing knowledge and resources for improved products/services to increase market share in the short run. By utilizing both explorative and exploitative innovation capabilities, SMEs operating in high-risk countries can remain competitive and achieve organizational performance. In this concern, our chapter strengthens the theorization of explorative and exploitative innovation interlinkage with SME performance, by specifying organizational resilience (Gölgeci et al., 2020; Iborra et al., 2020; Jia et al., 2020) as a key contingency factor especially in high-risk contexts. We show that organizational resilience is a vital operational capability that enables SMEs operating in risky environments to bounce back and reorient themselves for developing competitive advantage. Such operational capability interacts with dynamic capabilities—explorative and exploitative innovation capabilities and enhance organizational performance. Specifically, we propose that organizational resilience strengthens the impact of explorative innovation and exploitative innovation capabilities on organizational performance. At high levels of organizational resilience, SMEs in high-risk economies can utilize higher levels of explorative innovation and exploitative innovation capabilities for greater organizational performance. Hence, our chapter conceptually shows that dynamic and operational capabilities in a combinative way influence organizational performance significantly more than individually (or separately).

For the managerial audience, our findings provide guidance on how to use explorative innovation capability and exploitative innovation capability to realize organizational performance in high-risk economies' context. This is essential for the long-term viability and growth of SMEs originating from institutionally weak and uncertain markets. Our work shows that for an SME to attain superior performance, it is vital to utilize explorative innovation and exploitative innovation capabilities. This highlights the need for SMEs' managers in such circumstances to develop their technical skills and exploit explorative and exploitative innovation capabilities to achieve organizational performance. Having clear aims as to how to capitalize on their different roles to generate explorative and exploitative innovation is crucially important for employees to make the most out of their technical skills.

For the policymakers, it is important to evaluate the extent to which SMEs (in their country) engage in R&D efforts, which will enable the availability of government funding for such firms to support their explorative and exploitative innovation efforts, thereby leading to economic development. Also, it is in the best interest of the policymakers to support SMEs in fine-tuning their internal capabilities and technology skills since these are important means to gain a return on explorative and exploitative innovation activities. Further, emerging economy SME managers especially in relatively risky contexts should strengthen the interplay between organizational resilience, explorative innovation, and exploitative innovation where organizational resilience facilitates both types of innovation capabilities. Also, the external crises like COVID-19 pandemic and geopolitical events like the ongoing Ukraine war are a reality of the current business climate. Therefore, it is vital for managers to understand how SMEs can achieve resilience, survive, and bounce back; it can inform managers how to deal with stressful events while emphasizing innovation efforts for performance gains.

Limitations and Future Research Directions

Our chapter also has several limitations like any other academic study. Firstly, the current chapter is conceptual, and the developed propositions have not been tested. Hence, generalizability is limited. Risk dynamics are contextual and in different emerging (Asian) economies, it can manifest itself differently in relation to innovation capabilities and SME resilience. Future studies can build on the arguments presented in our chapters and undertake both qualitative and quantitative empirical assessments in different Asian economies so that specific implications can be drawn on these issues. Secondly, our chapter focused on explorative and exploitative innovation capabilities as determinants of organizational performance. As SMEs often rely on external networks to gain access to resources (Díez-Vial et al., 2022; Kim et al., 2018; Neyens et al., 2010), future studies could consider the role of collaborative explorative and exploitative innovation activities to improve organizational performance by taking an entire network view. Thirdly, we considered organizational resilience as the only contingency factor. There might be other moderating factors that can hinder or promote the impact of explorative and exploitative innovation capabilities on organizational performance. For example, certain environmental factors can influence innovation capabilities, including institutional specificity, government R&D support, and institutional enforceability. Also, there might be some other organizational factors to promote the innovation capabilities of SMEs like leaders' attributes, R&D teams, asset specificity, and so on. As such, future studies should consider additional moderating factors for explorative and exploitative innovation capabilities and organizational performance relationships.

Conclusions

The purpose of this chapter was to offer a conceptual discussion on the specific role played by the explorative and exploitative innovation capabilities for SME performance in high-risk contexts. The conceptual discussion presented established that both explorative (such as discovery of new opportunities, technologies, and markets) and exploitative (improving and optimizing existing products, processes, and business models) innovation capabilities are critical for SME performance (and success) in high-risk contexts (especially in emerging economies). It is important to stress that the joint influence of these innovation capabilities is more beneficial for SME performance compared to their individual influences. Also, for both explorative and exploitative innovation capabilities' influence on SME performance is strengthened by the presence of organizational resilience. Hence, the discussion offered in this chapter established organizational resilience acts as a contingency factor to support the linkage between explorative and exploitative innovation capabilities and organizational performance.

References

Afshar Jahanshahi, A., & Brem, A. (2020). Entrepreneurs in post-sanctions Iran: Innovation or imitation under conditions of perceived environmental uncertainty? *Asia Pacific Journal of Management, 37*(2), 531–551.

Amankwah-Amoah, J., Khan, Z., & Wood, G. (2021). COVID-19 and business failures: The paradoxes of experience, scale, and scope for theory and practice. *European Management Journal, 39*(2), 179–184.

Amit, R., & Schoemaker, P. J. H. (1993). Strategic assets and organizational rent. *Strategic Management Journal, 14*(1), 33–46.

Bank, A. D. (2020). *Asia Small and medium-sized enterprises monitor 2020*. Manila, Philippines: Asia Development Bank Retrieved from https://www.adb.org/sites/default/files/publication/650251/asia-sme-monitor-2020-volume-2.pdf

Bank, W. (2021). *Small and Medium Enterprises (SMEs) Finance*. The World Bank.

Benner, M. J., & Tushman, M. L. (2003). Exploitation, exploration, and process management: The productivity dilemma revisited. *Academy of Management Review, 28*(2), 238–256.

Bianchini, M., & Kwon, I. (2021). *Enhancing SMEs' resilience through digitalisation: The case of Korea*. OECD Retrieved from. https://doi.org/10.1787/23bd7a26-en

Brown, R., & Cowling, M. (2021). The geographical impact of the Covid-19 crisis on precautionary savings, firm survival and jobs: Evidence from the United Kingdom's 100 largest towns and cities. *International Small Business Journal, 39*(4), 319–329.

Burhan, M., Salam, M. T., Hamdan, O. A., & Tariq, H. (2021). "Crisis management in the hospitality sector SMEs in Pakistan during COVID-19". *International Journal of Hospitality Management, 98*, 103037.

Cao, Z., & Shi, X. (2021). A systematic literature review of entrepreneurial ecosystems in advanced and emerging economies. *Small Business Economics, 57*(1), 75–110.

Colclough, S. N., Moen, Ø., Hovd, N. S., & Chan, A. (2019). SME innovation orientation: Evidence from Norwegian exporting SMEs. *International Small Business Journal, 37*(8), 780–803.

Cooper, R. G. (1993). *Winning at new products*. Perseus.

Damanpour, F. (1991). Organizational Innovation: A meta-analysis of effects of determinants and moderators. *Academy of Management Journal, 34*(3), 555–590.

Darvishmotevali, M., Altinay, L., & Köseoglu, M. A. (2020). The link between environmental uncertainty, organizational agility, and organizational creativity in the hotel industry. *International Journal of Hospitality Management, 87*, 102499.

Duarte Alonso, A., Kok, S. K., Bressan, A., O'Shea, M., Sakellarios, N., Koresis, A., Buitrago Solis, M. A., & Santoni, L. J. (2020). COVID-19, aftermath, impacts, and hospitality firms: An international perspective. *International Journal of Hospitality Management, 91*, 102654.

Donbesuur, F., Owusu-Yirenkyi, D., Ampong, G. O. A., & Hultman, M. (2023). Enhancing export intensity of entrepreneurial firms through bricolage and international opportunity recognition: The differential roles of explorative and exploitative learning. *Journal of Business Research, 156*, 113467.

Dubey, R., Gunasekaran, A., Childe, S. J., Bryde, D. J., Giannakis, M., Foropon, C., Roubaud, D., & Hazen, B. T. (2020). Big data analytics and artificial intelligence pathway to operational performance under the effects of entrepreneurial orientation and environmental dynamism: A study of manufacturing organisations. *International Journal of Production Economics, 226*, 107599.

Eggers, F. (2020). Masters of disasters? Challenges and opportunities for SMEs in times of crisis. *Journal of Business Research, 116*, 199–208.

Eisenhardt, K. M., & Martin, J. A. (2000). Dynamic capabilities: What are they? *Strategic Management Journal, 21*(10–11), 1105–1121.

Exposito, A., & Sanchis-Llopis, J. A. (2018). Innovation and business performance for Spanish SMEs: New evidence from a multi-dimensional approach. *International Small Business Journal, 36*(8), 911–931.

Fath, B., Fiedler, A., Sinkovics, N., Sinkovics, R. R., & Sullivan-Taylor, B. (2021). International relationships and resilience of New Zealand SME exporters during COVID-19. *Critical perspectives on international business, 17*(2), 359–379.

Ferreira, J., Coelho, A., & Moutinho, L. (2020). Dynamic capabilities, creativity and innovation capability and their impact on competitive advantage and firm performance: The moderating role of entrepreneurial orientation. *Technovation, 92–93*, 102061.

Figueiredo, P. N., Larsen, H., & Hansen, U. E. (2020). The role of interactive learning in innovation capability building in multinational subsidiaries: A micro-level study of biotechnology in Brazil. *Research Policy, 49*(6), 103995.

Gölgeci, I., Arslan, A., Dikova, D., & Gligor, D. M. (2020). Resilient agility in volatile economies: Institutional and organizational antecedents. *Journal of Organizational Change Management, 33*(1), 100–113.

Gölgeci, I., & Kuivalainen, O. (2020). Does social capital matter for supply chain resilience? The role of absorptive capacity and marketing-supply chain management alignment. *Industrial Marketing Management, 84*, 63–74.

Harries, T., McEwen, L., & Wragg, A. (2018). Why it takes an 'ontological shock' to prompt increases in small firm resilience: Sensemaking, emotions and flood risk. *International Small Business Journal, 36*(6), 712–733.

Huang, S., Ding, D., & Chen, Z. (2014). Entrepreneurial leadership and performance in Chinese new ventures: A moderated mediation model of exploratory innovation, exploitative innovation and environmental dynamism. *Creativity and Innovation Management, 23*(4), 453–471.

Hughes, M., Chang, Y.-Y., Hodgkinson, I., Hughes, P., & Chang, C.-Y. (2021). The multi-level effects of corporate entrepreneurial orientation on business unit radical innovation and financial performance. *Long Range Planning, 54*(1), 101989.

Iborra, M., Safón, V., & Dolz, C. (2020). What explains the resilience of SMEs? Ambidexterity capability and strategic consistency. *Long Range Planning, 53*(6), 101947.

Jansen, J. J. P., Van Den Bosch, F. A. J., & Volberda, H. W. (2006). Exploratory innovation, exploitative innovation, and performance: Effects of organizational antecedents and environmental moderators. *Management Science, 52*(11), 1661–1674.

Jia, X., Chowdhury, M., Prayag, G., & Hossan Chowdhury, M. M. (2020). The role of social capital on proactive and reactive resilience of organizations post-disaster. *International Journal of Disaster Risk Reduction, 48*, 101614.

Khan, H., Zahoor, N., Arslan, A., & Khan, Z. (2023). Market exit and re-entry in a volatile emerging economy: A case study of Yamaha motorcycles in Pakistan. *Multinational Business Review*. Ahead of print article available online at https://doi.org/10.1108/MBR-09-2022-0132

Khan, Z., Lew, Y. K., & Marinova, S. (2019). Exploitative and exploratory innovations in emerging economies: The role of realized absorptive capacity and learning intent. *International Business Review, 28*(3), 499–512.

Kyriakopoulos, K., Hughes, M., & Hughes, P. (2016). The role of marketing resources in radical innovation activity: Antecedents and payoffs. *Journal of Product Innovation Management, 33*(4), 398–417.

Levinthal, D. A., & March, J. G. (1993). The myopia of learning. *Strategic Management Journal, 14*(S2), 95–112.

Li, B., Zhong, Y., Zhang, T., & Hua, N. (2021). Transcending the COVID-19 crisis: Business resilience and innovation of the restaurant industry in China. *Journal of Hospitality and Tourism Management, 49*, 44–53.

Li, Y., Li, X., Liu, Y., & Barnes, B. R. (2011). Knowledge communication, exploitation and endogenous innovation: The moderating effects of internal controls in SMEs. *R&D Management, 41*(2), 156–172.

Limaj, E., & Bernroider, E. W. N. (2019a). The roles of absorptive capacity and cultural balance for exploratory and exploitative innovation in SMEs. *Journal of Business Research, 94*, 137–153.

Liu, Y., Chan, C., Zhao, C., & Liu, C. (2019). Unpacking knowledge management practices in China: Do institution, national and organizational culture matter? *Journal of Knowledge Management, 23*(4), 619–643.

Liu, Y., Ndubisi, N. O., Liu, Y., & Barrane, F. Z. (2020). New product development and sustainable performance of Chinese SMMEs: The role of dynamic capability and intra-national environmental forces. *International Journal of Production Economics, 230*, 107817.

Loon, M., & Chik, R. (2019). Efficiency-centered, innovation-enabling business models of high tech SMEs: Evidence from Hong Kong. *Asia Pacific Journal of Management, 36*(1), 87–111.

Lopes de Sousa Jabbour, A. B., Ndubisi, N. O., & Roman Pais Seles, B. M. (2020). Sustainable development in Asian manufacturing SMEs: Progress and directions. *International Journal of Production Economics, 225*, 107567.

Love, J. H., & Roper, S. (2015). SME innovation, exporting and growth: A review of existing evidence. *International Small Business Journal, 33*(1), 28–48.

Lu, S., Shan, B., & Fei, Y. (2022). Exploring an inverted U-shaped relationship between entrepreneurial experience and Chinese new venture performance: The moderating role of environmental uncertainty. *Asia Pacific Business Review, 28*(4), 518–535.

March, J. G. (1991). Exploration and exploitation in organizational learning. *Organization Science, 2*(1), 71–87.

Marcucci, G., Antomarioni, S., Ciarapica, F. E., & Bevilacqua, M. (2022). The impact of Operations and IT-related Industry 4.0 key technologies on organizational resilience. *Production Planning & Control, 33*(15), 1417–1431.

Mazzucchelli, A., Chierici, R., Tortora, D., & Fontana, S. (2021). Innovation capability in geographically dispersed R&D teams: The role of social capital and IT support. *Journal of Business Research, 128*, 742–751.

Najafi-Tavani, S., Najafi-Tavani, Z., Naudé, P., Oghazi, P., & Zeynaloo, E. (2018). How collaborative innovation networks affect new product performance: Product innovation capability, process innovation capability, and absorptive capacity. *Industrial Marketing Management, 73*, 193–205.

O'Reilly, C. A., & Tushman, M. L. (2013). Organizational ambidexterity: Past, present, and future. *Academy of Management Perspectives, 27*(4), 324–338.

Ortiz-de-Mandojana, N., & Bansal, P. (2016). The long-term benefits of organizational resilience through sustainable business practices. *Strategic Management Journal, 37*(8), 1615–1631.

Oura, M. M., Zilber, S. N., & Lopes, E. L. (2016). Innovation capacity, international experience and export performance of SMEs in Brazil. *International Business Review, 25*(4), 921–932.

Purnomo, B. R., Adiguna, R., Widodo, W., Suyatna, H., & Nusantoro, B. P. (2021). Entrepreneurial resilience during the Covid-19 pandemic: Navigating survival, continuity and growth. *Journal of Entrepreneurship in Emerging Economies, 13*(4), 497–524.

Raymond, L., Bergeron, F., Croteau, A. M., Ortiz de Guinea, A., & Uwizeyemungu, S. (2020). Information technology-enabled explorative learning and competitive performance in industrial service SMEs: A configurational analysis. *Journal of Knowledge Management, 24*(7), 1625–1651.

Rosenbusch, N., Brinckmann, J., & Bausch, A. (2011). Is innovation always beneficial? A meta-analysis of the relationship between innovation and performance in SMEs. *Journal of Business Venturing, 26*(4), 441–457.

Ryan, P., Geoghegan, W., & Hilliard, R. (2018). The microfoundations of firms' explorative innovation capabilities within the triple helix framework. *Technovation, 76–77*, 15–27.

Saleem, H., Li, Y., Ali, Z., Mehreen, A., & Mansoor, M. S. (2020). An empirical investigation on how big data analytics influence China SMEs performance: Do product and process innovation matter? *Asia Pacific Business Review, 26*(5), 537–562.

Saridakis, G., Idris, B., Hansen, J. M., & Dana, L. P. (2019). SMEs' internationalisation: When does innovation matter? *Journal of Business Research, 96*, 250–263.

Schoenherr, T., & Swink, M. (2015). The Roles of supply chain intelligence and adaptability in new product launch success. *Decision Sciences, 46*(5), 901–936.

Shashi, Centobelli, P., Cerchione, R., & Singh, R. (2019). The impact of leanness and innovativeness on environmental and financial performance: Insights from Indian SMEs. *International Journal of Production Economics, 212*, 111–124.

Shin, H., Lee, J.-N., Kim, D., & Rhim, H. (2015). Strategic agility of Korean small and medium enterprises and its influence on operational and firm performance. *International Journal of Production Economics, 168*, 181–196.

Singh, S. K., Giudice, M. D., Tarba, S. Y., & Bernardi, P. D. (2022). Top management team shared leadership, market-oriented culture, innovation capability, and firm performance. *IEEE Transactions on Engineering Management, 69*(6), 2544–2554.

Su, F., Khan, Z., Kyu Lew, Y., Il Park, B., & Shafi Choksy, U. (2020). Internationalization of Chinese SMEs: The role of networks and global value chains. *BRQ Business Research Quarterly, 23*(2), 141–158.

Sulistyo, H., & Siyamtinah. (2016). Innovation capability of SMEs through entrepreneurship, marketing capability, relational capital and empowerment. *Asia Pacific Management Review, 21*(4), 196–203.

Teece, D. J. (2007). Explicating dynamic capabilities: The nature and microfoundations of (sustainable) enterprise performance. *Strategic Management Journal, 28*(13), 1319–1350.

Teece, D. J. (2014). The foundations of enterprise performance: Dynamic and ordinary capabilities in an (Economic) theory of firms. *Academy of Management Perspectives, 28*(4), 328–352.

Teece, D. J., Pisano, G., & Shuen, A. (1997). Dynamic capabilities and strategic management. *Strategic Management Journal, 18*(7), 509–533.

Velamuri, S. R., & Liu, W. (2017). Ownership structure, insider behavior, and IPO performance of SMEs in China. *Small Business Economics, 48*(3), 771–793.

Wang, C. L., & Ahmed, P. K. (2007). Dynamic capabilities: A review and research agenda. *International Journal of Management Reviews, 9*(1), 31–51.

Wu, Z., & Peng, X. (2020). Exploratory versus exploitative innovation: SME performance implications of managerial ties and empowering leadership in China. *Asian Journal of Technology Innovation*, 1–29.

Xiao, S. S., Lew, Y. K., & Park, B. I. (2020). International network searching, learning, and explorative capability: Small and medium-sized enterprises from China. *Management International Review, 60*(4), 597–621.

Yang, H., Dess, G. G., & Robins, J. A. (2019). Does entrepreneurial orientation always pay off? The role of resource mobilization within and across organizations. *Asia Pacific Journal of Management, 36*(3), 565–591.

Yang, X., Li, J., Stanley, L. J., Kellermanns, F. W., & Li, X. (2020). How family firm characteristics affect internationalization of Chinese family SMEs. *Asia Pacific Journal of Management, 37*(2), 417–448.

Zahoor, N., Khan, Z., Arslan, A., Khan, H., & Tarba, S. Y. (2021). International open innovation and international market success: An empirical study of emerging market small and medium-sized enterprises. *International Marketing Review, 39*(3), 755–782.

Zahoor, N., Golgeci, I., Haapanen, L., Ali, I., & Arslan, A. (2022). The role of dynamic capabilities and strategic agility of B2B high-tech small and medium-sized enterprises during COVID-19 pandemic: Exploratory case studies from Finland. *Industrial Marketing Management, 105*, 502–514.

Zahoor, N., Tarba, S., Arslan, A., Ahammad, M. F., Mostafiz, M. I., & Battisti, E. (2023). The impact of entrepreneurial leadership and international explorative-exploitative learning on the performance of international new ventures. *Asia Pacific Journal of Management*. Early view available online at https://doi.org/10.1016/j.ibusrev.2021.101800

Zhang, M., & Hartley, J. L. (2018). Guanxi, IT systems, and innovation capability: The moderating role of proactiveness. *Journal of Business Research, 90*, 75–86.

Dr. Nadia Zahoor is a Senior Lecturer in Strategy at the Queen Mary University of London, UK. She is also an affiliate researcher at InnoLab, University of Vaasa, Finland. completed her Ph.D. in Management at the University of Huddersfield, UK. Her research interests are strategic alliances, global strategy, innovation, and organizational resilience. She is particularly interested in the context of small and medium-sized enterprises in emerging markets. Her research has been published in mainstream journals, including the *Journal of Product Innovation Management, Global Strategy Journal, British Journal of Management, Technovation, International Journal of Management Reviews, International Business Review, International Marketing Review, International Small Business Journal, Business Strategy and the Environment*, among others.

Prof. Ahmad Arslan is currently working as a Professor at the Department of Marketing, Management, and International Business, University of Oulu, Finland. He is also affiliated with

InnoLab, University of Vaasa, Finland, and also holds the position of Honorary Chair at the Business School, University of Aberdeen, Scotland, UK. His earlier research has been published in prestigious academic journals like *British Journal of Management, Human Resource Management (US), IEEE Transactions on Engineering Management, International Business Review, International Journal of Human Resource Management, International Marketing Review, Journal of Business Research, Journal of International Management, Journal of Product Innovation Management, Production Planning & Control, Public Management Review, Supply Chain Management, and Technological Forecasting and Social Change,* among others. Finally, he holds several editorial board memberships and is currently an Associate Editor of the *International Journal of Entrepreneurship and Small Business.*

Dr. Domnan Miri is a Senior Lecturer in Business at Teesside University International Business School. He earned a Doctor of Philosophy (Ph.D.) in Business and Management from the University of Huddersfield. Domnan's research interest cuts across the fields of Strategy, and Entrepreneurship, with particular interests, which are Organizational Structures, Dynamic Capabilities of Small and Medium Enterprises (SMEs) and Social Enterprises (SEs) within Emerging and Developing Economies. His work has been published in the Technological Forecasting and Social Change.

Prof. Zaheer Khan is a Professor in Strategy & International Business at Business School, University of Aberdeen, UK. He is also a visiting professor at the University of Vaasa, Finland. He is a Fellow of the Academy of Social Sciences (FAcSS). His research focuses on global technology management with a particular focus on knowledge transfer through FDI to emerging markets. His work has appeared in leading journals such as the *Journal of International Business Studies, Journal of World Business, Global Strategy Journal, International Business Review, Management International Review, Industrial Marketing Management, Long Range Planning, Human Relations, British Journal of Management, Journal of Corporate Finance, Journal of Business Ethics, International Small Business Journal,* and *Technological Forecasting & Social Change,* among others.